מסורה

ArtScroll® Series

Rabbi Nosson Scherman / Rabbi Meir Zlotowitz

General Editors

Published by

Mesorah Publications, ltd

The Maggid at the Podium

Stories and practical ideas
from the lectures of

RABBI PAYSACH J. KROHN

FIRST EDITION
First Impression ... November 2013
Second Impression ... November 2013
Third Impression ... February 2013

Published and Distributed by
MESORAH PUBLICATIONS, LTD.
4401 Second Avenue / Brooklyn, N.Y 11232

Distributed in Europe by
LEHMANNS
Unit E, Viking Business Park
Rolling Mill Road
Jarow, Tyne & Wear, NE32 3DP
England

Distributed in Australia and New Zealand
by **GOLDS WORLDS OF JUDAICA**
3-13 William Street
Balaclava, Melbourne 3183
Victoria, Australia

Distributed in Israel by
SIFRIATI / A. GITLER — BOOKS
Moshav Magshimim
Israel

Distributed in South Africa by
KOLLEL BOOKSHOP
Northfield Centre, 17 Northfield Avenue
Glenhazel 2192, Johannesburg, South Africa

ARTSCROLL® SERIES
THE MAGGID AT THE PODIUM
© Copyright 2013, by MESORAH PUBLICATIONS, Ltd.
4401 Second Avenue / Brooklyn, N.Y. 11232 / (718) 921-9000 / www.artscroll.com

---

ISBN 10: 1-4226-1453-0 / ISBN 13: 978-1-4226-1453-2

Typography by CompuScribe at ArtScroll Studios, Ltd.
Printed in the United States of America
Bound by Sefercraft, Quality Bookbinders, Ltd., Brooklyn N.Y. 11232

דוד קאהן

ביהמ"ד נבול יעבץ
ברוקלין, נוא יארק

ב"ה

יהי' היש (?) חסת ולש של ג'ונא

נה שכת הוזעת לי שכתיב יצא מאור חה תורר מחק

ותקרא מינן מכתב רובה:

כ"ק רב' מאיר היה אד"ק צאוא א צבה כאסוקר
ותואא ק'ב טחפים שהסא ת הצבם אקעצר כניחיות.
וג'צע גדולות שאק חסת ולש אקעוים עם אצאתק
בקראם שהר' אואר קעולה'ק ל'קח' היגן (כ"סת ופהי
הצה'חת ע' נשואין קקרב ולערר ולק' ברות וג'ק
שק ע' תורר' הה' נתולס עגב שאים.

ויהי' אברק אותק לתעשק ברכין ע נ"ע של שלא.

אוהבק ודולך שלוא
דוד קאהן

יה אדאון קכ'ץ

Tel. (718) 520-0115
Fax (718) 268-0186

קהל נחלת יצחק ד'הומנא

CONGREGATION NACHLAS YITZCHOK

141-43 73rd AVENUE
Kew Gardens, Hills, N. Y. 11367

בס"ד

NOACH ISAAC OELBAUM
Rabbi
AUTHOR OF SEFORIM
MINCHAS CHEN

נח אייזיק אהלבוים
בעהמח"ס מנחת חן
רב ואב"ד דקהק נחלת יצחק
בקיו גארדענס הילס, נ.י.

יום חמישי לסדר "שא נא עיניך וראה דנו ואת ביתי" תשנ"ב

הסכמה. וצעת הסבוריים הא'מ'יס'לו א'י'דל מו ומ'
ה'א'ב'יס'ל. אשר נא אלא ויבא נירבד אלה מלאי אשלו ומקדמ,
הרב ה'ש'ל' אדם, ואצא הלמיים ואשבה אלה הרבה לא'י' איני'ק
אהלבוים. פ'א'ת אודה אסם ה'פ' שלם ק'ר'שלין א'ל'א'ל.

הלומד לעבד ולעשה היא לי עבוד ס'פ'ל ונתעלו
הטלמד להולך ה'ב'א'ת ל'מ'ע'מ'ם, ל'פ'י ה'מ'ב'ם, ועבד יצא
ה'ט'ל'מ'ם רוח לאש הראשון לש'ע'ל'א ה'ע'ו'לם אלה'ל'א'ל ולום הבים
א'ה'ל'י דן ישראל לע'ב'ד'ים שלומים.

 והנני מעל להרבון שובה לה'א'ל'ם ה'ה'ל'ת
הס'ל'א אהלם הגולת ה'מ'ו'ל' א'ל'א'ל'א'ל ו'ל'ה'ר'בים
אס'ל' הס'ל'ולא אהלת מלאה ולאת. ה'א'ס'ל'א ת'ל'ד
ול ה'ס'מ'ב'ל'א צד נ'ט'ל'א א'ל'א'ל צדק ה'ל'ל.

הבוא ל'ק'לא ונ'ה'ל'ד ול'א'ל'י'

Table of Contents

AUTHOR'S PREFACE

אוֹדֶה ה' מְאֹד בְּפִי וּבְתוֹךְ רַבִּים אֲהַלְלֶנּוּ:
*I will thank Hashem exceedingly with my mouth
and amid the multitudes I will praise Him.*
(Tehillim 109:30)

I t is with a deep sense of gratitude to Hashem that I present this second book of lectures to the reading public. As we approach the upcoming *Yom Tov* of Chanukah, we are reminded that the halachah follows Beis Hillel, who hold that we add an additional candle to the menorah every night: from the first night when we light only one, until the eighth night when we light eight. This process, מוֹסִיף וְהוֹלֵךְ, *adding and carrying on,* is also a lesson in how we should lead our lives. One should never remain with the status quo; one should always try to accomplish more, seek to further enhance the lives of fellow Jews, and find additional ways to enrich the world. I hope the addition of this new work to the vast array of ArtScroll/Mesorah *sefarim/ books* will indeed add inspiration to the lives of thousands.

A maggid is an itinerant speaker who inspires people wherever he travels, with stories and parables as the basis of his speeches. The first maggid I ever saw was Rabbi Sholom Schwadron, known as the Maggid of Yerushalayim. He came to America for the first time in 1964 and stayed in my parents' home for six months! (See *Introduction* to *The Maggid Speaks* and "An Appreciation" in *Echoes of the Maggid*.) He mesmerized his audiences. He delighted them with his wit, he moved them to tears with his sensitivities, but more than anything else he motivated them to look inward and change. There was incredible excitement and anticipation before he rose to speak. Which story would he tell? What *gadol* would he quote? What era would he depict? Which *Chazal* or *pasuk* would he expound on? And then when he made his way to the pulpit, it was magical and thrilling. Rabbi Schwadron was not only a great speaker but an illustrious *talmid chacham*, eminent *yarei Shamayim,* and *oheiv Yisrael*. He was the ultimate "Maggid at the Podium."

In those years, when I followed him to many of his *drashos*, I asked my father, Rabbi Avrohom Zelig Krohn, if it was possible to be a maggid in America. His answer surprised me. He said convincingly, "In America you can be anything you want to be."

Who could have imagined how *Klal Yisrael* would change in the next 50 years? Orthodoxy would blossom into a vibrant entity with yeshivos, Bais Yaakovs, *batei midrash*, *shuls*, *kollelim*, and seminaries flourishing throughout America, Europe, South America, and, of course *Eretz Yisrael*. This created a great thirst for inspiration and guidance, and thus a plethora of conferences, conventions, Shabbatons, symposiums, and *Yom Tov* programs began to sprout everywhere.

I am fortunate to be one of the cadre of speakers who travel far and wide to hopefully inspire, motivate, and nurture growth in people's behavior in *bein adam laMakom* (between man and Hashem) and *bein adam laChaveiro* (between man and man). Over the last number of years, I have been privileged to lecture in several countries, and audiences today are responsive. It is remarkable to see how many people come to *drashos* today; such is the yearning to grow in *Yiddishkeit*. Every speaker in his own way, in his personal style, according to the needs and mores of his audience, longs to accomplish what Rav Sholom did in his illustrious career. Every speaker strives to be *The Maggid at the Podium*.

━━►●◄━━

I was recently asked which I thought was the more effective way of transmitting ideas: the written word or the spoken word. To me, the dynamic speech with its inherent raw power and passion is certainly more effective in the short term. When I think of ideas that I have asked people in lectures to consider and accept, I find that when they've heard it in person (or on a recording afterward) they have more often absorbed and undertaken them.

However, there is an eternity to the written word; indeed, "The written word is forever." Moshe Rabbeinu instructed the people, וְכָתַבְתָּ עַל הָאֲבָנִים אֶת כָּל דִּבְרֵי הַתּוֹרָה הַזֹּאת בַּאֵר הֵיטֵב, *You shall inscribe on the stones* [הָאֲבָנִים] *all the words of the Torah well clarified* (Devarim 27:8). Rabbi Zvi Ryzman wrote that the word אֶבֶן is an allusion to three words, אָב, בֵּן, נֶכֶד, *father, son, grandson.* It is this transmission of Torah that assures the continuance of Torah. And to do this, the written word is necessary.

We are called the *Am HaSefer,* the People of the Book, because the legacy of Torah and *mitzvos* that has been passed on through the generations has come to us through our holy Books of Torah. *Rabbeinu HaKadosh* understood that even *Torah Sheb'al Peh* (Oral Torah) had to be committed to writing to become, in a sense, *Torah Shebiksav* (Written Torah). That's why he redacted the Mishnah, which led to the Gemara being written as well.

But even the written texts must be taught and expounded by verbal teaching. Thus the spoken and the written word are for Jews imperative and inseparable.

I am therefore forever grateful to Rabbi Meir Zlotowitz and Rabbi Nosson Scherman for giving me the opportunity to have my lectures published in book form so that the ideas and insights that I have expounded verbally will be made available to readers as well as listeners. I ask Hashem that both my written words and spoken words will always be acceptable and encouraging. As David HaMelech expressed it in his prayer to Hashem, תָּבוֹא לְפָנֶיךָ תְּפִלָּתִי הַטֵּה אָזְנְךָ לְרִנָּתִי, *Let my prayer come before You, incline Your ear to my song* (Tehillim 88:3).

Acknowledgments

As the now world-renowned *Zman* magazine was in its early planning stages, Rabbi Yaakov Astor, the General Editor, called me and asked if I would allow his staff to transcribe my speeches so that they could be used as monthly articles. I was thrilled that they would consider it and of course I consented. It is now three years later and *baruch Hashem*, every issue since its inception has contained a transcribed and edited speech as the lead essay in a column called "Perspectives." *Zman* soon gained popularity throughout the Jewish world (they now have a glossy monthly Hebrew edition), and one *Motza'ei Shabbos*, Rabbi Gedaliah Zlotowitz suggested that perhaps a book of those essays could be published by ArtScroll. When Rav Gedaliah's father, Rabbi Meir, and Rabbi Nosson Scherman okayed the idea we went to work to produce the book *PERSPECTIVES OF THE MAGGID*, which was published in February 2012. I am grateful to both Rabbi Yaakov Astor and Rabbi Gedaliah Zlotowitz for creating this idea and bringing it to fruition.

This book, like the first, would not be what it is except for the deft stylistic editing of Mrs. Felice Eisner. Her rearranging a sentence, her clever choice of words, her paraphrasing a thought are genuine artwork. It is an honor to work with her.

Throughout my speaking career there have been many who have afforded me wondrous opportunities. I thank once again Rabbi Elazar Boruch Bald (Irgun Shiyurei Torah), Rabbi Leibish Becker and Rabbi Avrohom Nisson Perl (Agudas Yisrael), Sholom Ber Eber (Brooklyn), Joseph Kerzner (Toronto), Rabbi Yitzchok Meyer Landau (Khal Veretsky), Mr. Michael Rothschild (Chofetz Chaim Heritage Foundation), and Mr. Eli Slomovitz (Founder of E&S Tours). They each have called on me countless times and I am awed and humbled by their accomplishments. I thank Yossi Kornfeld for acting as the liaison between *Zman* and ArtScroll/Mesorah.

My speaking career has been enhanced by the opportunities that the following individuals have given me: Yosef Davis (Torahanytime. com), Rebbetzin Dina Fink (Le'chu Venailcha), Rabbi Warren Goldstein (Chief Rabbi, South Africa), Dov Harris, (London PAL), Shmully and Sarah Rivka Kohn (LINKS), Yaniv Meirov (Chazaq), Shea Rubenstein (Marine Park), Ari Scharf (Project Mesorah), Rabbi Shlomo Singer (PTI Passaic), Mrs. Shonnie Stefansky and Mrs. Bryndee Halberstam (Samcheinu), and Rabbi Moshe Tussia (Mexico). I have spoken often for their organizations and I am a better person because I know them and their sacred work.

Rav Dovid Cohen is my connection to Har Sinai. I have had the indescribable *zechus* to learn with him for all these years as he has been to me a rebbi, father, *moreh derech*, sounding board, and *posek*. May he and his wife Rebbetzin Leah see *nachas* from all their descendants.

My dear friend Yaakov Salomon is among the most talented and accomplished people I know. I treasure his unconditional friendship and his wise counsel, which often guides me in my *drashos*.

Once again Eli Kroen has displayed his artistic brilliance with a stunning cover. I thank Mr. Joel Berkowitz for the use of his photograph of the New West End Synagogue in Bayswater, England. He has photographed more than 1000 synagogues the world over.

Mendy Herzberg shepherded this book from start to finish. Miss Rivky Plittman typeset the manuscript; Mrs. Estie Dicker provided technical assistance; Mrs. Faygie Weinbaum and Mrs. Esther Feierstein diligently proofread. I thank them all for their help in producing this volume.

I thank Imanuel Natanelov for relieving me of a great deal of the driving during my hectic days; because of him, I am able to use the precious hours spent traveling to write these speeches.

My wife Miriam is the anchor of my life. I thank the *Ribono Shel Olam* that I love what I do, be it performing a *bris*, writing a story, or giving a *drashah*. At times my commitments feel as if they will overwhelm me. Because she efficiently manages all aspects of our home, I can be available to do what I do. My gratitude toward her is boundless.

May my wife and I see *nachas* and *berachah* from our dear children, precious grandchildren, and, *b'ezras Hashem*, cherished great-grandchildren and may you see the same from yours.

שָׁמַע ה׳ תְּחִנָתִי ה׳ תְּפִלָתִי יִקָח

Paysach Krohn   Chai Cheshvon 5774
Kew Gardens, NY 11418   October 2013

> The publisher takes this opportunity to thank Mr. Robert Vegh for his longtime friendship, and for his assistance in initially locating the appropriate photograph gracing the cover of this book.

A Life
of
Elevation

Being a Blessing

We are living in a time of crisis. Jews throughout the world are suffering. But a Jew is never allowed to be broken. If he finds himself in a difficult spot, he must seek encouragement to build himself up. When *Klal Yisrael* is in a precarious position, we must join together to be *mechazek* one another. The question is: How can we encourage one another, or ourselves, when the situation seems so dire?

Anyone who has survived a national or personal tragedy should realize that survival is a blessing, and being together with other Jews is a blessing.

In the beginning of *Parashas Lech Lecha*, Hashem speaks to Avraham Avinu. In addition to telling him to leave the house of his father, Hashem tells him, וֶהְיֵה בְּרָכָה, *and you shall become a blessing* (*Bereishis* 12:2). According to Rabbi Samson Raphael Hirsch, this is a directive. It is not, as many people mistakenly believe, a promise. It does not mean that Hashem is promising to bless Avraham with fame and wealth. Rather, Rav Hirsch says, Hashem is instructing Avraham in how to live. Avraham is to "become a blessing" by giving *chizuk*, inspiration, and happiness to others. He is to make himself into someone who brings blessing to others.

Let me give you a perspective on what you really are and what you can accomplish.

Being a Blessing

Each of us has experienced challenges and difficulties. Nobody gets away scot free. That's what *galus* is all about. If you think someone else has it easy, that their life is perfect, that's just because you don't know what their life is really like. Nobody has a perfect, easy life.

Think of a challenge that you have overcome, whether it was financial, emotional, or physical. You survived it. Now you can go out and look for someone experiencing a similar challenge, put your arm around that person, and tell him that you understand how he feels because you went through it too. Share with him whatever tactics and support you used.

If you have never (*baruch Hashem*) had a heart attack, you have no right to enter a cardiac unit and reassure patients that they will be fine. You aren't a prophet, you're not the doctor, and you don't know how they feel. But if you have survived a heart attack, then you *are* the person who can — and should — go to the hospital and tell cardiac patients your experience, what helped, what didn't.

If you have never experienced a long period of unemployment, if you have never gone through your savings because you had no income for so long, then you won't understand your neighbor who is ashamed to come to shul because he can't afford an *aliyah*, much less make tuition payments. You won't understand the man who can't *even* get an interview because he's been out of work for too many years. But someone who finally did find a job, someone who rebuilt himself financially, can speak to that neighbor.

Many people are struggling to find a *shidduch*. Some women are frantic that their daughters are so old — already 22! — and not married yet. You may know that I helped push the idea that boys date girls older than they are, and *baruch Hashem*, it's taking off. Girls come back from seminary thinking they are Rachel Imeinu, and they need some time to recover. Older girls make better wives, better mothers, and better money. But a girl who got married at the age of 28 should be calling other girls and telling them not to worry, not to settle, not to rush. She can tell them to wait, as she did, until they meet the right one. She should be giving *chizuk* to other girls still looking.

When you were in those straits, didn't you welcome *chizuk*? So many people around us are broken. They don't need you to break them further; they need you to build them up. Make whoever comes into your life feel special.

We may face a different type of challenge, as well. Sometimes we need to be a blessing for ourselves. We may be going through a difficult time and need *chizuk*. The best thing is to give *chizuk* to yourself, to inspire yourself with the courage to continue despite your difficulties. Sometimes you might need to go to a Rav or a therapist. There's nothing wrong with going to a therapist; they can sometimes be very helpful.

Recently, a young man visited my home and shared an emotional experience. He had been through a traumatic divorce and felt destroyed. It had taken him many years to find a *shidduch* and after he finally married, it was over in less than a year. Now he had to start all over again. He had spoken to many people and gone to many *rabbanim* and therapists for help in getting his life back on track, but nothing seemed to work. Then one night he heard this insight from a Rav:

> The Rebbe Reb Zisha was once asked what he thought about as he said the *berachah* of שֶׁעָשָׂה לִי כָּל צָרְכִּי, *He provides for all my needs*. This refers to having shoes. Shoes are a real blessing. Without them, we can't go to shul, to school, to work, or to shop. Indeed the *Shulchan Aruch* (O.C. 41:1) writes that originally, before the *berachos* were organized to be said in the order we follow today, one recited this blessing when donning his shoes. Reb Zisha was so poor, he didn't own shoes. He was too poor even to borrow shoes. So what did he think about during this *berachah*?
>
> Reb Zisha answered, "Imagine that a king had a very expensive suit. He wanted to sell it, so he offered it at a much lower price than he had spent. If a man

were to try it on and it was a little too big, he could get a tailor to take it in. No problem. If it were too small, the tailor could let it out. But if the king wanted to sell a pair of his shoes, and they were a little too big or a little too small, the man could not take them to a shoemaker to adjust the size. Shoes have to fit exactly. That is the meaning of this *berachah*. Whatever situation I am in, it was designed to fit me exactly, like a pair of shoes."

Reb Zisha was not thinking about shoes. He was thinking about the concept of shoes. We have to realize that whatever difficulties we experience are a test designed specifically for each one of us. Hashem wants to know how we will relate to Him in difficult times. Don't focus on the negative. Don't forget it, but don't think only of your suffering. Focus on the positive. Focus on what you can do because of your experience.

Sharing the Burden ...

The *Mishnah* in *Avos* 6:6 is very important. It tells us all the different paths by which a person can acquire Torah. The 37th path is, נוֹשֵׂא בְעֹל עִם חֲבֵרוֹ, *carrying the burden of his friend*. The *Tiferes Yisrael* (note 103) elaborates that there are four ways to carry our friends' burdens. The first two are obvious, but the other two bear discussion.

The first is טִרְחַת הַגּוּף, *physical labor*. If you see an older person building a *sukkah*, help him build it, put on the *schach*, hang the decorations, etc. You see someone having trouble changing a tire, go help. Your friend can't find a babysitter? Go and watch their kids. That's giving physical assistance. The second method is הוֹצָאוֹת מָמוֹן, *financial assistance*. Help your friend get a job or a loan. Those two we can readily understand.

The third category is בְּצַעַר נַפְשׁוֹ; literally, "the pain of the soul." Your soul should feel your friend's pain. I believe it means you should *daven* for them.

Some of you are old enough to remember 1976. It was a great year in America, the bicentennial year, when America turned 200 years old. Every day there was another form of celebration, especially on July 4. At every *bris* I did in that year, I gave the baby a red-white-and-blue *yarmulke*.

Do you remember what else happened on July 4, 1976? The week before, on June 27, a plane was hijacked out of Israel and taken to Entebbe Airport in Uganda. The country was headed by Idi Amin, a *rasha merusha*, who threatened to kill every Jew on the plane. Everyone in *Eretz Yisrael* knew someone who knew someone who was on that plane. Everyone was nervous, because Amin was crazy enough to do it. He had already killed tens of thousands of Ugandans. In *Eretz Yisrael*, they decided to make a *yom tefillah*, a day of *davening*. It was to be held at Mirrer Yeshivah, led by Rav Chaim Shmulevitz. Rav Chaim was quite old by then and lived in a small apartment right across from the *beis midrash*.

Rabbi Moshe Zucker, who was a *talmid* in Mir at the time, told me that Rav Chaim waited until the *beis midrash* was full before coming out. He paused at the door, looked around the crowded *beis midrash*, and, overcome by emotion, entered and took a seat — and cried. Everyone was silent, watching and listening to him. Finally, he rose and walked over to the *aron hakodesh*. He kissed it, turned around, looked at the people, and again began to cry. Dramatically, he said one sentence, "*Daven* as if it was your father or your mother or your brother or your sister on that plane!"

That is how you are supposed to *daven*. The next time you say "*Refa'einu*" for someone, pretend it's your family member with an incurable illness. The next time you *daven* in "*Baruch Aleinu*" for someone's *parnassah*, pretend it's your brother who has nine kids and no income and who is embarrassed to show his face in public. The next time you *daven* for an elderly acquaintance, pretend he is your own father who is in a nursing home and cannot walk unassisted. Think about each person whose name you are saying.

Why does Hashem answer our *tefillos*? Because He cares about us. If He sees us *daven*, and sees our sincere pain for a friend, He sees our goodness and He will help the friend for our sake. When a Rebbe *davens* for someone, it is not magic. Hashem loves *tzaddikim*, and when the *tzaddikim daven* for us they are in genuine pain because of our situation. Hashem will answer their *tefillos*. We might not be worthy, but our *tzaddikim* are.

So when we *daven*, we have to show Hashem that we are in pain. We can't just read off names with no emotion. It would seem to me it's better to *daven* for two or three people as you envision their suffering and pain rather than to rattle off 25 names as though you are reading a roll call. Imagine yourself or a loved one in the same situation.

———❖———

The fourth element is, כְּשֶׁחָסֵר שֶׁכֶל לַחֲבֵירוֹ בְּעִנְיָינִים זְמַנִּיִּים אוֹ נִצְחִיִּים, לֹא יָחוּשׁ מִלְּהַטְרִיחַ אֶת עַצְמוֹ לְיַעֲצוֹ, *When your friend is missing wisdom, temporarily or eternally, don't hesitate to give advice.* If someone needs advice in matters of *ruchnius* or *gashmius*, help him get it. Giving advice is one aspect of feeling the pain of another.

I was once asked by Partners in Torah to speak in Los Angeles. Rabbi Dovid Schustal also spoke, and he said something incredible. He said that he himself had a learning partner: his own second cousin, who was married to a non-Jew.

What about our cousins? When was the last time you called your non-*frum* cousin? Their souls are waiting! Eventually, Rav Schustal's cousin became *frum*. Don't give up on your non-religious relatives. Sometimes it takes years to see the effect you may be having, but you have to be there for them. *Kiruv* is not only for "professionals." If someone is lacking in *ruchnius*, you have to help them.

Eishes Chayil

How will we react to life's difficulties? We must react with constant faith; still *davening*, still doing *mitzvos* just as we did before.

It always puzzled me why in *"Eishes Chayil"* it says nothing about lighting candles Friday night. Isn't that the quintessential *mitzvah* for women? Actually, though, candles and women are mentioned in verse 9: טָעֲמָה כִּי טוֹב סַחְרָהּ, לֹא יִכְבֶּה בַלַּיְלָה נֵרָהּ, *She senses that her business is good, and her candle does not go out at night.* She knows what she is doing is important and she works diligently late into the night.

It occurred to me that one can understand the *pasuk* in a different way. "Night" also refers to a time when a situation is dark and full of problems. The great woman does not lose her light, her upbeat attitude, when things get dark. Men are convinced that they are the strong ones, but really it is the women who are. They determine the attitude in the house. Men can be broken for many reasons, but if the woman stays upbeat and cheerful, then the house will stay a happy place. And so I say to all of the women who have gathered here, don't let your candle go out in times of crisis. Remain enthusiastic, remain cheerful, be there for your household. You can do that better for your husband than he can for you. You can do it for your children.

Remember Their Pain

I would like to mention another group whose members have become a blessing to all of us by their shining example: Holocaust survivors. Have you ever noticed elderly people, some of them bent over with age and infirmity, and thought, *Look what they went through, and they are here*? Whatever they experienced, they are here, part of the community. When you see an elderly person, it is hard to imagine that they were ever young and vibrant. But look at all the Bais Yaakov students and *yeshivah bachurim* around us. When Holocaust survivors were only as young as these students, they went through such suffering. Yet they emerged still believing in Hashem.

I led a group of about 35 adults on a tour in Poland, organized by Ari Scharf of Project Mesorah. We stood there at the Auschwitz death camp, outside the barracks in the freezing cold, dressed in our warm coats with hoods and warm boots and warm gloves, and I said, "Don't go into the barracks yet. Stand here for a minute and think about how cold you are feeling, even dressed as you are. Imagine how it must have felt to someone standing out here in a lineup at 5 in the morning dressed in almost nothing, or to someone working in the fields in one thin piece of clothing. We are going to leave here soon and get on a comfortable heated bus to a nice warm hotel, with lots of warm water to wash with and cold water to drink and we're going to eat a warm, filling meal. Here in the camps, people had barely any water. Some used their scarce ration of water to wash *netilas yadaim*, rather than to drink. They suffered through so much, yet they remained *frum*. What excuse can any of us have?"

We cannot forget them, because they are our inspiration. From these survivors came the society we have today. If we were to count all the descendants of the Holocaust survivors, the sum would be in the millions, *baruch Hashem*. Those survivors are greater than any of us can hope to be. They endured *Gehinnom*, yet they remained loyal Jews. They continue to *daven*, to do *mitzvos*, light *Shabbos* candles — they became a blessing for us all.

The Amazing Pesach Seder

Lady Amélie Jakobovits would tell this story every year at her *Seder* table.

> Gertie lived in Nuremberg, Germany in the 1930s. People realized that the atmosphere in the country was souring when one day the Nazis announced that every public building was required to fly the Nazi flag. Eventually Gertie and her family fled to Paris, where her father was able to get a job. This respite was short-lived, though, as her father was soon taken to serve in the French Army. The Germans invaded France, and many of the French people collaborated with them.
>
> Gertie, her mother, and her three siblings fled by train from town to town, trying to stay ahead of the Nazis. These trains were so crowded that often Gertie and her family members were pushed away from one another. Usually they managed to get back together quickly. But one day the crush was so great that Gertie was forced off the train and could not get back on. She could not find her mother or her siblings. No other train came that day. She went from street to street looking for a friendly face but could not find even one. She slept in the forest that night.
>
> In the morning, she *daven*ed, then decided to knock on the first door she came to and hope for the best. She reached a farmhouse. The farmer opened the door, looked at her, and said, "Come in, my child.

I understand where you are coming from. I will protect you. Go down to my cellar; there is another little girl there. I will bring you food."

This farmer was not Jewish, and he was risking his life for these children. Over the next few months, three more Jewish children found refuge in his cellar, with one small window near the ceiling. At first, they were afraid to talk to each other, but as time passed trust developed. Every day the farmer sent down food, always careful that the children would not be seen or heard by anyone else.

One morning one of the children realized that the sun coming through the window seemed much brighter than usual. Then they noticed grass growing near the cellar window. "Spring must be almost here! That means Pesach must be soon!"

But how could they make Pesach? They had no calendar and did not know the date, but they decided on a specific date on which they would celebrate. They asked the farmer for a newspaper, matches, some water, and some flour. They were going to make matzah for their *Seder*.

The farmer was able to give them everything right away, except the flour. A few days later, he did manage to get them a small amount. The boys lit the paper and the girls mixed the flour and water into dough. Remembering that it had to be done in 18 minutes, they tried to be quick. Then the girls held the dough in their hands above the little fire until the matzah was baked. It was an unusual-looking matzah, but it was theirs.

Then they began their *Seder*. They had no wine, no *Seder* plate, no silver candlesticks, no fancy tablecloth. They switched clothes with each other so that everyone would have "new" clothes for the holiday. The oldest boy made *Kiddush*, the youngest girl said the *Mah Nishtanah*; they sang "*Dayeinu*" and whatever else they could remember, through "*Chad Gadya.*" Then they *davened* that just as the Jews were freed from Egypt, they would be saved from their confinement.

When Lady Jakobovits told this story, she would say, "May the children of *Klal Yisrael* never experience that again, but may they merit to have a *Seder* as holy as the one those children made." The children each became a blessing: for each other at that time, and for us through their story.

iPad Generation

Many today are familiar with three popular gadgets: the iPod, the iPad, and the iPhone. One can't help but notice that these names are always written with a lowercase "i." This strikes me as no coincidence. The term "Me Generation" has often been used to describe the current generation, but I call it the "I Generation," because many people focus only on themselves — "I must, I want, I need." If so, they are indeed "lowercase" personalities.

> Many are familiar with three popular gadgets: the iPod, the iPad, and the iPhone. One can't help but notice that these names are always written with a lowercase "i."

However, I feel that we must transform ourselves: to take the selfishness represented by the lowercase "i" in iPod, iPad, and iPhone and elevate ourselves into a different type of person; into people who say, "I care, I help, and I do," and become uppercase personalities.

Remembering 9/11

There's a *pasuk* that strikes me as the antithesis of the "I Generation." However before I present it, I would like to share with you a very personal, painful story that led me to think about the message in the *pasuk*.

It was the day of 9/11. Most of us remember where we were on that terrible, tragic morning. I had performed a *bris* that morning and was on my way home to get ready to fly to Toronto to speak that evening when I received a frantic call from my wife, Miriam, telling me not to go to the airport.

"Why not?" I asked.

She told me to turn on the radio, that I wouldn't believe the news: a plane had just crashed into one of the Twin Towers and the airports were closed. I tuned in just as the second plane was crashing into the second tower. Tragically thousands of people would die that day.

Later that afternoon I received a call from Mrs. Rochel Reifer, principal of Shevach High School for girls in Queens. She asked that I come the next morning to speak to the students and give them a Torah perspective on the day's calamitous events. I told her that I was as frightened and confused as everyone else and didn't know what one could say. Mrs. Reifer appealed to me that I come (I had spoken in Shevach many times before), because, as she said, everyone needed the proper *hashkafah* about this cataclysmic day. Reluctantly, I consented. I then called *rabbanim* and looked in *sefarim* searching for ideas. By late evening I had some ideas. The next morning I went to Shevach.

As principal, Mrs. Reifer got up to speak first and said something incredible. I don't remember most of what I said that morning, but I will never forget her talk, which lasted only three or four minutes.

She said that at the end of *Aleinu*, after *v'al kein nikaveh*, there are three *pesukim* many people probably never notice. The first pasuk says, אַל תִּירָא מִפַּחַד פִּתְאֹם, *Do not be afraid of sudden terror*, וּמִשֹּׁאַת רְשָׁעִים כִּי תָבֹא, *and the calamity of evildoers when it comes* (*Mishlei* 3:25). In the second *pasuk*, it is as though the Jewish nation is speaking to those who plan evil against them: עֻצוּ עֵצָה וְתֻפָר, *Plan a conspiracy but it will be annulled*, דַּבְּרוּ דָבָר וְלֹא יָקוּם כִּי עִמָּנוּ קֵל, *Come up with your [evil] plans but they will not endure, for Hashem is with us* (*Yeshayahu* 8:10).

I was so taken by those *pesukim* as she applied them to the moment. *We should not be afraid of sudden terror … for Hashem is with us … evil plans will be annulled ….* That day I undertook to say those *pesukim* after *Aleinu* so that they are a constant source of *chizuk*.

Years later, in October 2006, a week after Succos, on a Friday night in Monsey, Mrs. Reifer was hit by a car and, tragically, lost her life. Her family, friends, colleagues, and students were completely devastated. I felt particularly crushed because I am on the board of Shevach High School and had helped hire Mrs. Reifer. They asked me to speak at the *sheloshim*.

After talking about how she was revered by all who knew her, I told the story of what had happened on the morning after 9/11 and how her words encouraged me to say daily the three *pesukim* after *Aleinu*. I suggested that as a *zechus* for the *neshamah* of Rochel Perl bas Yitzchok everyone should always say those *pesukim* after *Aleinu*.

However, I explained, that the third *pasuk* intrigued me. The prophet Yeshayahu (46:4) is quoting Hashem, who says the word "I" no less than five times: וְעַד זִקְנָה אֲנִי הוּא וְעַד שֵׂיבָה אֲנִי אֶסְבֹּל אֲנִי עָשִׂיתִי וַאֲנִי אֶשָּׂא וַאֲנִי אֶסְבֹּל וַאֲמַלֵּט.

What is the significance here? What does this *pasuk* mean?

וְעַד זִקְנָה אֲנִי הוּא : Don't worry, Hashem is telling us. *I will be with you until your old age,* I remain unchanged; I will protect you. וְעַד שֵׂיבָה, *when you become elderly,* אֲנִי אֶסְבֹּל, I will carry you. אֲנִי עָשִׂיתִי, *I made you,* וַאֲנִי אֶשָּׂא, *I will bear you,* וַאֲנִי אֶסְבֹּל, *and I will carry you,* וַאֲמַלֵּט, *and I will save you.*

Hashem is teaching us what "I" is all about; that is the "I" that we have to become: I care, I do, and I will help. It is the antithesis of the "I Generation." In my *siddur* I have the repeated words אֲנִי underlined. When I say this verse three times a day, I try to remember the care and concern I should have for others. I believe that none of us should ever forget to say this small paragraph in our *davening* after *Aleinu*. It will help us focus on how we relate to others.

Moshe and Aharon

Let me share with you three stories that reflect what it means to be selfless, to care for others.

Imagine this scene. Moshe is beside the burning bush and Hashem says, "וְאֶשְׁלָחֲךָ אֶל פַּרְעֹה וְהוֹצֵא אֶת עַמִּי בְנֵי יִשְׂרָאֵל מִמִּצְרָיִם, *I will send* you to Pharaoh to take Bnei Yisrael out of Mitzrayim" (*Shemos* 3:10). Hashem is giving Moshe the most important job in history. What does Moshe say? "מִי אָנֹכִי, *Who am I?* [i.e., I'm not worthy]" (ibid 3:11).

Chazal (Rashi, ibid. 4:10) teach that Hashem and Moshe debated this for seven days! Moshe insisted that he wasn't capable of speaking and so Hashem told him, "מִי שָׂם פֶּה לָאָדָם, *Who makes a mouth for man?*" (ibid. 4:11). Still, Moshe refuses. Why? Because he wants Hashem to send his brother Aharon instead of him.

The *Midrash* explains (see Rashi, ibid. 4:14) that Moshe was concerned that because Aharon was the elder brother, he might feel hurt that his younger brother was given this important job and he wasn't. Incredibly, Moshe is commanded to undertake the greatest role in history, yet what is on his mind is that his older brother might be upset by it!

In wrath, Hashem tells Moshe that he just does not understand the nature of his brother. Aharon will actually be thrilled: וְגַם הִנֵּה הוּא יֹצֵא לִקְרָאתֶךָ וְרָאֲךָ וְשָׂמַח בְּלִבּוֹ, *he is going out to meet you and when he sees you he will rejoice in his heart* (ibid. 4:14).

Think about it. If your younger brother or sister suddenly received tremendous recognition, would you be happy for him/her? If your younger brother suddenly became rich and famous, would you be overjoyed or would you feel a little jealousy? *Why not me? I'm older, smarter, better.*

But that's not what Moshe felt. He worried about his older brother feeling bad. Hashem had to tell him that, to the contrary, Aharon would feel proud and happy. As a matter of fact, *Chazal* (*Shabbos* 139a) teach us that because Aharon had genuine heartfelt happiness for his brother, he merited that the *Choshen* rested over his heart.

Aharon was not a member of the "I Generation." He was happy when someone even younger than he had such a vital task to accomplish. Moshe was not a member of the "I Generation." He was worried about an older brother's feelings.

The Beis Yosef and the Rema

The second story took place in the 16th century. The Beis Yosef, Rav Yosef Caro, was born in Spain in 1488. In 1492, he and his family fled to Turkey; they eventually settled in *Eretz Yisrael*. He died in 1575 at the age of 87.

In the same generation, in the city of Krakow, Poland, another great Jew was born. His name was Rabbi Moshe Isserles, the Rema. Tragically, he lived a very short life. He was born in 1530 and died 1572, only 42 years old.

Rav Yosef Caro wrote the *Shulchan Aruch*, codifying all laws pertaining to our daily lives, which include daily *mitzvos*, *Shabbos*, *Yomim Tovim*, *kashrus*, marriage, business, etc., stating the final *psak halachah* in each situation so that everyone could know how to live as a Jew. However, as the *gadol* of the Sefardim, his work represented the view of Sefardic Jewry. Ashkenazic Jewry had different traditions in many cases, which resulted in different final halachic viewpoints.

Meanwhile, in Krakow, the Rema was also writing. He didn't know the Beis Yosef had written a *Shulchan Aruch*, but he also wanted to record and simplify the full compendium of Torah law. After putting enormous effort into his work, he heard what Rav Yosef Caro had done. When he found out, he had a choice to make. The Rema could have said to himself, *Ashkenazim are not going to use the Shulchan Aruch of the Beis Yosef. It's for the Sefardim. I'll publish my own Shulchan Aruch separately and that will benefit the Ashkenazic communities.*

But that was *not* what he did. Instead, he decided that since Rav Yosef Caro had called his work *Shulchan Aruch*, "The Set Table," he would present his compendium as glosses on the *Shulchan Aruch* and call it *HaMapah*, "The Tablecloth."

By doing so, the Rema, in his genius and selflessness, united the entire *Klal Yisrael*. Today, every Jew, whether Sephardic or Ashkenazic, learns the same *Shulchan Aruch*. The Beis Yosef's words are the basic component of the *Shulchan Aruch* and if there is any difference in Ashkenazic law, the Rema adds the words (printed in a different typeface) and records the Ashkenazic ruling.

He did this because he was not a member of the "I Generation." He was content to be an addendum to the work of Rav Yosef Caro. To him, it was more important that *Klal Yisrael* be united in their Torah study than that he should have the glory of knowing he wrote an entire *Shulchan Aruch*.

Rav Pam

The third story took place at the end of the 1950s when Rav Avraham Pam lived in the East New York section of Brooklyn. There was a shul there called the Young Israel of New Lots. Rav Pam was not a *rav* in any of the shuls there, but every night he gave a *shiur* to the *baalei batim* in those neighborhoods who would gather in the Young Israel.

One freezing cold, snowy night Rav Pam was putting on his coat when his rebbetzin asked him where he was going. He told her he was going to give his *shiur*. She said no one would be going out in a snowstorm on a freezing cold night like that. Rav Pam said that he had a responsibility to go even if only one person would be there.

So he bundled up in his coat, put on his gloves and galoshes, and walked eight long blocks to the Young Israel of New Lots. He opened the door and there was one man inside, Benzion Rephael Lasker. He wasn't even one of the regulars. Interestingly, not one of the regulars came. Rav Pam asked Mr. Lasker why he had come this particular night.

"Rav Pam," he answered, "I knew you would come. And if you were coming, I knew it would not be nice for you to walk so far and not be able to give the *shiur*."

Both Rav Pam and Mr. Lasker were selfless. Rav Pam thought about that one person who might come, Mr. Lasker thought of Rav Pam. They thought about others besides themselves. They were people who were not part of the "I Generation."

Exhibit A

The question is: How do we become unselfish, caring people? How will we broaden our perspectives? How can we become people of "I care, I do, and I help"?

I think one of the ways is working on our *hakaras hatov*, our recognition of all the wonderful things people do for us, and say "thank you" to them. Then all of a sudden we realize that we're not in this world alone.

One of the exercises I want you to try is to make an extra effort to thank people as often as possible this week. Text them, even though that is the most impersonal way; or email them, or call them, or write a letter (not that anybody does that anymore). The idea is that there are many people out there who do favors for you. If you go to a store and the salesperson was wonderful to you, write a thank-you note. If you had a family *simchah* and the caterer was wonderful, write him a note or call to thank him. Everyone from the plumber and the computer technician to the teacher and rebbi — if they helped you, write a letter or make a call and say thank you.

> A lawyer came up to me and said, "Rabbi Krohn, I have to show you something. You were exhibit A in a court case."

Let me tell you what can happen when you write a letter. I once came to a shul to perform a *bris* when a lawyer approached me and said, "Rabbi Krohn, I have to show you something. You were exhibit A in a court case."

"Oh really?" I said.

He told me that he's a lawyer for airline employees. A few years ago, a clerk — let's call him Donald — was behind the counter at LaGuardia Airport checking people in who were going to Canada on a holiday weekend. There was a mad rush and people were pushing and shoving. Suddenly, a man ran up from the middle of the line, yelling, "Put me on right away!"

"Who do you think you are?" Donald said.

"I'm a major shareholder of this airline and you had better put me on the flight right now."

Donald replied, "Please get back in line."

The passenger let out some nasty, off-color words, and Donald replied with some equally nasty, off-color words, until suddenly it occurred to Donald that the fellow might really be someone important. He paused and said, "Okay, come here and give me your passport."

However, in grabbing the passport quickly with disgust, Donald ripped half the page! The man was furious. When he came back home, he put in a grievance and Donald was fired. He really was an important person to the airline.

Donald took his case to this lawyer. The lawyer told him that *every* airline employee has a file and asked if there were any letters from customers in his file. Donald didn't know, so they went through his file and sure enough there was a letter … from me!

I don't remember writing it, but it was my handwriting on my stationery, and I suddenly remembered what had happened years earlier. I was trying to get to Toronto, and for some reason the flight was canceled 10 minutes before boarding was to begin. There was an uproar, but Donald, the man behind the counter, was cool as a cucumber. He cracked jokes and calmed everybody down until they got everyone on different planes. I did not write anything exceptional, just a few lines such as, "Donald was wonderful. He has a great sense of humor. He calmed a potentially volatile situation."

That letter was exhibit A, and eventually he got his job back. To be sure there were many other exhibits in Donald's favor, but that thank-you letter surely helped Donald's cause.

A thank-you letter will not always have these dramatic results but it can make an impression on the recipient and can make you a better person, an "uppercase" person.

Let's make a commitment this week to thank people for something they have done for us. Don't wait to bump into them in the street. Call, write, email, or text them.

Paysach Fell on Succos

On Simchas Torah 2011 in *Eretz Yisrael*, I missed a step as I walked into the street, fell, and ripped the quadriceps in both my legs. I couldn't stand up. I came back to New York on a stretcher and was operated on in Manhattan's Hospital for Joint Diseases. *Baruch Hashem* I had a wonderful surgeon, Dr. Marc Silverman; a fabulous physical therapist, Adi Gedali; and a brilliant pain-control specialist, Dr. Isaac Pinter. However, I had to wear braces and use crutches for months.

While I was in the hospital, I decided to write down the names of every doctor, nurse, and orderly who was kind to me, and when I got home I wrote a letter to the director of the hospital listing them all individually. Two weeks later, I received a letter from him. He had sent a copy of my letter to each of the 26 people I had mentioned. They were so happy that someone took the time to say, "Thank you."

My hospital experience also reminded me how at times people unwillingly can be insensitive. A joke at an inappropriate time is not appreciated and sometimes painful. Somebody called me while I was hospitalized and said, "You know, it was really *kedai* (well worth it) that you fell in *Eretz Yisrael*. Because now people can say, 'Paysach fell on Succos!'"

> **Somebody called me and said, "You know, it was really *kedai* that you fell in *Eretz Yisrael*. Because now people can say, 'Paysach fell on Succos!'"**

Today I can laugh at that comment, but when I was in the hospital, being shot up with morphine, and taking injections so no infection would set in, this was not funny. How many times do we make insensitive jokes knowing that everyone will laugh — except for that one person who is the butt of the joke?.

We have to be better than that. We can't be lowercase people, people of the "I Generation." Next time when you say *Aleinu*, say that "I" *pasuk* — where *Hashem* says, "I care, I'll save, I'll protect" — with *kavannah*. Say it and really mean it.

Let's become uppercase people, people who care for and are sensitive to each other.

Making Tefillah Meaningful

M^{any} years ago, when I was a *talmid* in Yeshiva Torah Vodaath, a young married fellow, Rabbi Shmuel Rubenstein, wrote and illustrated a magnificent pamphlet on *tefillin*. He came to the *beis medrash* to sell it to the rebbis and *talmidim*. Nowadays there are numerous books and pamphlets about *tefillin*, but his was among the first. He produced pamphlets on many other subjects as well. Decades later, after I began writing the *Maggid* books, he passed away. During the *shivah*, his wife told me a remarkable story about him.

When he was about 11 years old, in the early 1950s, his father passed away. His mother, Pesha Rubenstein, was raising him as best she could and wanted him to have a yeshivah education. There were not many yeshivos in those days, so although they lived in the Bronx she sent him to Torah Vodaath, all the way in Brooklyn. What a schlep every day!

He never complained about the trip, but one day he was not feeling well and she took him for a checkup. The doctor told his mother that Shmuel had developed rheumatic fever, which affects the nervous system and the heart. The doctor advised her that she could no longer allow young Shmuel to travel such a distance every day; the trip would kill him. She replied that she would not send her son to public school.

"Look," he said, "I'm your doctor, not your rabbi. I can't tell you what to do, but I'm telling you your son's heart can't take a round trip like this every day."

The woman looked around for a yeshivah closer to home and discovered that the Bobover Rebbe, Rav Shlomo Halberstam, had recently arrived from Europe and had opened a small yeshivah in Manhattan. She was not *Chassidish*, but she figured that such a yeshivah was better than public school, so she enrolled her son there. In those days, there were not many *bachurim* in Bobov, and this boy became like a son to the Rebbe and the Rebbe became like a father to him.

Shmuel's bar mitzvah was approaching, and so was Succos. Mrs. Rubinstein did not have much money, but she bought him a *lulav* and *esrog*. It was a kosher set, but one night Shmuel got to thinking that the Rebbe must have a really special *lulav* and *esrog*. Maybe the Rebbe would let him make a *berachah* on his set? But then, he thought, *What if I drop the Rebbe's esrog? That would be terrible!*

After agonizing for a while, he decided he would go to the Rebbe the next morning. When he arrived, the Rebbe was surprised to see him because it was not a school day. Shmuel told the Rebbe why he had come.

"You traveled all the way just for that? You are a dear child," the Rebbe said. Glowingly, he then took his *lulav* and *esrog* from his desk and handed them to Shmuel, explaining, "You are supposed to take the *esrog* first upside down, along with the *lulav*, and then turn the *esrog* right side up after you make the *berachah*."

The boy was so nervous that as he held the *lulav* in one hand and tried to turn the *esrog* with the other, he dropped the *esrog*. It rolled away and hit the wall,

The boy was so nervous that as he held the *lulav* in one hand and tried to turn the *esrog* with the other, he dropped the *esrog*. It rolled away and hit the wall. Shmuel just wanted the earth to open up and swallow him. His worst fear had come true.

The Rebbe watched his *esrog* hit the wall. Then he picked it up and brought it over to the boy. "Shmuel, look," he said. "The *pitom* did not break. This is a *siman* (sign; message) from *Shamayim* (Heaven) to you; Hashem is sending you a message."

"What message, Rebbe?" Shmuel asked.

"You know that the *arba minim* (the Four Species) represent different parts of the body. The *lulav* represents the spine, the *hadassim* represent the eyes, the *aravos* represent the mouth, and the *esrog* represents the heart. Shmuel, you have rheumatic fever. You are worried that your heart will not be strong. Hashem is showing you that the *esrog*, which represents the heart, is strong. It fell but the *pitom* did not break. You too will be strong, just like the *esrog*."

Shmuel was stunned. What had been a nightmare 20 seconds ago had suddenly become an amazing blessing.

Shmuel never told anyone this story — until 32 years later, when he was sitting in his *succah* with his own family. Why on that day? Because the word לֵב, "heart," has the *gematria* (numerical value) of 32. His heart had been strong for 32 years.

Three weeks later, he died.

That is when his family called me. They understood the Rebbe's message. The Gemara (*Taanis* 2a) asks, "How do you serve Hashem with all your heart? Through prayer." The service of the heart is prayer. Rabbi Shmuel Rubenstein learned — and epitomized — the real meaning of being strong of heart, of connecting to Hashem through the service of the heart. We, too, have to learn how to make our hearts strong, because that is how we connect to Hashem.

Davening by Rote

Many years ago, when the first large Siyum HaShas was held in Madison Square Garden, two unforgettable things happened. Let me mention the second thing first. Rabbi Moshe Sherer had arranged that an electrical sign would flash right after the program, "Only one united *minyan!*" He did not want it to be like at a wedding when there are 20 different little *minyanim*. He wanted the 19,000 people there to *daven* altogether. And *daven* they did as I never heard people *daven* before. To hear 19,000 men, women, and children crying out in unison, "*Shema Yisrael*" was astounding! The whole evening would have been worthwhile just for that.

However, earlier, the Philadelphia Rosh Yeshivah, Rav Elya Svei, quoted something from his Rebbe, Rav Aharon Kotler, that was remarkable: "When you *daven*, you are talking to Hashem. When you learn, Hashem is talking to you." In other words, when you *daven* you are telling Hashem what you want from Him. We need *chachmah*, we need *refuah*, we need *parnassah*, etc. But when we are learning, be it *Chumash*, Halachah, Gemara, etc., Hashem is telling us what He needs and wants from us. If that is the case, why is it that so often our bodies are here but our minds are someplace else?

It could be because we do it so often that it is easy to become rote. If you are *davening* three times a day, that's more than 1,000 times a year. Doing something 1,000 times a year is going to make it less interesting. Additionally, we are supposed to make 100 *berachos* a day, 365 days a year; that's 36,500 *berachos* a year. The Gemara says there are four things for which we need *chizuk* or they will fall by the wayside, and one of those things is *tefillah*. [Interestingly the Gemara is on *Berachos* 32b, Daf לֵב (heart), and the service of the heart is *tefillah*.]

Rav Aharon Kotler once asked (*Mishnas Rav Aharon* 2:92), Why do we have to *daven*? Doesn't Hashem know what we need? The reason we *daven* is not to tell Hashem what we need. It is to strengthen our recognition that everything comes from Hashem. *Davening* is for us. When we *daven* that Hashem send us *parnassah* or *refuah* or a *shidduch*, that means we are giving ourselves *chizuk* and teaching ourselves that only through Hashem do all these things come.

The Satmar Rebbe, Rav Yoel Teitelbaum, was a guest at a wedding. A *badchan* was entertaining the crowd there and asked the Rebbe permission to imitate him. The Rebbe gave permission and the *badchan* took a *tallis* from his bag, covered his head with it, and started imitating the Rebbe perfectly. Everyone was laughing — except for the Rebbe. The Rebbe sat there, astonished, then suddenly began to cry.

The **badchan** took a **tallis** from his bag, covered his head with it, and started imitating the Rebbe perfectly. Everyone was laughing — except for the Rebbe. The Rebbe sat there, astonished, then suddenly began to cry.

The *badchan*, a devoted *chassid* of the Rebbe, was watching the crowd and did not immediately realize that the Rebbe had been so affected. When he did, he stopped and apologized profusely, saying he had never intended to make the Rebbe cry.

"It's not you," said the Rebbe, "I was watching you, and you were imitating me so exactly that it occurred to me that sometimes, when I am *davening*, I am only imitating myself."

Sometimes we come to shul, but our minds are not focused there. We can't stand there doing nothing, though, so we *shuckle* (sway) and we say the words; we look involved, but we are just imitating ourselves. If the Rebbe can admit that sometimes even he was only imitating himself, what can we say for ourselves? How many times do we go to shul and just go through the motions?

Two Suggestions

How are we going to improve? How are we going to change?

There are two ways that our *tefillos* can be answered long before we even get into the shul. We have just started saying, מַשִּׁיב הָרוּחַ וּמוֹרִיד הַגֶּשֶׁם, *He makes the wind blow and He makes the rain descend,* because in *Eretz Yisrael* if it does not rain at this time there will be no crops. The Gemara (*Taanis* 25b) tells us about a severe drought in *Eretz Yisrael*. The people were *davening*, but it did not rain. The people went to Rabbi Eliezer to ask him to *daven* for rain. Rabbi Eliezer *daven*ed, but it did not help. Then the people went to Rabbi Akiva. Rabbi Akiva composed the *tefillah* "Avinu Malkeinu" and *daven*ed for rain, and the rain fell right away. Everyone concluded that Rabbi Akiva must have been a greater *tzaddik* than Rabbi Eliezer!

Then a *Bas Kol* (voice from heaven) announced, "It is not because one is greater than the other, but because Rabbi Akiva is *maavir al midosov*, he overlooks insults." If someone hurts him, he does not try to take revenge; he looks away. Someone who looks away when others hurt or insult him merits that Hashem looks away when he does something wrong.

All of us have done things we wish Hashem would overlook. We *daven* to Him, but if He looks at all we have done, He may not answer our *tefillos*. Nevertheless, Hashem says if you look away I will also look away.

The second way to success in *tefillah* is told by the Chofetz Chaim. He writes that when a person *daven*s or learns, every word that is said creates an angel, and that angel brings that word up to *Shamayim*.

Say you want to build a table, but your hammer has a loose handle. You can do the job, but not properly. Similarly, your mouth is a tool. Many people, writes the Chofetz Chaim, mistakenly believe that only *lashon hara* makes one's mouth impure. If you say an uncalled-for hurtful word to your spouse or to your child or to a co-worker or to a friend, then you cannot be building perfect *malachim*, because your mouth is an imperfect tool. For example, if someone starts an argument, or becomes angry, or makes fun of another person, it will be almost impossible for their *tefillos* to be answered.

If we are careful with our mouths, we build people up rather than breaking them down. Then we will build holy messengers who will take our *tefillos* directly to *Shamayim*, so Hashem will be able to answer us.

The Problem With Lateness

One of the most important things for success in *tefillah* is getting to the *minyan* on time. When a person is one of the first 10 to come to shul, thereby forming a *minyan*, he receives an additional special reward. Not only does he receive a reward for *davening* with a *minyan* but he gets an additional reward equaling the amount of *schar* that everyone else in shul receives for *davening* with a *minyan* (see *Berachos* 47b).

There is an amazing story of how one young man learned that lesson in a challenging way.

> He owned a store and opened it at 9 every morning. One day, at around 10 a.m., he smelled smoke. He ran downstairs and found the place on fire. He tried to put it out with his extinguisher, but it did not help. By the time he ran upstairs the fire had spread there too. Much of the merchandise was burning along with the building. By the time the fire department arrived, the place was gutted. They were able to hose down and save the store next door, but not his.
>
> A few days after the fire, the owner went to shul and told a friend that just a few days earlier a fellow

congregant had approached him and said, "You come to shul *every* day, but you always come late. Why?"

"What's the difference?" he had replied. "At the end, I come, right?"

Now, however, he understood the problem with coming late: "Hashem showed me the difference. At the end, the fire department came, too. But it was too late."

A man had approached him and said, "You come to shul every day, but you always come late. Why?" "What's the difference?" he had replied. "At the end, I come, right?"

Hundreds of people have started coming to shul on time because of this story. One Shabbos, a man introduced himself to me as the store owner in this story. I hugged him and told him how many people have changed because of his story.

The first thing a person who wants his *tefillos* answered needs to know is to get to shul on time. You have to be there at the beginning. If you come late you'll be skipping so much of the *davening* or saying words at a pace that you can't possibly comprehend their meaning.

Thank You!

Chazal (*Sanhedrin* 94a) tell us something frightening. Hashem wanted to make Chizkiyahu HaMelech the *Mashiach*, but the angels complained that he did not deserve the honor. They argued that David HaMelech, who had said so much praise of Hashem, had not been appointed the *Mashiach*, so certainly Chizkiyahu, who was otherwise a very great person but who had not properly thanked Hashem, was not worthy. That teaches us a great lesson. Those who are *makir tov*, those who express gratitude, will help bring *Mashiach*.

We learn from here that one of the most important aspects of prayer is saying "thank you." And the place to say it, and feel it in our hearts, is during *Modim* in the *Shemoneh Esrei*. However, most of us fly through *Modim* without thinking. After all, it is near the end. And it is "only" thanking Hashem, not asking for anything.

That is the wrong attitude. We have to remember that we have so much good in this world. If you have a spouse, a house, children,

Making Tefillah Meaningful | 45 |

grandchildren, a job, etc., thank Him. מוֹדִים אֲנַחְנוּ לָךְ, *We thank You, Hashem*.

While it's true that each of us is lacking certain things, we must though focus on what we do have. Everybody has challenges. Hashem should help that all our challenges are only a passing problem and not something permanent, *chas v'shalom*. But whatever it is, we must look at the positive and thank Hashem. That is what David HaMelech says: פִּתְחוּ לִי שַׁעֲרֵי צֶדֶק אָבֹא בָם אוֹדֶה קָהּ, *Open for me the gates of righteousness [the gates of the beis medrash and the gates of the shul] and I will come and say thank You (Tehillim* 118:19).

I have a good friend, Rabbi Aryeh Rodin, in Dallas, Texas. Reb Aryeh learned in Yeshivas Chofetz Chaim, which has a wonderful training program. The *bachurim* stay in *kollel* for a certain amount of time; then they must go out and accomplish something for *Klal Yisrael*. That's why there are so many Chofetz Chaim *kollelim* all over, and so many of their *bachurim* are serving *Klal Yisrael* in different capacities in so many different towns and cities.

Reb Aryeh wanted to build a shul in North Dallas. He started it in his own home. Once, when he was preparing a class for adults in his living room, a stranger came to his house and introduced himself as Leonard Fruhman. He came to discuss religion. They talked for almost two hours. Mr. Fruhman was so impressed by their discussion that he told Reb Aryeh he was going to send him $2,000. A few weeks later, he sent, instead, $3,000. He started attending shul regularly, and encouraged his friends to go. Eventually, they helped raise enough money to build the Young Israel of North Dallas.

Unfortunately, Leonard Fruhman had never married, and when he was 49 he passed away suddenly of a massive heart attack. His mother stood up at the funeral and said, "I will match every penny that my son gave to this synagogue, because I am so grateful to Rabbi Rodin and to all of you in the community for what you did for my son." That day she gave the shul over $50,000 as *hakaras hatov*.

At the *sheloshim* memorial service, Rabbi Rodin got up to speak. He told the assemblage that the first time Leonard Fruhman had come to speak with him, he asked Leonard why he had chosen this little shul. Leonard answered that he had just returned from his first trip to

Eretz Yisrael. He had taken a tour of the country and on the last day the group went to the *Kosel.* He knew only his Hebrew name and *Shema Yisrael.* He saw people writing little notes and putting them in the cracks of the Wall, so he did also. He looked around and saw a praying man who looked so connected to Hashem. Leonard wished he could be connected to Hashem in that intense manner. He wanted to give the man some money, but he felt it wasn't proper because they were strangers, and the other man might feel uncomfortable. Therefore, when Leonard returned to Dallas, he went to the kosher bakery and asked the man behind the counter where he thought a man who prayed like the man at the *Kosel* prayed would choose to pray in Dallas. And the man told him he should go to Rabbi Rodin.

Imagine, continued Rabbi Rodin, when that man who was *davening* at the *Kosel* gets to *Shamayim.* He will be greeted as a *tzaddik,* and will be praised for building a shul in Dallas, which he might never have heard of. But it is true. He was a role model in his *davening,* which led to a man speaking to a rabbi, to getting his friends to go to shul, and to send their children to shul, which led to their becoming *frum* and sending their children to *talmidei Torah* and yeshivos and Bais Yaakovs.

And so that is the final lesson. We are all role models. When you *daven* in a shul, *beis medrash,* or yeshivah, don't think that people don't notice how you *daven.* They may not say anything to you, but they notice.

Going to shul is not only a privilege but a responsibility. We need to learn how to *daven,* and how to make sure others *daven* well too. If you *daven* aloud slowly and carefully, others will *daven* that way too. If you *daven* with your children near you and they, like you, take their *davening* seriously, others will do so too. If we come on time and *daven* from a *siddur,* others will do so as well. May Hashem help each of us learn how to make our *davening* meaningful so that it is easy for Him to answer our *tefillos.*

The Imperative of Kiruv

When we think of *kiruv*, we think of numerous great professional organizations. However, I feel that *kiruv* is not only for professionals. Each of us, regardless of the country we live in, is capable and, yes, even obligated to be involved in bringing our brothers and sisters closer to Hashem and *Yiddishkeit*.

The *Midrash (Yalkut Shimoni, Shmuel* 1:1) tells us that every year, Elkanah would take his family to be *oleh regel* by making the pilgrimage to the *Mishkan* in Shiloh. However, each year he would take a different route. One year he would travel the northern route, and when people asked him where he was headed, he would tell them he was on his way to celebrate the *Yom Tov* at Shiloh. He would invite them to come along and bring their friends and families. And indeed they came.

The following year he would travel the southern route and invite the families who lived along the way there to accompany him and his family to Shiloh. The year after that, he would travel yet another route where he once again inspired families to come along with him. Eventually everyone was *oleh regel*.

In reward, Hashem said to him, "Since you have influenced the masses to come close to Me, I will give you a child who will influence all of *Klal Yisrael* to come close to Me." That is how Elkanah merited being the father of the great prophet Shmuel; only because he made it a point to educate and be *mekaraiv* others.

We know that Avraham Avinu brought many of the men of his generation "*under the wings of the Shechinah.*" He taught and inspired them to believe in Hashem. Sarah did the same for the women. Rav Chaim Vital (*Shaar HaKedushah* 2:7) writes that Avraham became great in the merit of inspiring the masses. He then adds something frightening: "Every leader of every generation will either be punished or rewarded only because of how they inspired others [and brought them closer to Hashem]." Next he cites a *Zohar (Parashas Terumah)* which writes that if people would only know how important it is to go out and bring others to Torah and *mitzvos*, "They would run after it as one runs after life."

That is what *kiruv* is all about.

A Moroccan Father Returns

Rabbi Sholom Schwadron, *zt'l*, the Maggid of Yerushalayim, told me the following story. In a town north of Tel Aviv, there was a *madrich* (youth leader) who had a Shabbos group. This *madrich* inspired one of the secularly oriented teenage boys to attend a yeshivah in the Negev. However, the boy's father was very upset. He had come from Morocco where he had had a semblance of what a Torah life was, but in *Eretz Yisrael* he dropped everything. Reluctantly he agreed to let his son attend the yeshivah. His son, who loved his new surroundings, wrote him often, inviting him to spend Shabbos with him. However, the father always refused.

Finally, the father agreed to spend a day with his son in the yeshivah. He said he would come for the holiday of Shavuos, which in Israel is only one day. The son was so happy! His father would come and see what learning and Torah life were all about!

The father arrived, attended the festive night *seudah* with the boys, and then went to one of the community *shiurim* that was being given close to the yeshivah. He was told that after this night of learning, everyone would gather back in the huge *beis medrash* of the yeshivah where they would be celebrating with singing and dancing. Indeed, the father returned and joined the dancing with the students and staff of the yeshivah. It was a beautiful, warm experience.

After the dancing, the yeshivah did something unique. They recited the longest *perek* in *Tehillim*, 119, slowly and fervently. The *talmidim* and guests, including this man, were reading together. As he read, he began to get the chills. Every verse in that chapter makes a reference to the study of Torah or the observance of *mitzvos*. As one who spoke Hebrew, he understood most of the verses.

דֶּרֶךְ שֶׁקֶר הָסֵר מִמֶּנִּי
Remove from me the way of falsehood (v. 29).

פְּנֵה אֵלַי וְחָנֵּנִי
Turn to me and be gracious to me (v. 132).

פַּלְגֵי מַיִם יָרְדוּ עֵינָי עַל לֹא שָׁמְרוּ תוֹרָתֶךָ
My eyes shed rivers of tears because they did not keep Your Torah (v. 136).

קָרָאתִי בְכָל לֵב עֲנֵנִי ה׳
I called [to You] with all my heart, Hashem, answer me … (V. 145).

תְּהִי יָדְךָ לְעָזְרֵנִי
Let Your hand be ready to assist me (v. 173).

When they finished, the father suddenly became emotional and collapsed onto the floor. It caused quite a tumult. When he was revived, he insisted that he was fine. Everyone wanted to know what had caused his collapse. "It was the last *pasuk*," he told them, and he quoted: תָּעִיתִי כְּשֶׂה אֹבֵד בַּקֵּשׁ עַבְדֶּךָ כִּי מִצְוֹתֶיךָ לֹא שָׁכָחְתִּי, *I made a mistake, like a lost sheep; seek out Your servant, because I have not forgotten Your mitzvos (ibid., v. 176).*

Rav Moshe Mordechai Epstein, *zt'l*, the Rosh Yeshivah of Yeshivah Knesseth Yisrael in Slabodka, once gave a beautiful explanation of this *pasuk*. What is the difference, Rav Epstein asked, between losing a sheep and losing a wallet? If you lose a wallet, it stays in one place while you look for it. But when a sheep gets lost, it looks for the shepherd while the shepherd is searching for the sheep. The chances are greater that the sheep will be found, because both are searching.

That was David HaMelech's intent. Often when we make a mistake, we are like sheep, looking for our Master (in repentance) while our Master looks for us (to repent). That is what happened on that Shavuos in that yeshivah in the Negev. That man was looking for Hashem and Hashem, of course, was looking for him.

There are hundreds of thousands of Jews around the world who are searching, desperately, for some meaning in life. We must be there for them.

Sniffing Out the Inner Jew

Yeshayahu tells us about the qualities of *Mashiach*: וְנָחָה עָלָיו רוּחַ ה׳ רוּחַ חָכְמָה וּבִינָה רוּחַ עֵצָה וּגְבוּרָה רוּחַ דַּעַת וְיִרְאַת ה׳, *The spirit of G-d shall rest upon him; the spirit of wisdom and understanding; the spirit of counsel and might; the spirit of knowledge and of the fear of Hashem* (*Yeshayahu* 11:2-5). Then the *navi* adds, וַהֲרִיחוֹ בְּיִרְאַת ה׳; that is, *Mashiach* will be able to "smell out" fear of Hashem. What does that mean?

The prophet continues: וְלֹא לְמַרְאֵה עֵינָיו יִשְׁפּוֹט וְלֹא לְמִשְׁמַע אָזְנָיו יוֹכִיחַ, *Not with his eyes shall he judge, nor decide after the hearing of his ears*. He will not be swayed by how a person looks or by what a person says. He will understand that there is something to this person, no matter how long his hair might be or what he chooses to talk about. He will sniff him out. He will discern the inner Jew underneath.

I was once at a memorial service for a young woman. I was introduced to her family just prior to our *davening* Minchah. One of the boys saying *Kaddish* looked like and *davened* like a real *ben Torah*. Later, the boy told me about himself and his family. They were tennis stars, with their pictures often in the papers. Indeed, a brother had just won a championship. He showed me a family picture, but I didn't see him in it. Then he pointed: he was the one with long curly hair wearing a sweat suit. He, too, had been a tennis star. One would never guess it from his demeanor and dress that afternoon.

> I wondered how my friend who first was *mekaraiv* this boy recognized the G-d-fearing yeshivah student inside the tennis star. I would never have seen it.

I wondered how my friend who first was *mekaraiv* this boy recognized the G-d-fearing yeshivah student inside the tennis star. I would never have seen it.

I would have judged by what the boy looked like and by what he talked about: tennis. But a person in *kiruv* — professionally or otherwise — must have that quality of *Mashiach*. He must be able to sniff out *yiras Hashem*. He has to understand who a person is, disregarding the outer shell. He has to go straight to his heart.

Ben Buzi

In 1939, Rav Dovid Leibowitz, (the father of Rav Henoch Leibowitz) headed the Chofetz Chaim Yeshivah, originally on South 9th Street in the Williamsburg section of Brooklyn. It was the end of the Depression. The United States had not recovered financially and many were struggling. Rav Dovid could not pay the yeshivah's heating bill. It was so cold that the *talmidim* were not learning in the *beis medrash*, but rather in the kitchen where a big pot of soup on the stove sent out warm vapors.

Rav Leibowitz suggested to one of his beloved *talmidim*, R' Abba Zalka Gewirtz, that they go to Miami to try to raise funds. They reserved seats on a train — regular upright seats, not sleepers, because that would have cost extra — and set out on a Wednesday. They arrived on Friday and went directly to the home of one of their most prominent contacts, who happened to be a Rav.

When they met him, though, he abruptly said that he was too busy to help. He disregarded the prominence of Rav Dovid. The young *talmid* was incensed. His Rebbi had been humiliated, and they had been counting on this Rav to introduce them around the community. The Rebbi and *talmid* sat down outside the Rav's office. Abba Zalka turned to his Rosh Yeshivah and asked, "How can you take that terrible humiliation?"

"That wasn't humiliation," answered Rav Dovid. "That was honor."

Rav Dovid then told him a *Midrash* (*Vayikra* 2:8). The Torah tells us that Yechezkel was the son of Buzi, but בּוּזִי was not his father's real name. It comes from the word בּוּז, which means "embarrassment." Yechezkel was willing to embarrass himself for the sake of Torah. He did not care if he was shamed, as long as he was able to teach *Klal Yisrael*. He was thus memorialized in *Tanach* because of his greatness and was called Yechezkel ben Buzi.

"Now, we are Yechezkel ben Buzi's people," the Rosh Yeshivah said. "That's a great honor!"

That is what each of us has to know. Sometimes it is embarrassing or even humiliating to bring up the topic of religion, Hashem, or *mitzvos*. Sometimes we are looked upon as people from a different planet. But we must know we are Yechezkel ben Buzi's people, and we should be proud of it.

Rav Aharon Kotler, *zt'l*, in his *sefer Mishnas Rav Aharon* 3:176, writes, "The world exists only because of those who feel a responsibility for the community, not those who say they will do their *mitzvos* and not involve themselves with the rest of the people." He explains the *pasuk*: וַיִּגְדַּל מֹשֶׁה וַיֵּצֵא אֶל אֶחָיו, *Moshe grew to greatness, by his having gone out to his brothers* (Shemos 2:11). He became great *because* he went out and was concerned for others. You can't just go into your little corner and ignore everybody else.

If you want to be great, go out among your brothers. Learn and absorb as much Torah as you can, then go out and share your knowledge. Become a *talmid chacham* for the sake of *Klal Yisrael*. Care for others. Don't stay only in your own *daled amos*. Women as well can serve as inspirational individuals to their sisters in *Klal Yisrael*.

One-Minute Kiruv

As I said at the beginning, *kiruv* is not limited to the professionals. In fact, we are all *kiruv* workers. It's just that some of us do it professionally.

> **We are all *kiruv* workers. It's just that some of us do it professionally.**

Sometimes you can do *kiruv* without even having to say a word, by just being a wonderful caring Jew who thus makes an impression on others. You may have contact with someone for just a fleeting moment, yet what you do or say during that short time may stay with that person forever.

When the Klausenberger Rebbe, Rav Yekusiel Yehudah Halberstam, passed away in 1994, his family sat *shivah* in Netanya. A woman came in, carrying a bag, and sat down next to the Rebbetzin. The Rebbetzin asked her name. The woman told her but the name was unfamiliar. Then the woman explained why she was there.

After the war, when the Rebbe had gone to the DP camps to give encouragement to the survivors, he overheard two young girls speaking Yiddish. He went over to them and asked one of them why she was not wearing socks. Didn't she know that wearing socks was more modest and appropriate for young Jewish women?

"I should wear socks?" the girl answered, "Do you think I have socks? I don't even have bread to eat? I have nothing!"

Immediately, the Rebbe sat down right there in the street, took off his own socks, and gave them to the girl.

The woman now talking to the Rebbetzin opened her bag and took out a pair of socks. She handed them to the Rebbetzin, saying, "These are the Rebbe's socks. I was that girl."

All those years, she had held onto those socks. She had only met the Rebbe once in her life and yet his care and concern remained with her. That's *kiruv*.

Rav Usher Weiss from Jerusalem told me that on an Erev Yom Kippur, also just after the war, as the Rebbe was home preparing for the fast, a girl knocked on his door.

"Rebbe," she pleaded, "please give me a *berachah*. My father used to give me one every year but now he is gone."

The Rebbe said, "I'll be your father," and he placed

his handkerchief over her hair, put his hands over it, and blessed her. She left feeling wonderful.

A few minutes later, another young girl knocked at his door with the same request. She had heard what had happened with the first girl. She came in to the Rebbe's house and he blessed her, too.

The word spread. That afternoon, no less than 87 orphaned girls came to receive a *berachah* from the Rebbe. They kept coming until it was time for *Kol Nidrei*. That was the Rebbe's preparation for Yom Kippur that year.

Could any of those girls forget what the Rebbe had done for them in those few minutes? He was there when they needed him. That's *kiruv*.

Share the Mitzvah

Kiruv is multifaceted. It is not only what you teach others directly, but what others learn from you even indirectly; for example, when you talk of the *mitzvos* you are involved with.

When the Kovno Rav, Rabbi Yitzchak Elchonon Spektor, passed away in 1896, he instructed his family to make sure that when he was eulogized, mention should be made of the various good things he was involved with in his lifetime.

"Not that I need to be glorified," he explained, "but rather so that others who hear of the good that was done will be inspired themselves to become involved in good things."

———⊱⚬⊰———

In the teachers' room of Shevach High School, where my wife Miriam is associate principal, two women were talking. One said, "I'm going to Loehmann's this afternoon. Would you like to come along?"

The other woman responded that she would love to go, but she was occupied that afternoon driving for Bikur Cholim, taking chemotherapy patients who didn't have their own transportation to their appointments. The first teacher had not known there was a need for such volunteering.

"Do you think they need more volunteers?" she asked. And because of that she joined Bikur Cholim as a regular driver.

How did that come about? The first teacher could have just answered, "I'm busy." She didn't have to elaborate on the *mitzvah* she would be doing. However, because she verbalized what *mitzvah* she was doing, another teacher also became involved in the same *mitzvah*. That is a form of *kiruv*. *Kiruv* means inspiring others, the non-observant and the observant.

Explain that you are going to a *shiur* or going to be *menachem avel* or are helping to set up for a *kiddush* or a *shalom zachor*. Share the *mitzvah*. Others will be inspired.

A Life-Changing Siddur

In Hungary, for the first time after the fall of Communism, a new Jewish school was opened. Two wonderful Jews, Mr. Albert Reichmann of Toronto and Mr. Dovid Moskowitz of Brooklyn, hired Mr. Michael Cohen of London, a respected educator, to head it. They expected 50 to 75 students, at most. At registration, 450 children showed up!

The administrators quickly called Israel, Europe, and the United States to find more teachers. They had rented two rooms, but now they needed an entire building.

After a few months, Mr. Michael Cohen called a meeting of the parents of the fourth-grade children. At the meeting, he asked if they were satisfied with the education their children were receiving. After their various answers, he asked each couple why they had enrolled their children in this school. Each parent offered a different answer. One said it was because he had attended a *cheder* as a child and wanted his child to have a Jewish education. Another said it was because of his grandfather. Another was dissatisfied with the secular school system. Only one man, sitting way in the back, did not answer.

Mr. Cohen noticed it and thus asked him directly, "Why did you send your child to this school?" The man replied that it was very difficult for him to discuss it. Mr. Cohen said he understood that, but still if he could muster the courage to explain his reason, it would surely make a great impression on all who were present. How right he was! Here is his story:

In 1944, when this man was only 9 years old, his family found out that the Nazis were coming to Hungary. Everyone, especially the children, was terrified. Everyone knew that many Hungarian Jews would be taken to slave labor camps and others would be sent to death camps. The fear was palpable.

One night, the boy heard his parents shouting at each other. He ran downstairs to listen, but the door to the living room was closed. He looked through the keyhole. He saw his father yelling, "Why are you worried? We don't look Jewish. We don't act Jewish. We don't seem Jewish. No one will come to take us. Don't worry!"

His mother answered, "Maybe there is a list somewhere. Maybe someone will say we are Jewish to save himself, so he will be spared."

His father countered, "So what? Even if they come here, they will find nothing. We have nothing Jewish in the house."

"Suddenly my father stopped talking," this parent said. "Instead, he slowly looked up to the top bookshelf. Lying there was a *siddur*. My mother now looked up as well. It was the *siddur* that her mother had given her on the day of her wedding. She took it down and opened it."

The parent said that as a little boy he was horrified. His mother was standing right near a lit fireplace. He was so afraid of what he was sure she was about to do.

Suddenly, she said to her husband, "You're right. What do we need this for?" and she threw it into the flames.

The boy ran to his room, crying bitterly. He cried for an hour, without understanding why. He only knew that his mother had done something terribly wrong.

"After all those years, I can still picture those pages burning," the man now told Mr. Cohen. "When I heard that you were opening a Jewish school, I knew I had to bring my child here. Here I can give my child a *siddur*."

People With Answers

Rabbi Abraham J. Twerski, M.D. once questioned the common definition of the term *baal teshuvah*, usually given as "a returnee to Judaism." He asked: How can they be *returning* to something they never had? Instead, he explained, the term comes from the word *teshuvah*, meaning "answer." A *baal teshuvah* is a person with an answer; a seeker whose thirst for fulfillment has been quenched because he or she has found an answer. Hence, the term *baal teshuvah* means the one who possesses the answer.

> A *baal teshuvah* is a person with an answer; a seeker whose thirst for fulfillment has been quenched because he or she has found an answer.

Jews all over are looking for answers. They may not look the part. They may not even realize it themselves. But their hearts are yearning. Their souls are searching. And it's only proper and fitting that we should be there for them. May we all merit to see the days when all Jews from all over feel close to Hashem so that He, in turn, will grant us, His beloved children, *Mashiach* in our time.

To See the Good

Over the past 10 years, I've had the opportunity to travel with hundreds of people to Eastern Europe, to places such as Poland and Lithuania, to cities and towns where *Yiddishkeit* once flourished. One of the most moving places we go to in Poland is the town of Lizhensk, to the gravesite of the Rebbe Reb Elimelech.

It is so special to *daven* there. I don't know what it is, but when I go there, it is almost like *davening* at Kever Rachel. The Rebbe Reb Elimelech once said that whoever prays at his gravesite will not die before doing *teshuvah*. That alone is incentive. You enter a room housing the *tzion*, and there is a huge laminated poster of a *tefillah* that Rebbe Elimelech wrote. Every year I tell the group with me, "Do not say that prayer until I tell you the whole story about Reb Elimelech, his life, his compassion for others, his caring."

After I tell the story, we say the *tefillah* together. It is so moving! Each of us is pouring his heart out to Hashem. As we near the end, we reach certain words that have become so famous that they have been made into a song. Listen to them carefully:

אַדְּרַבָּה תֵּן בְּלִבֵּנוּ שֶׁנִּרְאֶה כָּל אֶחָד מַעֲלוֹת חֲבֵרֵינוּ וְלֹא חֶסְרוֹנָם

To the contrary [Hashem], please put into our hearts that we each may see the virtues of our friends and not their faults.

Every person has good qualities and every person has faults. We *daven* that we should see the good in other people. That is our topic, לִרְאוֹת טוֹב: *To See the Good* (*Tehillim* 34:13). To see the good in the people we meet every day, in our spouses, in our children, in our teachers. It is obvious that Reb Elimelech understood that that is not our natural reaction. Unfortunately, we live today in a world of criticism and cynicism, and we get caught up in that negativity.

Sometimes, we just look for the negative in others. When visitors departed, Rav Yosef Chaim Sonnenfeld, the Rav of Yerushalayim, always used to tell them a *pasuk* written by David HaMelech: וּרְאֵה בְּטוֹב יְרוּשָׁלָ֫ם, *see the good in Jerusalem* (*Tehillim* 128:5). That seems incredible. How could you not see the good of Yerushalayim? It is the most beautiful, holy city in the world. But Rav Yosef Chaim understood, as Reb Elimelech did, that seeing the good is not the natural inclination.

Even a person coming from Yerushalayim might find some fault — in the people, in the city, in whatever he saw in the street. Rav Yosef Chaim wanted him *liros tov*, to see the good in Yerushalayim. It's so important in life.

Seeing With Both Eyes

I remember the first time I was in England. My wife and I took a five-day trip there because I had some speaking engagements. For five days it was foggy and rainy. I said to my wife, "The people here are so lovely. When we go home, let's not talk about the weather. Let's talk about the goodness of the people, the interest and friendship that they showed us. That's what's important."

In every situation you will find good and bad. The Boyaner Rebbe, Reb Mordechai Shlomo Friedman, came to the Lower East Side of New York after 1926. He started a shul there and soon everyone came to appreciate the greatness of this *tzaddik*. He was very close with Rav Moshe Feinstein, he was a member of the Moetzes Gedolei

HaTorah, and soon all kinds of people, not just *Chassidim*, flocked to the Boyaner Rebbe.

It made no difference to him what sort of beard the person had (if he had one at all), what size *yarmulke* he wore (or didn't wear), whether or not he was a *talmid chacham*. The Boyaner Rebbe loved and cared for *every* Jew. He once said a phenomenal insight on the *Mishnah* in *Negaim* (2:3): כֹּהֵן הַסּוּמָא בְּאַחַת מֵעֵינָיו ... לֹא יִרְאֶה אֶת הַנְּגָעִים , a *Kohen* who is blind in one eye is not allowed to check if a person has tzaraas.

The Boyaner Rebbe asked: Why not? The *Kohen* can still see out of the other eye. The symbolism here is important, he explained. A person's natural inclination is to look for the negative. When you see someone who has a skin blemish, that blemish is usually the first thing to make an impression on you. Therefore, you need a second *eye* to see the positive in the person, to see his potential. The Boyaner Rebbe remarked that if someone comes to him, or any other Rebbe, for a *berachah* or for encouragement, the Rebbe has to look at him with both eyes. The Rebbe may know that the person has certain faults, that he has done certain sins, but that cannot be the only way the Rebbe looks at him. The Rebbe must look at him with both eyes and see the greatness that lies within, and then he will be able to encourage him and bless him.

Covering an Inferiority Complex

When we look at people, it is vitally important not to judge them with preconceived notions. The Gemara in *Taanis* (29a) tells us that the day the spies returned and gave a negative report to *Klal Yisrael*, causing them all to cry and despair, was *Tishah B'Av*. They took away the hope of the people with their *lashon hara*.

The *Mishnah* tells us: That day was *Tishah B'Av*. Hashem said to them, "You cried for no reason. I will establish this day for crying for generations."

Rav Chaim Shmulevitz asks: We know that the *Bnei Yisrael* were punished with 40 years in the Wilderness in return for the 40 days that the spies were in *Eretz Yisrael*. But, Rav Chaim points out, they only spoke *lashon hara* once, on that particular day. Why were we punished for 40 years?

His answer: Because for those 40 days, all they did was see the bad. All they did, he stresses, was see the negative.

The *Mesillas Yesharim* (Ch. 11) makes a remarkable correlation. Why did they speak evil against the land? Because they were worried that perhaps their honor would be diminished when they entered *Eretz Yisrael*, for then they would no longer be the leaders. Others might take their places.

Imagine that. They knew before they entered the land that if all the people succeeded in reaching *Eretz Yisrael*, they might lose their prominence. And with that preconceived notion, they sought out the country's flaws.

How often do we do that? We meet a certain type of person and think, *Oh, he belongs to that group? They're not nice; they're cheap, they're nasty, they're always late.* Automatically, because we have a preconceived notion of "that group" we will see the bad in this person. There is no way we can see the good because the negative is already entrenched.

For Yourself

Let me share with you a question that has always bothered me. Every day, three times a day, in *Krias Shema* we say the third chapter of *Shema*. We say the paragraph about *tzitzis*, וְלֹא תָתוּרוּ אַחֲרֵי לְבַבְכֶם וְאַחֲרֵי עֵינֵיכֶם, *Don't explore after your heart and your eyes.*

To me, the order of the *pasuk* seems unusual. Don't you first see something and then want it? Shouldn't the *pasuk* put eyes before heart, reading, וְלֹא תָתוּרוּ אַחֲרֵי עֵינֵיכֶם וְאַחֲרֵי לְבַבְכֶם?

The answer, I believe, is that your eyes see what your heart wants them to see. That is the language of the *Tosafos* in *Avodah Zarah* (28b): רְאִיַּית הָעַיִן תָּלוּי בַּהֲבָנַת הַלֵּב, *the vision of the eye depends on the understanding of the heart.*

If someone really wants to see something good, he'll see it. If someone really wants to see something bad, he'll see that. That is why the Torah tells us not to go after the desires of our hearts, because that is where it all begins.

And maybe that is the reason we look for the bad in other people: because deep in our hearts, we have low self-esteem and we are constantly deriding ourselves, criticizing ourselves, demoralizing ourselves, and demeaning ourselves: *I am not good to others; I'm not treating them right,* etc. We are so negative about ourselves that unfortunately we look at others and think they are like that too.

We have got to change. We have got to look for something good so that we can say something nice. Rav Yerucham Levovitz, the great Mashgiach of Mir, once said, "It is important for a person to know his faults, so that he knows what to fix. But it is even more important for a person to know his virtues, so that he knows what he can accomplish."

> Rav Yerucham: "It is important for a person to know his faults, so that he knows what to fix. But it is even more important for a person to know his virtues, so that he knows what he can accomplish."

In other words, look for the good, even in yourself!

It is very important for us to know our faults, because we must improve. No one is perfect. But what is more important is to know our virtues, to know what we can accomplish. In fact, the *Tzidkas HaTzaddik* tells us just that. He says that a Jew must believe in three things: Hashem, the Torah, and himself. When you believe in yourself and you recognize your virtues, then you can accomplish.

When you look at the good in yourself, you are doing *liros tov* not only for others but for yourself, and it will follow automatically that you will look for the good in others. Self-confident people, people who feel that they can accomplish, will not feel threatened by others. He can accomplish and they can accomplish.

Making Others Feel Tall

A number of years ago, unfortunately, a man who was a tremendous *talmid chacham* passed away in a terrible bus accident. His name was Rabbi Eliezer Geldzahler. Some of you may know his father-in-law, Reb Michel Twersky of Milwaukee. This *leibedike* young man, only 46 years old, was a rosh yeshivah who imbued his *talmidim* with love of Torah and Hashem.

About two years after he passed away, his daughter, Chana Malka, was driving on the Garden State Parkway. She pulled into a gas station. The attendant who came out to pump her gas was a dwarf. While the tank was filling up he washed her windows. As he glanced inside her car, he saw a picture of Rabbi Geldzahler. The attendant asked her if she knew that man. Yes, she said, he was her father.

"He was your father?" the man cried. Tears were streaming down his face.

"You knew my father?" the woman asked.

"I've been waiting for him for the last two years," the dwarf replied. "You see, I come here every day. Most people who come to get gas here don't look at me, because they are uncomfortable with my appearance. But one day your father came here, and he looked me straight in the eye, as nobody else had ever done. And he said to me, 'You are an inspiration! You were born with something that many people would consider to be a tremendous handicap, but you didn't accept that. You didn't allow yourself to become a victim. You get up every morning and come to work to earn an honest living; you're a role model. You know, I head a very big school in Brooklyn. I'm on my way there now, and today I am going to tell my students about you. You are an example from whom we should all learn."

> **The man began to cry again. "Your father was so special," he said, "he made me feel tall."**

The man began to cry again. "Your father was so special," he said, "he made me feel tall."

Rabbi Geldzahler made that man feel tall. Why? Because *liros tov*, he saw the good. When you see the good in people, you build them up. You make them feel special. You carry them for years. Two years later that gas station attendant was still waiting for Rabbi Geldzahler to appear again and give him *chizuk*.

The $2 Million Loss

I want to share one more story, of someone close to me, someone who also looked for the good.

This gentleman owns a construction company, and he builds power lines throughout the United States.

The way the business works is, if a city needs transmission lines, they call this man. He gets an architect to design it, and the estimator has to give the client a bid.

Many years ago, a city council called him saying they needed seven miles of transmission lines, and they had an architect. The estimator went there, determined the bid, and presented it. The way this field works is that once a bid is entered it cannot be rescinded. This particular bid was so low that of course this company got the job. The estimator returned to his office, wondering why his bid was so much lower than the others. Soon he realized that he had made a terrible mistake. When he had picked up the architect's drawings, he had not picked up all the pages. This was before computers. He had put in the bid on five-and-a-half miles of cable, not seven.

But the bid had been placed and accepted, and it could not be taken back. The man was heartbroken, because he loved his boss and had just cost him $2 million. The next morning he went into the boss's office, and he was crying.

"I'm here to resign," he said.

"Why?" asked the surprised boss.

"I can't explain it, but I didn't pick up all the architect's drawings, and I gave a bid on only a portion of the contract. You stand to lose $2 million because of me. I can't stay here."

The boss looked at him and said firmly, "I do not accept your resignation. You are one of the best people we have here, and you will never make that mistake again. That's why I want you here: because you won't make that mistake again."

The man was stunned. He had just caused the loss of $2 million, but the boss saw something good in him. The boss saw that he would be the best estimator the company could ever have. And that's exactly what happened. He stayed on at the company and when the chief estimator left, this man moved up into that position.

What would most people do? "Two million dollars?!" If he cost us $200, most of us would have thrown him out. But that is not what that boss did. He looked for the good, he saw it, and kept the employee on.

From Spaced Out to Spaced In

There is a wonderful third-grade rebbi in Brooklyn who asked to remain anonymous, so I have to respect his wishes. He does a wonderful thing with his students at the end of every year. Throughout the year he takes pictures with each boy, and on the last day of the year he hands each student a large envelope with the pictures inside. Onto the pictures he has stapled an index card, and on the card he writes words of encouragement to each boy. Everybody knows that this rebbi does this on the last day of yeshivah.

> One little boy, as he continued on through fourth, fifth, sixth grade, became very quiet and withdrawn. He became such a loner that people began calling him a "spaced-out loser." Unfortunately, when a child is called a name, it often becomes a self-fulfilling prophecy. The more people called him a spaced-out loser, the more he became one. As time went on, he often missed school entirely. His parents were absolutely exasperated.
>
> When he turned 17, he came to his mother one day and said, "Ma, I want to change. I want to start again. I want a new beginning. Find me a yeshivah. I'm going to change."
>
> His parents enrolled him in an out-of-town yeshivah where nobody knew him, and he began to flourish. A few days after he left, his aunt went into his bedroom. She had never seen such a mess. There was no bedding, no sheets or blankets on the bed;

instead, it was covered with CDs, books, and other things. The pillows and blankets were on the floor. However, on the desk, in the only neat corner, stood a picture of her nephew with his third-grade rebbi. When she saw the index card, she realized that it had been read many, many times, for it was frayed at the edges. She turned the card over and on the back she read, "Ari, you asked such wonderful questions this year! Keep it up. You CAN do it! Love, Rebbi."

It is hard to say that that card is what carried the boy throughout the years, but it was obvious that he must have read it 1,000 times, and eventually it went into his *neshamah*. Because the rebbi was *liros tov*, he saw the good in this child. He heard his questions and realized that his inquisitiveness showed intelligence. The good that the rebbi found within him carried him until he changed. That boy became an extraordinary young man.

The Secret of Meod

One of the most inspirational thoughts I've heard on this theme is from Rav Yitzchak Hutner, Rosh Yeshivah of Yeshivas Chaim Berlin. He was a student of the Alter of Slobodka, Rav Nosson Tzvi Finkel, and the Alter's philosophy of *gadlus ha'adam*, the greatness of man.

Rav Hutner pointed out that the Torah says (*Bereishis* 1:31), "Hashem saw everything that He had done and it was '*tov meod*' (very good)." The *Midrash* says (*Bereishis Rabbah* 9:12), הוּא מְאֹד הוּא אָדָם (man). What does that mean? מְאֹד actually means "very." The two words are spelled with the same letters, מ־א־ד and א־ד־ם. Any child can see that. Do we need a *Midrash* to tell us that?

Rav Hutner explained that everything in life can be measured: the depth of the sea, the distance between the earth and the sun, the speed of sound and light. The only thing that cannot be measured, he said, is a person's potential. If a person believes in himself, there is no limit to what he can accomplish. Adam; i.e., a person is מְאֹד, "very," because there is no end to his potential.

When you believe in yourself and feel that you can accomplish anything, when you look for your virtues, then you will look for the virtues in others and seek to help them accomplish as well. Good people want other people to be good. Only those who are negative, who do not accomplish in life, will look at others and criticize.

We must begin looking at ourselves in a positive way, and then we can be positive toward others.

We must begin looking at ourselves in a positive way, and then we can be positive toward others.

Being a Mentsch

The *Mishnah* in *Avos* (2:9) relates that when Rabbi Yochanan ben Zakkai asked his students to pick the best character trait, each student offered a different one. Rabbi Elazar said a person should have an עַיִן טוֹבָה, *a good eye* (be happy for others). Rabbi Yehoshua said one should be a חָבֵר טוֹב, *a good friend.* Others gave different answers. Rabbi Eliezer ben Aruch said that a person should have a לֵב טוֹב, *a good heart.*

Rabbi Yochanan declared that "a good heart" was the best answer, since it included the characteristics mentioned by the others. All good *middos* stem from a *lev tov.*

The *Bnei Yissaschar* (*Chodesh Iyar, Maamar* 3:1) points out that the *gematria* of the word לֵב is 32. The *gematria* of the word טוֹב is 17. Together they equal 49. There are 49 days of *Sefirah.* During these 49 days, each of us is supposed to gain that "good heart," because in so doing we are readying ourselves for Shavuos and receiving the Torah.

Perhaps, one might add, this is an allusion to the famous *Chazal,* "*Derech eretz kadmah l'Torah,*" that is, attaining proper character traits precedes the study of Torah (see *Vayikra Rabbah* 9:3).

Let us take time now to learn what it means to have a "good heart."

Be a Mentsch

Rav Chaim Ozer Grodzinsky was recognized as a genius even as a child. Once, Rav Yisrael Salanter, the great *talmid chacham* and father of the Mussar (ethical character) movement, came to his town. Rav Yisrael delivered a *shiur* and posed a very difficult question, one to which no one had an answer. Afterward, the 10-year-old Chaim Ozer approached him and said, "Would the Rav mind if I presented an answer to the question?" He then proceeded to do so.

Rav Yisrael could hardly believe that the boy had understood the question he posed, let alone attempted to give an answer. However, the young Chaim Ozer indeed gave a brilliant answer. Rav Yisrael Salanter was amazed. Putting his hand on the boy's head, he kissed him and said, "May you be *zoche* to get a wonderful *shidduch!*"

Years later, Rav Yisrael Salanter received a letter telling him that someone was suggesting R' Chaim Ozer Grodzinsky as a *shidduch* for his granddaughter (his daughter's daughter). Rav Yisrael wrote back that he knew for certain that the young man was a great *talmid chacham*. He had been one at 10 years of age. "But," Rav Yisrael added cleverly, "it says in *Devarim* (22:16): אֶת בִּתִּי נָתַתִּי לָאִישׁ הַזֶּה, *I give my daughter to this* אִישׁ, this *mentsch*. Before finalizing the *shidduch*," he concluded, "be sure that he is a *mentsch*."

Of course, they confirmed it and the *shidduch* went through. However, it is obvious from Rav Yisrael Salanter's reply that a person can be a *talmid chacham* without necessarily being an *ish*, a *mentsch*. Frightening!

R' Moshe Shimon Mendlowitz, nephew of Rav Shraga Feivel Mendlowitz, *zt'l*, once told me that the first day he came to Telshe Yeshivah, he heard Rav Mottel Katz deliver a *shmuess* (a Torah discourse). It was the same *shmuess* he would deliver the first day of every *zman*. (He actually said it twice every year: the first day of the semester and once in *Parashas Vayechi*, because the *pasuk* he was quoting was in that week's *haftarah*.) Here is the gist of his *shmuess*:

When David HaMelech was going to die, he wanted to give advice to his young son, Shlomo, who was about to become king. The first thing he told him was, "אָנֹכִי הֹלֵךְ בְּדֶרֶךְ כָּל הָאָרֶץ, *[I know] I am going the way of all mankind;* וְחָזַקְתָּ וְהָיִיתָ לְאִישׁ, *be strong and become an ish,* a man — become a *mentsch*" (*I Melachim* 2:2).

That was the first requirement for becoming king. Similarly, Rav Mottel told the *bachurim,* the first thing a boy has to know when he comes to a yeshivah is that he must have *mentschlichkeit.* After that, Torah and *middos* can grow.

Learning to become a *mentsch* is not only how boys prepare for the *zman,* but how a person prepares for life.

A Readers' Digest Survey

Readers' Digest, during July 2006, conducted a survey on courtesy. They designed three tests. They sent people to 35 different cities worldwide and performed these tests 60 times.

In one test, someone walked into an office building carrying a heavy package and observed how many people held the door open for him. The second test took place in the middle of a busy store: A person would "accidently" drop a stack of papers on the floor and note how many people stopped to help him pick them up. The third test was to see if, after they purchased an item, the clerk would say, "Thank you for shopping here," or express a similar sentiment.

> **Believe it or not, the city that was voted the most courteous was New York!**

Believe it or not, the city that was voted the most courteous was New York! (Zurich was #2, Toronto #3, Vienna #14, London #18, Paris #19, Moscow #30 — and the worst city was Mumbai, India.)

And I (who love New York) think that if New York was voted #1, we are all in trouble!

In all seriousness, the work of becoming a *mentsch* is never done. Even the most refined people need to work on their *middos.* Rav Avrohom Pam kept an index card near him at all times with a quote from the Vilna

> **The work of becoming a *mentsch* is never done.**

Gaon from the *sefer Even Sheleimah*: "The main function of a person in this world is to correct his *middos.*"

Imagine! If Rav Pam was worried that he had to be reminded constantly to correct his character, what should we say?

Why do so many people lack *mentschlichkeit*? If we would truly understand this definition of *mentschlichkeit* — and if we thought about it every time we were about to say or do something — we would act in a totally different way.

I believe that *mentschlichkeit* should be defined as the act of being a kind, sensitive, caring person who thinks of others, not only of him/herself. That is the essence of this article. The rest is commentary.

Learn to Say Thank You

Perhaps the most basic characteristic of a being a *mentsch* is the *middah* of *hakaras hatov*, having a continual sense of gratitude. A *mentsch* continually feels thankful for all the good he receives and thus never wastes an opportunity to express his thanks.

Make a list of how often during the day you say "thank you." If you have not said it five or ten times a day, you are probably a person who thinks others owe you everything.

Train yourself to say "thank you." Say thank you to the person behind the counter who served you. Of course he/she is getting paid to do so, but he/she performed a service for you. Say thank you to the grocer who stocked his store with all those kosher products. If not for him, you would have to travel miles away.

Shelly Lang, the musician, has a son named Shneur. At the *bris* he was asked why he chose that name. He answered that at every wedding at which he played that Rav Shneur Kotler attended, Rav Shneur came up to the band and thanked them for the music.

The Manchester Rosh Yeshivah, Rav Yehuda Zev Segal, wrote letters to those who wrote *sefarim* that he appreciated. He learned *mishnayos l'ilui nishmas* the Chofetz Chaim, the Chovos HaLevovos, the Mesillas Yesharim, and others. He felt that because he had learned and grown from their *sefarim,* he had to show his appreciation.

When Rav Pam spoke at a parlor meeting, he would always personally thank the hostess for all her efforts. One hostess related that Rav Pam even complimented her on the paintings on the wall. At an

Agudah convention, before he left, Rav Pam went into the kitchen to thank the cooks. Who thanks the cooks? Who even thinks about the cooks?

In the 1970s, when he was still a rebbi in Torah Vodaath, Rav Pam was offered a prestigious position as a Rosh Yeshivah in a new yeshivah opening in *Eretz Yisrael*. He turned it down because he felt that he owed everything to Torah Vodaath. He had learned there. They had given him a job when he was starting out. They had been good to him. He had such *hakaras hatov* that he turned down an ostensibly better position.

The Best Thank-You

A *mechanech* in an out-of-town yeshivah finally had a child after many years. The baby was healthy, but premature, and was required to stay in the hospital for many weeks. When the baby was ready to leave, the parents wanted to give a gift to the nurses. The father had once learned in Philadelphia, so he contacted Rav Elya Svei and explained the situation. Rav Svei told him not to buy anything. The father was flabbergasted. He wanted to show *hakaras hatov* toward the hospital staff!

Rav Elya told him to see what the Torah says about the nurses Shifrah and Puah (Yocheved and Miriam), who took care of the Jewish babies: וַיֵּיטֶב אֱלֹקים לַמְיַלְּדֹת ... וַיַּעַצְמוּ מְאֹד, *Hashem did good for the midwives … they [the people] became strong (Shemos* 1:20). The greatest thing Hashem could do for the nurses was to make the children grow strong. Rav Elya suggested that instead of buying a gift for the nurses, the father should take his child back to the hospital *every* year on his birthday. Let the staff *see* how the child they had helped was growing strong.

And that is what the father did. He took the child back on his birthday for the first seven years of his life. Then it became difficult to manage the trip and he stopped. However, when the boy became bar mitzvah, the father decided that it would be nice to do it again, so he took him back to that out-of-town hospital and showed them his son.

Not long afterward he received a letter from one of the non-Jewish nurses:

Dear Rabbi,

I am a nurse in the High-Risk Unit at [Out-of-Town] Hospital. As you well know, your son was born at this hospital many years ago. I was not employed by the hospital at that time, but at orientation, when I came on staff, they told us about you, how you always brought your child back every year. Although I was not one of the nurses who tended to your son, I want you to know how much we appreciated your visits. Candy and flowers are a nice sentiment, but what you and your family do helps us make it through the rough days.

That is what Rav Elya understood. A genuine thank-you — heartfelt and meaningful: that is the true thanks that the nurses wanted.

When we say "thank you," it has to be done genuinely, so that the recipient understands that we truly mean it.

Thoughtful Thanks

Rav Eliyahu Dessler was once walking in Gateshead with Rav Betzalel Rakov (the Rav of the city) and they passed a children's clothing store. The store was having a sale, and Rav Dessler started taking notes. Rav Rakov was surprised. Rav Dessler explained that while he had no need for such clothes, he was often invited out for Shabbos meals, and this way he could show some *hakaras hatov* by telling the hostess that there was a sale at this store. She might appreciate the news.[1]

Rav Dessler also put thought into what he might discuss at his host's table well before he actually went there. In the fifth volume of *Michtav Me'Eliyahu* (page 507), there is a letter he wrote, thanking his host for the cake and tea the hostess had made for him. That is genuine thanks.

I was once flying to Canada from LaGuardia. I don't have to tell you what the terminal was like: hundreds of busy people going in all directions. I went through security, into the waiting area, and suddenly two serious-looking security guards appeared, searching for someone. Then they started walking — straight to me! My heart was pounding.

---

1. *Rav Dessler* by Yonason Rosenblum, p. 228 (ArtScroll Mesorah Publications, NY).

"Sir, is this yours?" one of the guards said as he pulled out a cell phone.

I was shocked. "Yes, it is my phone. How did you get it?"

"When you went through the security check, you left it in one of the bins," he replied.

"Thank you very much," I said, "but there are close to a thousand people here. How did you find me?"

"Well," the guard said, "when you went through security, you said something to us that made us take notice of you. You said, 'Thank you for being here. I feel safer that you fellows are here.' Thousands of people go through security every day and no one says 'thank you.' You said 'thank you' and so we were determined to find you."

Let's make a *kabbalah* now that at least five times a day we will say "thank you." At least once a week we will write a thank-you note. With email it is so easy. Don't say you don't have time. You somehow make time for things you consider important.

Sensitivity

Another component of being a *mentsch* is becoming sensitive to the feelings of others. If we would only learn this we would not make nasty comments, take away parking spots designated for the handicapped, answer cell phones where we shouldn't (e.g., at a *chuppah*, during a speech, or next to someone who is *davening*), cut into lines, and the like.

The Torah (*Devarim* 22:10) forbids us to harness an ox and a donkey together. Why? Because the ox chews its cud, and it seems as if it is eating again, causing the donkey to feel bad that it has nothing to eat (see *Daas Zekeinim* ibid.). If the Torah requires us to worry about the feelings of a donkey, then certainly we have to worry about the feelings of people.

Every Erev Rosh Hashanah Rav Yehuda Zev Segal would call certain people, who had once been wealthy and had since lost their money, to wish them a good year. When asked why he bothered, he explained that in years past the whole world had been calling these people, and now almost no one did.

When was the last time you called a widow before Shabbos or *Yom Tov*? Life will never be the same for her. *Mentschlichkeit* means that if you were close to the family when things were busy and lively at her home, you will remain close now as well.

Training to Be a Mentsch

There are several tried and true ways to train yourself in *mentschlichkeit*.

First: *daven* for other people every day. Not one *Shemoneh Esrei* should go by without a *tefillah* for someone else. When you *daven* for a *choleh*, think about what the ill person and his/her family are going through.

Another way to train yourself in *mentschlichkeit* is to do a *chesed* a day for someone, anyone. Don't go to bed until you have helped someone, somehow. Keep a notebook and write down one *chesed* you did that day. You will see that after a month that notebook will become one of your most treasured possessions. In his *sefer*, *Ahavas Chesed*, the Chofetz Chaim extols the importance of not letting even one day go by without having done a *chesed* for others.

Here is another beautiful thing to do. Keep a *simchah* calendar. You can't go to every *simchah*, but at least write down the date of each *simchah* you have been invited to. If you can't attend, make sure to call the *baalei simchah* the day before the event and wish them *mazel tov*. They will be so touched and pleased! To the *baalei simchah*, the world revolves around their joyous occasion; your call shows you care.

We all need to give *mussar* to each other at one point or another. But learn from the Torah how to give it. Hashem was disturbed that Aaron and Miriam spoke *lashon hara* about Moshe. How did Hashem introduce His *mussar* to them? שִׁמְעוּ נָא דְבָרָי, **Please** listen to My words (*Bamidbar* 12:6). Even though Hashem was giving them *mussar*, He still said, "*Please* listen."

The *Sifsei Chachamim* (ibid.) explains that even though Hashem was angry at them, He spoke softly and kindly to them. Rav Henoch Leibowitz often cited this *Sifsei Chachamim* to teach the method of giving rebuke.

Mentschlichkeit means that even when we have to give *mussar*, we speak in a kind way. Never call someone "stupid." If anything, say "that was a stupid thing to do." We all do stupid things at times. But calling a person names does more harm than good. Try to *always* speak with kindness and softness.

Why Before Shavuos?

I always wondered why Rabbi Akiva's students, who died because they did not treat each other with the proper respect, passed away in the days between Pesach and Shavous. If Hashem wanted to teach us a lesson about *middos*, wouldn't it have had a greater impact if they had died during, say, Elul?

The answer is: דֶּרֶךְ אֶרֶץ קָדְמָה לַתּוֹרָה, *Derech eretz kadmah l'Torah* (*Midrash Vayikra Rabbah* 9:3). Proper behavior comes before learning Torah.

Of course, if it had occurred during the *Aseres Yemei Teshuvah,* it would have made a tremendous impact. But the idea of learning about *middos*, of self-improvement, of preparing ourselves for receiving the Torah, was more important. Rav Aaron Kotler writes that the students died before the holiday of *Kabbalas HaTorah* to show that those without the proper *derech eretz* are not the ones who can transmit Torah to the next generations (*Mishnas Rav Aharon* 3:13, *Yemei HaSefirah*).

The Maharal asks: What is the *middah k'negged middah* (the *measure for measure*) involved in the death of Rabbi Akiva's students? What did they do to make death an appropriate penalty? The Maharal answers that giving *kavod* to each other, treating each other with the proper respect, is the essence of life. When you deprive another of his due respect, you deprive him of life. (See his commentary on *Yevamos* 62b.)

Let us, in the 49 days of *Sefirah*, understand that we are here to develop a *lev tov*, a good heart. Let us try to build our *middos* and our *mentschlichkeit*. Let us remember that *derech eretz kadmah l'Torah*, proper behavior is a prerequisite for learning Torah. In that *zechus*, may we merit to be *mekabel* and be *mekayeim* the entire Torah and merit to transfer it to the coming generations.

> **When you deprive another of his due respect, you deprive him of life.**

Rebbetzin Kanievsky

Rebbetzin Batsheva Esther was blessed with extraordinary genealogy. She had the most extraordinary grandfather, Rav Aryeh Levin, *zt"l*. She had the most extraordinary father, Rav Yosef Shalom Elyashiv, *zt"l*. She had the most extraordinary husband, Rav Chaim Kanievsky, *shlita*, one of the *gedolei hador*. And she had the most extraordinary father-in-law, the Steipler Gaon, Rav Yaakov Yitzchak Kanievsky, *zt"l*.

Imagine such genealogy! She learned from each of these great people and became the Rachel Imeinu of our generation. Every pain, every anguish, every heartache came to her door. She received each visitor with a smile and gave them *chizuk*. She made her lifework healing the brokenhearted.

> She became the Rachel Imeinu of our generation. Every pain, every anguish, every heartache came to her door. She received each visitor with a smile and gave them *chizuk*. She made her life work healing the brokenhearted.

True Freedom, True Wealth

The Rebbetzin once said that every person is allotted a certain amount of *agmas nefesh* (aggravation). However, whenever we feel someone else's pain, we have some of our personal *agmas nefesh* lifted from our shoulders.

Think about that. If we feel aggravation on someone else's behalf, we are spared our own personal aggravation. David HaMelech wrote that Hashem is הָרוֹפֵא לִשְׁבוּרֵי לֵב, *The healer of the brokenhearted* (*Tehillim* 147:3). It is interesting to note that the first letters of the three Hebrew words are הַלֵּל, *praise*. In other words one who has the capacity to heal broken hearts is praiseworthy. That was the Rebbetzin and that is what we should strive to be like.

> **Every person is allotted a certain amount of *agmas nefesh*. However, whenever we feel someone else's pain, we have some of our personal *agmas nefesh* lifted from our shoulders.**

People who saw the Rebbetzin's kitchen, dining room, etc. saw that she lived in poverty, or something very close to it. Nevertheless, she was always happy and able to give *chizuk* to others.

Much of that came from her grandfather, Rav Aryeh Levin. She used to accompany him on his walks and when he went to visit the prisoners. That was before 1948, when the British ruled Palestine and jailed many, many Jews.

> The story is told how on one Chol HaMoed Pesach, Rav Aryeh went to the prison and asked the Jewish prisoners if they had been able to have a *Seder*.
>
> "Yes," they said, "we had almost everything."
>
> "*Almost* everything?" he asked.
>
> "Yes. We were given wine for the four cups, as well as *matzah* and *marror*."
>
> "Then what didn't you have?
>
> "Well," they answered, "for *shefoch chamascha* we wanted to open the front door, but we weren't allowed to."
>
> Rav Aryeh smiled and said, "You think you are prisoners because the front door isn't open? That isn't what makes a prisoner. A prisoner is someone who, in his heart, has no control over himself."

If someone is obsessed with material gains to the point that he has no control, he is a prisoner … of his desires. A free man is someone who is in control — who does not lose himself with anger or frustration when he does not have what he wants or thinks he needs.

That is the way the Rebbetzin and her family lived. They were the freest, happiest, wealthiest people in the truest sense — despite external trappings that to outsiders appeared just the opposite.

Her Piety

I have the great *zechus* to be somewhat friendly with Rav Chaim Kanievsky's son-in-law, Rav Yitzchak Kolodetzky. I asked Rav Yitzchak Kolodetzky to tell me the outstanding qualities of his mother-in-law. Three things immediately came to mind: First was the Rebbetzin's *tefillah*.

Do you know how long it took for the Rebbetzin to *bentch licht*? An hour! It is an *eis ratzon* and she took full advantage of it. She would *daven* and cry — for her children and for the children of others.

The Rebbetzin *davened* three times a day with a *minyan* and woke up early to *daven vasikin* (the earliest time for *davening*, at dawn). My daughter told me that when my granddaughter was in seminary and she and her friends wanted to see the Rebbetzin, they went to Lederman's Shul to *daven* Minchah, because everyone knew that after Minchah they could speak to the Rebbetzin as she left shul. She was approached by so many visitors at that time that it took her half an hour to walk the 125 feet from the shul to her home.

One day, as the Rebbetzin came out of the shul, a *kallah* stepped out of a taxi. She was wearing her wedding dress and was accompanied by a photographer. She was on her way to her wedding and wanted a *berachah*, a hug, a kiss, and a picture with the Rebbetzin. Many other young women also did that.

> During *shivah* for his Rebbetzin, Rav Chaim cried. He said, "I used to see mothers bring their children to the Rebbetzin, and they would hug her and thank her for *davening* on their behalf when they had been sick. Hundreds streamed in and she had strength and

patience for all of them. I'm thinking of all those souls she saved with her *tefillos*. Who will do it now?"

The Rebbetzin was known for giving *berachos*, but was very humble about it. I remember the first time I met her. I went into that little kitchen with my children and asked if she would mind giving me a *berachah*.

"Oh," she said, "why do you want with a *berachah* from me? Go to my husband. He'll give you a *berachah*."

"Rebbetzin," I said. "The Gemara says (*Shevuos* 30b), אֵשֶׁת חָבֵר הֲרֵי הִיא כְּחָבֵר, *the wife of a talmid chacham is like a talmid chacham*, so I am asking for a *berachah* from you." She smiled and gave me a *berachah*.

A few days after the *shivah*, so many people were going to the Kanievsky apartment for *berachos* that Rav Chaim asked, "Who will give *berachos* now?"

He designated his daughter Leah Kolodetzky to come to her mother's kitchen and give *berachos* in her place, and guaranteed that her *berachos* would be fulfilled.

Learning Is Life

The Rebbetzin's father, Rav Elyashiv, was the most incredible *masmid*. He would rise very early in the morning, about 2 or 3 a.m., and his wife would also get up to make him a hot drink. Sometimes their children would offer to wake up and serve their father, but Rebbetzin Shayna Chaya Elyashiv would always refuse, saying it was her *mitzvah*. She didn't want to give the *zechus* to anyone else. She would go back to sleep afterward, but she would not give up that opportunity.

Rebbetzin Kanievsky would do the same thing. When Rav Chaim would rise early in the morning to learn, she would get up with him and make him a hot drink. But she did one thing differently. She did not go back to sleep. She would learn as well: she would recite *Perek Shirah*, or read the Letter *(Iggeres)* of the Ramban, or study two *halachos* of *shemiras halashon*.

The Rebbetzin lived in a world of incredible *ahavas Torah*. Those around her viewed Torah as life itself. To her, there was nothing greater than the fact that her husband and her children were learning.

A remarkable story is told by Rav Yisrael Brill.

> In Ponovezh Yeshivah, there was a 15-year-old *bachur*, the son of a wealthy man who worked not far from Bnei Brak. Every day the father would come to the yeshivah to learn with his son for two hours. What greater *nachas* can a father have?
>
> These were the days before cell phones. One day the father came to learn and saw a tumult in the hallway. A crowd had gathered together and everyone was in animated conversation. Somehow he got the feeling that something was wrong. He ran over to the crowd and asked what was going on. The students told him that they had been trying to reach him because his son was in the hospital; he had been hit by a bus about 30 minutes earlier. The father rushed to the hospital. *Baruch Hashem*, although he was badly bruised, his son was alive. For three days, the parents stayed in the hospital with their son.
>
> After three days, when the boy was out of danger, the father sent a message to Rav Kanievsky asking what he could do to show Hashem *hakaras hatov* for saving his son. Rav Chaim answered that in *every* big yeshivah there are boys who slip through the cracks; the *mashgiach* and the rebbis cannot take care of everybody there. Rav Chaim recommended that if the man had the means, he should find a boy who was not learning well, who was in danger of slipping away, and pay an older boy or a *yungerman,* a kollel fellow, to learn with him — because learning is life, and as Hashem had given life to his son, the father should give life to another boy.
>
> The man almost fainted when he heard this, because that was what he was already doing. One of the

mashgichim had called him asking if he could pay for a boy's tutor, and the man had given six postdated checks — and on that very day when his son was spared, the first check was scheduled to be cashed. When Rav Chaim heard that, he said, " He paid for life and got life in return!"

A Visit From Eliyahu HaNavi

The Rebbetzin grew up among *malachim* (angels) — her father, her grandfather, her husband, her father-in-law. To appreciate a little bit the type of holy environment she was born into, consider the following story she often told.

> Her grandfather, Rav Aryeh Levin, was a tremendous *tzaddik*, and he was very, very poor. The family had no crib for any of his babies; they slept on the bed with the other children. Their home had no running water. They would go down to the well, fill up a tub of water, and keep the tub in the apartment. One day Rebbetzin Levin had to run out to do an errand, and so she put her baby daughter, Shayna Chaya, on the bed while she ran downstairs. Just outside, she was stopped by a man who told her he was extremely thirsty, and asked if she could please get him a drink of water.
>
> She told him she was just on her way to the store for a minute. If he waited, she would give him a drink as soon as she returned. The man begged her to get the drink right away; he would die of thirst if he had to wait. So Rebbetzin Levin ran back upstairs — and found that her daughter had rolled off the bed and was in the tub of water! She grabbed the girl, dried her off, and moved her to a safer room. Rebbetzin Levin filled a glass with water and ran down to give it to the man, but he was gone.

That little girl grew up to be the wife of Rav Elyashiv and the mother of Rebbetzin Kanievsky. When Rebbetzin Levin told this story to her sister-in-law, the wife of Rav Tzvi Pesach Frank, Rav Frank said that surely the man had been Eliyahu HaNavi, and the child had been saved because she must have a wonderful future. And we know whom she married and who her children were.

An Uncanny Ability

Once, a young woman was brought to the Rebbetzin by her distraught parents. She had become secular and was engaged to a non-Jew. Nobody could dissuade her. The Rebbetzin hugged and kissed the girl and made her feel like she was really something special. She spoke to the girl about the importance of building a *bayis ne'eman b'Yisrael*, and the girl seemed really moved.

Nonetheless, at the end of the meeting, the girl announced that she still intended to marry the man. However, in honor of the Rebbetzin, she would take upon herself any *mitzvah* the Rebbetzin requested of her.

If you were the Rebbetzin, what would you have said?

With only moments to think about it, the Rebbetzin asked the girl to say one chapter of *Tehillim* every day. The girl agreed. The Rebbetzin said, "Good, let's start right now."

She took out her *Tehillim,* opened it at random to Chapter 43, and read the first verse: שָׁפְטֵנִי אֱלֹקִים וְרִיבָה רִיבִי מִגּוֹי לֹא חָסִיד מֵאִישׁ מִרְמָה וְעַוְלָה תְפַלְּטֵנִי, *Judge me, Hashem, and fight my battles against an impious non-Jew; deliver me from a man who is deceitful and unjust.* The Hebrew words in the *pasuk* she read say "רִיבָה רִיבִי." The girl was in shock, because her name was Reva. The Rebbetzin was in shock as well, because she had not planned that. The two of them cried on each other's shoulder. They did not let go of each other's embrace. When they both stopped crying they looked at each other in amazement and the girl said to the Rebbetzin, "I will not marry him."

Her Middos

Here is the second thing that Rav Kolodetzky said about the Rebbetzin. She was *maavir al midosov.* She looked away from taking offense at anything anyone might have done that hurt her.

Countless visitors came and burdened her unnecessarily. This included frustrated people and people who did not have all their mental faculties intact. At times some of them said inappropriate things. Yet, she never answered back. She was *maavir al midosov*. That is what the *Mesillas Yesharim* tells us (Chapter 19): If someone does not want to look away, how can he possible expect Hashem to look away from his own shortcomings? Rather, Hashem will judge him exactly as he judges others.

Therefore, the antidote to being judged harshly by others is to be *maavir al midosav*, to let insults go by without response. That was the Rebbetzin.

The third thing Rav Kolodetzky mentioned was *tznius*. After the Rebbetzin's passing, Rav Chaim said that for anyone who undertakes any additional stricture in *tznius*, the Rebbetzin will be a *meilitzas yashar* (heavenly advocate). That is a promise from Rav Chaim.

Savlanus

The Rebbetzin passed away on Shabbos. It was Chol HaMoed Succos, so *shivah* could not begin until after the holiday. On Shabbos afternoon all the children went to be with their father. They were sitting alone with him and asked him an interesting question: What would he say was their mother's greatest *middah*?

What would any of us have said? *Ahavas Yisrael*, *tznius*, *tefillah*, *shmiras halashon*?

Rav Chaim answered that his wife's greatest *middah* was *savlanus* (patience). What a great insight. What an idea worth absorbing into our own lives — especially those of us who live in New York. Have you ever driven down a busy New York street? People are constantly leaning on the horn of their cars. There's an expression: "Patience is something you admire in the driver behind you, but not in the one in front of you."

We have to have patience with others. We also have to have patience with ourselves.

Rav Shimon Schwab said that *Mashiach* is called a צֶמַח, *flower* (Zechariah 3:8): כִּי הִנְנִי מֵבִיא אֶת עַבְדִּי צֶמַח, *I will bring my servant Tzemach*. That is, *Mashiach*. Every day we say, "צֶמַח דָּוִד עַבְדְּךָ." Rav

Schwab explains that *Mashiach* is called a flower because the final redemption does not happen overnight. *Mashiach's* coming is a long, slow process, just as a flower takes time to grow. Everything good in life takes time and you have to have patience.

The Rebbetzin had patience. We have to have it too. Both in *ruchnius* matters and in *gashmius*.

For example, someone wants to finish a *masechta*, but it's taking so long that he stops. He should realize that not reaching the intended goal becomes more frustrating than having lost patience in the process and thereby stopping his progress. Anything in life that is worthwhile takes time.

If, for example, a person wants to lose weight, it takes patience. You're on a diet, you've lost some pounds, but it's taking forever and the next day you go out and get a doughnut because you've lost patience with the process. It just defeats your purpose and delays your achieving your goal.

Rebbetzin Kanievsky was a *savlan*; she was patient with others. The amount of patience you have in daily life and relationships can determine how much you enjoy life. Say you are standing in line in a store. It's taking the person in front of you so long to check out. Well, take it easy! Don't get so stressed out. Think of the Rebbetzin who had time for everyone. She didn't judge quickly. She was not harsh with others or with herself. Learn from her. Take it easy. Be a *savlan*.

Family Life

What touched me most about the Rebbetzin was her family life. She had five daughters and three sons. Her grandchildren were already grandparents. She was a great-great-great-grandmother. Rav Chaim and the Rebbetzin always wanted their family to live close to them. I was told that the furthest any of their descendants lived from them was a ten-minute walk. These children came to the Rebbetzin once a week. She knew each one's name, what school they attended, and what they were up to.

That is what family life was to her. That is what made her so special. Her public role did not interfere with her private role.

In his younger years, when his mother was still alive, Rav Chaim used to go to his parents' house every morning. His mother would make him a little breakfast — after all, he may have been the *gadol hador*, but he was still her son. When his mother passed away, Rav Chaim stopped visiting; he didn't expect his father to make breakfast for him.

One day Rav Chaim met his father, the Steipler, in the street. The Steipler said to him, "I also enjoyed your visits." Rav Chaim was upset; he had thought that his visits might disturb his father when he would rather be learning. From that day on, Rav Chaim went every day to have breakfast with his father.

Rav Chaim has a sister, Rebbetzin Ahuvah Barzam, who was widowed at a very young age. After their mother passed away, Rebbetzin Barzam moved into her parents' home and took care of her father. After the Steipler was *niftar*, Rav Chaim continued to visit his sister every day, until his age made it too difficult for him to go out so often. Thereafter, he visited her once a week.

That is what family is all about. That is the Rebbetzin's final lesson. No matter what you do for the public, don't forget about your family. To be involved with the whole world and not with your family would be a terrible sacrifice.

That is what family is all about. That is the Rebbetzin's final lesson. No matter what you do for the public, do not forget about your family. To be involved with the whole world and not with your family would be a terrible sacrifice.

May Hashem help that we are able to bring all these wonderful lessons we have learned about the Rebbetzin into our own lives.

Derech Eretz —
A Path for Life

The Torah tells us that the Jews were counted numerous times during their sojourn in the desert on the way from Egypt to *Eretz Yisrael*. The Ramban (*Bamidbar* 1:45) underscores that the Jews had to be counted בְּכָבוֹד וּגְדוּלָה, *with honor and distinction*.

He writes that Hashem warned Moshe: "You shall not [simply] say to the head of the family, 'How many [men] are in your family; how many sons do you have?' Rather they shall pass before you with awe and respect and you shall count them." From verses 1:2,3 (ibid.) it seems that the Ramban contends that they were counted by the "telling of their names." Every man stated his name as he gave his *machtzis hashekel* as an act of individual recognition.

The First to Say Hello

The Gemara (*Berachos* 17a) says that Rabbi Yochanan ben Zakkai always greeted someone first, whether the person was Jewish or non-Jewish. Rav Eliyahu Dessler (*Michtav Me'Eliyahu* 4:246) amplifies this

Gemara and writes, "Let's think for a moment who Rabbi Yochanan ben Zakkai was. *Chazal* say he basically knew everything: *Mikra, Mishnah, Halachah, Gemara, Dikdukei Torah*, etc. He even knew the language of the *malachim*. Not only that, but he was the *Nasi*. Every important question came to him. Rabbi Yochanan ben Zakkai had the concerns of *Klal Yisrael* on his shoulders." Yet, the Gemara tells us, he was never too busy to say hello to someone first, even a non-Jew. Can we imagine what kind of *kavod habriyos* (respect for people) Rabbi Yochanan ben Zakkai had?

Thus when the mail carrier brings your mail, be the first to say hello. When the janitor cleans up in school, be the first to say hello. When you walk into a store, be the first to say good morning to the proprietor. When you step on the bus, be the first to say hello to the bus driver.

That's what Rabbi Yochanan ben Zakkai would have done. Be first. That's *derech eretz*.

Saved by a "Hello"

Some of you might not have had the experience of being in a *shlachthois*, a slaughterhouse. It is usually a complex of barns and buildings, each with a different function. In one area, the animals are fed; in another, the animals are slaughtered. There's a building where the meat is cut and packed. Another area contains a big walk-in freezer where the meat is stored, as well as a business office and a locker room where the workers changed their clothes.

In Argentina the slaughterhouse opened very early every day at 5 in the morning and it closed about 5 or 6 in the evening. The owner, Zev,* would stay until about 8 at night. He would turn off the lights, drive to the guardhouse, say good-night to Pedro,* the security officer stationed there, and then each of them would leave in his own car. One night, at 8, Zev stopped at the guardhouse as usual and said, "Time to go home, Pedro."

"We can't go," Pedro replied.

"What do you mean? Why not?"

Pedro told Zev that someone hadn't left yet.

"How do you know?" Zev asked. "It's two hours after closing time. Everybody's gone."

"No," Pedro responded, "not everyone."

"Who is still here?"

Pedro told him that Rabbi Berkowitz, one of the *shochtim,* hadn't left yet. Zev doubted him, but the guard was insistent. So Zev and Pedro went back into the plant to look for the missing *shochet.*

The first place they checked was the locker room. Not there. They went to the business office. Not there. They went to the meat-packing plant. Not there either. Finally, they unlocked the door to the huge walk-in freezer. As they walked in, they were stunned to see Rabbi Berkowitz, rolling around on the floor trying to stay warm. He had accidentally locked himself in the freezer and no one had known about it. Had he been there overnight, he would have frozen to death. (Today they have a phone installed inside.)

After they helped Rabbi Berkowitz out and made sure he was warm and not injured, Zev asked Pedro, "How did you know he hadn't left yet?"

"That rabbi," Pedro replied, "always says 'Good morning' to me when he arrives, and every night before he leaves he says, 'Good night, have a pleasant evening.' And I wait for it, because almost no one else pays attention to me, because to them, I'm 'just' the security guard. But this rabbi makes me feel important, so I wait for his 'Good night' blessing. I knew he was here this morning, and I knew that he hadn't left yet."

Because of a simple "hello, good morning, good evening," Rabbi Berkowitz's life was saved. Now, that doesn't mean that every time you say hello your life will be saved, but we see how far reaching *derech eretz* can be.

Reflection in the Pupil

Rabbi Avraham Chaim Feuer once took his father-in-law, Rav Mordechai Gifter, *zt'l,* the Rosh Yeshivah of Telshe Yeshivah in Cleveland, to a well-respected eye doctor in Brooklyn, Dr. Sam Cohen. Since Rabbi Feuer had just written his *sefer* on *Tehillim,* he said, "Doctor, I want to tell you something very interesting that I saw recently by the Radak on a *pasuk* in *Tehillim* (17:8). David HaMelech says to Hashem, שָׁמְרֵנִי כְּאִישׁוֹן בַּת עָיִן, *Watch me like the pupil of an eye.*

Rav Feuer asked Dr. Cohen, "Why is the pupil of the eye called אִישׁוֹן? Where does the word come from?" He continued, "The Radak (ibid.) says that אִישׁוֹן comes from the word אִישׁ, *man*. If you look very closely into the pupil of the *eye* of another person, whom do you see? Yourself. Not only that, but the suffix ון indicates 'a small one.' *Yeled* is a child; *yaldon* is a little child. *Ish* is a man; *ishon* is a little man. When you look at the pupil of the eye of another person you will see *ishon*, a little man. You will actually be seeing yourself."

Rav Gifter heard this and exclaimed, "What a great *mussar haskel* (moral lesson) we can learn from this *Radak!* Most of the time when one person talks to another, the person talking thinks he's the big man; that others have to listen to him because he's the important one. But here's a great lesson: when you look at somebody else, you are supposed to look at that reflection in his eye and see yourself as the little man, and view the person you are speaking to as the important one, the big one."

That's *derech eretz*: looking at someone else and seeing yourself as a little person; giving the other person the feeling that he is important. Everyone is special for a different reason. Most of the time we focus on why we ourselves are special. However, the lesson of *ishon* is that we should view the other person as the significant one and "bigger" than we are.

A Mad Rush

It seems that everybody is in a rush these days. When we're rushed, we don't think about the other person. But the essence of *derech eretz* is this: Don't just think about yourself; think about somebody else.

Listen to this story.

> A fellow who works for Hatzolah gets a call at 2 in the morning. He knows that if someone is calling at that hour there is a serious problem. He answers the phone and indeed there's someone whose life is in danger. He quickly dresses and runs down to his car — but there is another car blocking his driveway! Someone had parked there!

Frantic, he calls the dispatcher on his radio to have someone else handle the emergency. *Baruch Hashem*, the fellow was saved. The first Hatzolah fellow was so furious that he wanted to call the police to ticket the man who was parked in his driveway. But when he looked out the window, the car was gone.

Next time you want to block a driveway, think for a moment. What if it's a Hatzolah fellow and he's going to save your grandson, or your niece, or your child, or your mother? What right does anyone have to block someone else's driveway? Is it just because they don't want to walk

> **Just because your are in a trying situation (or lazy), the other person doesn't have to suffer.**

an extra block? Remember, just because you are in a trying situation (or lazy) is not a reason for somebody else to suffer.

The Fancy Dress Disgrace

The *Sefer HaChinuch* (338) teaches us something important regarding *derech eretz*: "Do not pain somebody else with words." An example might be not reminding a *baal teshuvah* or *ger* about his past. That is an *issur d'Oraisa*.

But how many of us are aware that this issue applies even when doing something as innocent as shopping in a store? The *Chinuch* tells us: "You are not allowed to go in and say to a storekeeper, 'How much is this?' if you have no intention of buying."

You're allowed to browse, of course, but then you must first tell the storekeeper and not keep him/her waiting, hoping to make a sale. A Rav told me the following incident that touches on this topic. It happened to a member of his shul.

> A woman went shopping in a high-end store looking for an expensive dress.
>
> "What's your return policy?" she asked. "How many days do I have to return something if I don't really like it?"

"We have a seven–day return policy," the sales-woman politely replied.

"Seven days? No problem. By then I'll know if I want to keep it."

Five days later, she returned the dress. Okay, she didn't like it. Nothing wrong with that, right?

Well, the next week another woman came in and tried on the same dress. She turned to the owner and commented, "I didn't know that you sell second-hand dresses."

Insulted, the owner replied, "Of course we don't."

The woman then said, "Really? I just found this card in the pocket, 'You are seated at Table 7.'"

The first woman wore it to a wedding, forgot to take her place card out of the pocket, and then returned the dress. I find this to be an outrageous act of chutzpah and lack of *derech eretz*. I would even venture to say there is an element of *geneivah* (stealing) involved here, but the total disregard of another's possessions is surely reprehensible.

A Stuttering Sensitivity

Let's think for a moment about sensitivity and *derech eretz*.

Rav Chaim Ozer Grodzenski was once walking with a *talmid* when a young man came over to them. This fellow stuttered terribly, and he asked the *talmid* for directions. The *talmid* told him. Then Rav Chaim Ozer instructed the *talmid* to go with the man to show him the way; the *rav* would wait for him to come back. The *talmid* did as his rebbi asked. When he came back, he asked Rav Chaim Ozer why he had him go with the man; his directions had been clear.

Rav Chaim Ozer answered, "A person who stutters is very self-conscious about it, and every time he has to begin talking to a new person, it is very embarrassing. Could you imagine how embarrassed the man must have been to have to come over to us and ask for directions? What if he was nervous? What if he didn't understand the directions? Then he would have to ask another person and suffer again. To avoid that, it was worth it to wait while you escorted the man to his destination."

That's *derech eretz*. That's sensitivity.

One more famous story about Rav Chaim Ozer:

> Rav Yechiel Yaakov Weinberg, a renowned *talmid chacham* from Switzerland who wrote *Sridei Eish*, was in Vilna for Succos and went to Rav Chaim Ozer's house, hoping he would be able to eat in Rav Chaim Ozer's *succah*. Rav Chaim Ozer wasn't feeling well, so he said to Rav Weinberg, "*Bekavod gadol*, you can eat in my *succah*, but I am an *oneis* (exempt). I'm not feeling well and won't eat in the *succah* tonight."
>
> Rav Weinberg took his food out to the *succah*. Ten minutes later, Rav Chaim Ozer came into the *succah* and sat down with him. Rav Weinberg asked, "Didn't the Rav say he was an *oneis* and *patur* from (not obligated in) the mitzvah of *succah*?"
>
> "I may be *patur* (exempt) from *succah*," Rav Chaim Ozer replied, "but I'm not *patur* from *hachnasas orchim* (hosting guests)."

"I may be *patur* from *succah*," Rav Chaim Ozer said, "but I'm not *patur* from *hachnasas orchim*."

After You, Sir

In New York, when Rudy Giuliani was mayor, there used to be a great little sign on highways that read "After You, Sir." That was meant to remind everybody to let the other person go first: at a toll booth, onto a bridge, or even into another lane of faster-moving traffic.

Imagine if people really lived that way.

We really should not have to imagine it, because that is part of *derech eretz,* which is a real obligation, especially toward people who are older. Let somebody else sit down first or deplane first. What's the rush to get off the plane? (Especially on international flights.) You're going to wait an hour for your luggage anyway. And if you don't have luggage, you'll wait at passport control. If you are going to wait some-place anyway, what is the rush?

If only we could learn and live by "After you, sir." We would be calmer, less stressed, and have a little more *derech eretz.*

Panim el Panim

When the *Kohanim* begin to *duchen,* they face the *aron kodesh,* just as the *chazzan* does. In the middle of their *berachah,* they turn around so that when they are finishing the last word of the *berachah,* which is *be'ahavah,* to bless *Klal Yisrael* "with love," they are facing the congregation, *panim el panim,* "face-to-face."

The *Mishnah Berurah* (225:2) says that if you haven't seen your friend for 30 days you are supposed to say the *berachah* of *Shehecheyanu.* If you haven't seen somebody in a year, you make the *berachah Mechayeh HaMeisim,* thanking *Hashem* for being the One "Who revives the dead."

What if you have a pen pal? You've been writing to this person for five years but you've never seen him. Now for the first time after all these years of writing to each other and feeling close to each other, you meet. Do you make this *berachah* of *Shehecheyanu* or not?

The *Mishnah Berurah* answers that even though people have been writing each other letters, and even though they are good friends, they nevertheless do not say the *berachah* because there has not been a face-to-face (*panim el panim*) connection. Only seeing some-one face-to-face generates the happiness that would obligate one to make the *berachah* of *Shehecheyanu.* The only way to have true love for another person is *panim el panim,* if you see them face-to-face.

That is the reason to have gatherings of *chizuk:* so that people can see each other. It is not enough only to listen to a recorded lecture. Seeing each other creates *ahavah* (love) and *achvah* (brotherhood).

We have to look each other in the face, *panim el panim*. We have to look at the other person and see the *ishon*, the little man that is us! We have to make the other person feel *chashuv*. And if we can learn that *derech eretz* is not just a nice idea, but an obligation, we will be *zocheh* to hear *Bircas Kohanim* in the *Beis HaMikdash* in our times.

However the *Midrash Tanchuma* (*Nitzavim* 1) teaches that *"Klal Yisrael will not be redeemed until we are one group."* It would seem to me that this can happen only when we have a mutual respect and tolerance for each other; and that all starts with *derech eretz*.

Public Eyes and Private I's

Reb Elimelech "Mike" Tress was an outstanding *oseik b'tzarchei tzibbur*, a community activist of the highest order. At the time of World War II, he worked day and night to bring thousands of refugees to America. One of them was HaGaon Rav Aharon Kotler and another was Rav Avraham Kalmanowitz. He obtained visas for many of the Mir students who were stuck in Shanghai and was in constant contact with Washington politicians to see to it that Jews could come to America. He opened the first Agudas Yisrael office in America; it was in Williamsburg at 616 Bedford Avenue. Many of the refugees lived on the top floor of that building.

In those days in Williamsburg, the revered Reb Shraga Feivel Mendlowitz was the *menahel* of Yeshivah Torah Vodaath. He delivered *shiurim* on *mussar* and *hashkafah* to the *talmidim* and local *baalei batim* who found him so inspirational. The following episode that happened at one of these *shiurim* was told to me by Dr. David Kranzler, who wrote a book about Reb Elimelech Tress.

One Motza'ei Shabbos, as many working men were gathered for his regular *Tehillim shiur,* Rav Shraga Feivel began by saying, "You know, *rabbosai*, today I had a dream." He continued, "I dreamed that *Mashiach* came … and that Rabbi Eliezer Silver came flying in from Cincinnati, Rav Kalmanowitz flew in from Washington, and the Boyaner Rebbe and the Kopycznitzer Rebbe came in from the Lower East Side. Everyone was making a tumult, clamoring to come up front to see *Mashiach*! And then, *Mashiach* came over to me and said, 'Who is that young man sitting in the back?' He was pointing to Elimelech Tress, who was sitting quietly by himself. And I told *Mashiach*, 'He is the man who brought you here.'"

> Rav Shraga Feivel began by saying, "You know, rabbosai, today I had a dream." He continued, "I dreamed that *Mashiach* came …."

Rav Shraga Feivel was teaching that a person who puts his entire heart and soul into the community's welfare has the merit to be able to bring *Mashiach*.

The Meaning of an Ish Elokim

There is an illuminating *Midrash* (*Bereishis Rabbah* 35:3) that brings out this point. "Rav Berachia says, 'Moshe Rabbeinu was more beloved to Hashem than Noach.'" We know this because at first Noach is described in the Torah with the words, נֹחַ אִישׁ צַדִּיק, *Noach was a righteous man* (*Bereishis* 6:9), but at the end of his life, the Torah writes, Noach was an אִישׁ הָאֲדָמָה, *a man of the earth* (ibid. 9:20). He started out as a *tzaddik* but degenerated into a man of the earth.

However, Moshe was different. At the start of his public life he is called an אִישׁ מִצְרִי, *an Egyptian man* (*Shemos* 2:19), but later in his life he was elevated and referred to as אִישׁ הָאֱלֹקִים, *a man of G-d* (*Devarim* 33:1).

Expounding on this *Midrash*, the *Meshech Chochmah* (*Parashas Noach* 9:2) says that there are two ways a person can be involved in *avodas Hashem*. One way is to lock himself in a room and grow in his own spirituality; another way is to be involved in *tzarchei tzibbur*, the needs of the community. And that, he says, was the difference between Noach and Moshe.

Many people think that if they divest themselves of all worldly involvement, they will be able to grow higher in *ruchnius*. However, no one was higher in *ruchnius* than Moshe Rabbeinu, and he reached his heights due to his involvement with *Klal Yisrael* with all his heart and soul. That is how one goes from being an אִישׁ מִצְרִי to being an אִישׁ הָאֱלֹקִים.

The Goat Story

The following amusing but instructional story was told to me by the noted teacher and *talmid chacham*, Rabbi Alter Metzger, from Crown Heights in Brooklyn.

A family from *Eretz Yisrael* called Rabbi Metzger. Their daughter was marrying an American boy and they needed a place to stay for a few weeks until after the wedding. He had an empty apartment on the first floor of his home, so he rented it to them. After the *sheva berachos*, Rabbi Metzger hosted a little *seudas preidah* (a goodbye party) for them before their return to *Eretz Yisrael*. As they were sitting and talking about marriage and the future, Rabbi Metzger told them a story that took place in a small town in Russia before the Revolution.

In the town, there was a *cheder* in a shul where a *melamed* taught many children every day. There was a boy in the class who was always wild and disruptive. One day this boy woke up early, took a baby goat from a local farm, arrived at the shul before anybody else, pushed the goat into the *aron hakodesh*, locked the door, and waited for everyone to show up.

After the *melamed* and the children arrived and started to *daven*, their voices frightened the goat, which started to bleat frantically from inside the *aron hakodesh*. When the *melamed* opened the door, the goat jumped out, causing a major disruption as children screamed and scampered all around the building.

The *melamed* immediately realized who the culprit was and took him to the local Rav. The Rav said that since the boy had repeatedly made trouble, he would be expelled from the *cheder*. As a matter of policy, the expulsion was referred to the person who was in charge of all the *chadarim* in the area, Rabbi Sholom Dov Ber Schneerson (the fifth Lubavitcher Rebbe, known as the RaSHaB, 1860-1920). The Rebbe agreed that based on his past behavior, this latest episode gave him no choice but to order the child to leave the *cheder* and never come back.

The boy listened intently and then, looking up at the Rebbe, exclaimed with seriousness beyond his years, "Rebbe, if you throw me out, you are throwing out my children, my grandchildren, and my great-grandchildren forever!"

The Rebbe was absolutely stunned by the remark. The viewpoint expressed by this seemingly reckless child bespoke thoughtfulness and maturity. His comment displayed a perception beyond his age. The Rebbe thought for a moment and decided that this boy deserved at least one more chance. The boy was taken back to the *cheder*, and after consultation with the Rav and the child's *melamed*, the child was reinstated.

> **"Rebbe, if you throw me out, you are throwing out my children, my grandchildren, and my great-grandchildren forever!"**

After finishing the story, Rabbi Metzger added hesitantly, "I am told that this boy eventually became a fine, upstanding fellow, but I really have no idea. I only said it over for its valuable message."

The father of the *kallah* from *Eretz Yisrael* then spoke and shocked everyone: "I do know it's true. My wife, the mother of the bride, is the granddaughter of that young boy in the story! We always thought it was a family secret in *Eretz Yisrael*. We never realized that the story was known in America as well!"

Every child is a link to the past and a link to the future. All of us know the expression, "a chain is only as strong as its weakest link." Our foremost responsibility and priority must be our children. We must dedicate our lives to making sure that the children Hashem has blessed us with will be strong links in the chain back to Har Sinai, and then become strong links to the chain leading to *Mashiach*.

On one hand, we have our great responsibility to each of our children and yet we must also be aware of our responsibility to community. How do we combine them?

Charity Begins at Home: A Deeper Meaning

Rav Aharon Kotler, *zt'l*, writes (*Mishnas Rav Aharon*, Vol. 1, p. 176) that part of our children's education is teaching them to have a strong sense of responsibility to the community.

We have all heard the expression, "Charity begins at home." How do we reconcile that with attending to the needs of the public? Most of us think the expression refers to giving charity; in other words, when you give of yourself and your resources, you usually start by giving at home. I think it has another meaning as well: Not only the giving of charity, but teaching charity, teaching concern — that's what begins at home. If your attitude is that only you and your family matter, then your children will never know anything about the community. Before you teach and preach to everyone else, teach your children the concept of "*achrayus to the klal*."

In America, we are obsessed with rights: animal rights, civil rights, squatter's rights, voting rights, pilot's rights, passenger's rights, tenant's rights, right to life, right to die. The American constitution is based on the Bill of Rights.

But where is the Bill of Duties, the Bill of Responsibilities?

A Jew is first supposed to live by a Bill of Responsibilities. How do we teach children that sense of responsibility? We do it by practicing it ourselves. If parents show that they care about others, then their children will learn to care.

And we can teach it in myriad ways. Here is one example. Every school has a snow list, which means that when school is canceled because of a snowstorm, person A is supposed to call person B; B is supposed to call C; C is supposed to call D, and so on. What if D's line is busy? So Mr. C may think, *I will call back in a minute.* However, think about it. What about the families of E, F, G, and the rest? Maybe

D's phone is broken or perhaps they are out of town. If you don't feel a responsibility to the community, you may satisfy yourself by having tried to call family D, but in the meantime others will suffer. Call the next person on the list. Make sure they don't needlessly trudge through the snow to get to a school that isn't open.

A wealthy man in our neighborhood had two wonderful sons, and they became, like their father, generous and very considerate. How did the father teach them to be generous? One son told me that two days before his wedding, his father called him in for a little chat. The father told him that they were spending a great deal of money on the wedding, but that they had no right to spend money only on themselves. He then took out the bills that had accrued because of the wedding and told his son to add up the sum. Then he sat down with his son and showed him that he was giving the same sum to *tzedakah*.

For his grandson's bar mitzvah, this wealthy man opened up a checking account for the boy and then told him he would give him $100 for the account, but the boy would have to write out 10 checks of $10 each to *tzedakah*. That's how he taught his grandson how to be generous.

Rav Yitzchak Hutner once said that there are certain people who bring guests when *Yom Tov* comes, but there are other people who bring *Yom Tov* when guests come. Some people love to have guests. No matter who they are, you can always learn something from guests. You've heard the expression, "Even a broken clock is right twice a day." That means everyone has something to teach: a *dvar* Torah, a life experience, a song. Therefore, when you have a guest and the children see that you welcome him and try to make him comfortable and happy, that is teaching — that is "charity begins at home."

> **Rav Hutner once said that there are certain people who only bring guests when *Yom Tov* comes, but there are other people who bring *Yom Tov* when guests come.**

Regardless of your financial or social status, your attitude toward others will be the foundation upon which your children will build their concern for the rest of the Jewish people.

The Dilemma

My dear friend, Rabbi Yaakov Salomon, is involved in many important activities; educational seminars, individual and marital therapy, and inspiring films and books. When his son Shmuel Salomon was young, he came home from school announcing that they finished *Chumash Bereishis* and would be having a *siyum*. As a dutiful father, Yaakov expressed joy for the wonderful accomplishment. However Shmuel then told his father that there would be a *siyum* celebration in class and that all the boys' fathers were invited. Shmuel was sure his father would go. Yaakov told him that actually he could not be there, because he was involved in Aish HaTorah's Discovery Program and had to fly to Boston that day to give a class that had been scheduled weeks in advance. Shmuel was devastated.

What should a parent do when faced with such a conflict?

Yaakov told his son that he was going to make a special *siyum* for him on the coming Shabbos, and he would invite all the boys in the class. He would even ask the Rebbi to come, too. The boys recited the *Birchas Yaakov* from *Parashas Vayechi* and everyone felt wonderful. Then, Yaakov told the boys something they would always remember. He explained to them how fortunate they were: they were able to finish *Bereishis*. But there were so many grown-ups who didn't even know what *Bereishis* was about, they never had an opportunity to learn *Chumash,* and it was his obligation to try to help them gain a desire for learning so that they too would one day start and finish *Bereishis*.

He knew he had to be out of town, but he told his child and his friends what he had to do and why he had to do it. The family and the class would never forget it.[1]

The Day Is Short

In *Pirkei Avos* (2:20, 21), Rav Tarfon says, רַבִּי טַרְפוֹן אוֹמֵר, הַיּוֹם קָצָר וְהַמְּלָאכָה מְרֻבָּה, וְהַפּוֹעֲלִים עֲצֵלִים, וְהַשָּׂכָר הַרְבֵּה, וּבַעַל הַבַּיִת דּוֹחֵק, *The day is short and the task is abundant; the laborers are lazy and*

---

1. See the wonderful story regarding Rav Moshe Feinstein's conflict in attending his grandson's bar mitzvah or being at the Agudas Yisroel Convention, told to me by his son Rav Reuven Feinstein, in *Perspectives of the Maggid,* p. 139).

the Master of the house [Hashem] is insistent [because there is so much to get done]. Then the next *Mishnah* tells us, הוּא הָיָה אוֹמֵר, לֹא עָלֶיךָ הַמְּלָאכָה לִגְמוֹר, וְלֹא אַתָּה בֶן חוֹרִין לְבָטֵל מִמֶּנָּה, *Rav Tarfon said,* "You are not required to complete the task, yet you are not free to withdraw from it."

There is no way that any of us can solve all the problems *Klal Yisrael* is confronted with: finances, health, social (marriages, children), but that is not an excuse for not doing whatever we can and thereby showing our children that we care. Don't feel guilty if you can't do it all. Some people feel overwhelmed because they can't do enough and they feel terrible about themselves. That's wrong. Take one or two organizations and make them your pet projects. Get involved and set an example. You can't fix the world. A child will understand. If you make it your business to be home at the child's bedtime, if you make it your business to be there to help with the homework or when a child is ill, the child will come to understand that there are other times a parent just has to be somewhere else.

Shlomo HaMelech writes, כַּבֵּד אֶת ה' מֵהוֹנֶךָ, *Honor Hashem with everything that He granted you* (*Mishlei* 3:9). Rashi explains that if you have a sweet voice, use that to honor Him. If you can sing, you have no right to refuse to *daven* for the *amud*. If you have a talent for writing, you have no right to hold it back from people. If you can sew, go out and offer to make clothing for those who can't afford to buy. If you can write plays or be a substitute teacher, volunteer to help in a school.

I remember Rav Avrohom Pam teaching us this frightening *Yalkut Shemoni* (*Mishlei* 3:932) about Navos HaYizreali on the aforementioned *pasuk*. Navos had a vineyard that King Achav wanted to purchase because it bordered on other land that the king already owned (see *I Melachim* 21:1). Navos refused to sell because he said it was a family inheritance toward which he had emotional attachment. When Achav's vindictive wife, Izevel, saw how distressed her husband was over not being able to procure the vineyard, she orchestrated an evil plan that resulted in Navos being killed.

However, the *Yalkut* explains, Navos had a beautiful voice. And every year he would go to Jerusalem for the holidays and people would be inspired by his melodious prayers. One year he refused to go and subsequently the evil plan was perpetrated against him and he lost his life.

The *Yalkut Shemoni* exclaims, "What caused this? Because he refused to go to Jerusalem and honor Hashem with the talent He had bestowed him with."

Being granted a talent (or wealth for that matter) is not only a privilege, it's a responsibility!

There are people who are wealthy in time. You know your time bankbook. If your children are older, or if the older ones can sometimes take care of the younger ones, then you are wealthy in time. Serve Hashem with what He has blessed you; one of those blessings is time. If you have time to tutor a new immigrant, teach him *alef-beis* or a *pasuk* of *Chumash*. If you have a wealth of knowledge, even if it is only that of knowing a *pasuk* that someone else does not know, you are obligated to help. (See *Mishnas Rav Aharon* 2:65, Elul.)

A Real Chesed

Sarah Schenirer, the founder of the Bais Yaakov movement, was a very devoted person. One night when she was up late, a student approached her and asked why she had not gone to sleep yet. She answered that every day she made a *din v'cheshbon* and wrote down everything she had done that day. That day, Sarah Schenirer said, she had been so busy that she had not done a *chesed* for anyone, and since at night the *neshamah* ascends to *Shamayim*, she was afraid that her *neshamah* would go up empty.

The student was astounded. "You mean that even this late at night you are waiting to do a *chesed* for someone?"

"That is right. Do you have a *chesed* I could do?"

The girl answered, "Yes, I have a great *chesed* you could do. You could go to bed now, so that tomorrow you will be refreshed and ready to teach us all."

Sarah Schenirer got up and gave the girl a kiss, saying, "You gave me life!" She said *Krias Shema* and went to bed.

We have to remember that even as we discuss our responsibility to the community, we cannot forget our responsibility to ourselves. We have to remember how to smile. We have to be healthy and take care of ourselves, because our children, spouses, and friends need us. Only if we are happy and smile will we have the ability to make others happy and make others smile.

May it be the will of Hashem that Rav Shraga Feivel's dream that "*Mashiach* came" becomes a reality. May the merits that all of us deserve for becoming involved in the community be the catalyst that brings *Mashiach*, and may we come to understand the proper balancing of our priorities so that we and our children as a unit see the ultimate *Geulah*. May it come in our day.

Criticism With Care

The Gemara (*Bava Basra* 8b) quotes a *pasuk* in *Daniel* (12:3): וּמַצְדִּיקֵי הָרַבִּים כַּכּוֹכָבִים לְעוֹלָם וָעֶד, *Those who teach right-eousness to the multitudes [shall shine] like the stars, for-ever and ever.* To whom is Daniel referring? The Gemara answers: *Eilu milamdim tinokos* — they are the [Torah] teachers of children.

They are the true stars of the generation, whether it is the rebbi, the parents, *mechanchim,* or *mechanchos.* The ones who teach Torah to children are like stars.

Why does the Gemara compare these people to stars? The Maharsha explains that it is because stars are not always visible. They can be seen at night, but not by day. The true barometer of a good and effective rebbi [or parent] is the one whose influence is felt by the student many years later, even when that rebbi can no longer be seen; even if the sun of that rebbi may have set and he is now in the *Olam HaEmes.*

Thus years after a child was in school, when he has to choose a partner in marriage, or a place to live, or a shul to *daven* in, or a business to go into, he will think back to his mentor and ask himself, *What would he say? What would he do? How would he advise me?*

That's the sign of a true star: having an influence even if he can no longer be seen.

What It Means to Be a Star

This role of a rebbi is not only a privilege, but a tremendous responsibility. We can learn this lesson from an incredible story.

Many years ago, in Vilna, there was an exclusive hotel where only the very wealthiest people made their weddings.

In Vilna there lived a shoemaker who was very poor but very diligent. He made money slowly but steadily and put as much of it aside as he could. After a while he was able to invest in other businesses, and after some years he had become wealthy. He kept a low profile, though, and most people did not know how well off he actually was. Eventually, his daughter became engaged, and he decided to hold the wedding in this expensive hotel.

When the wealthy people heard this, they were insulted. "This *shlepper* of a shoemaker is going to make a wedding in our exclusive hall? What a *bizayon* (humiliation)!" They decided to ridicule and embarrass him. After the *chuppah*, when the father was walking down the aisle behind the new couple, accepting *mazel tovs*, a few of the wealthy men each held out a dirty old shoe and said, "This shoe has no sole or heel, could you fix it for me?"

Everyone started laughing — except the shoemaker. He was humiliated. The prank was the talk of Vilna for the next few days.

At that time, Rabbi Yisrael Salanter was living in Vilna. His reaction to this story was frightening. "I am positive," he said, "that right now in *Shamayim*, the *gedolim* who lived here in the previous generation are being judged, for they had the opportunity to teach these people how to behave but did not."

In other words, those *gedolim* were being called to judgment in heaven and asked if they really did all that they could have done to set those people on the proper path. Indeed, it's possible that the *gedolim* would be judged favorably but nevertheless Rav Yisrael taught that there was going to be a judgment on them and their townsfolk. Did they exert the influence they could have? Or were the townsfolk so corrupt that the guidance of their teachers was to no avail?

Nevertheless, Rabbi Yisrael Salanter is teaching us that there is such a thing as giving a judgment and accounting on the ultimate Judgment Day, even years later, for not having a positive influence on those individuals whom you could have affected. People who have children or students under their influence are held liable for their actions even well after the former are gone.

Stealing From Yourself

A Jew who was not particularly religious came to speak with Rav Zalman Plitnick in Liverpool, England. The man's daughter was about to intermarry. The man approached the Rav and asked him to please speak to his daughter, to convince her to break off or at least delay her wedding. Rav Plitnick agreed. He ended up speaking to her for over an hour. After the girl left, the Rav called the father back into his office and told him that he had tried but was not successful; he could not change her mind.

The father felt terrible. Rav Plitnick then told him a story from the Chofetz Chaim. (Rav Plitnick was married to a daughter of Rav Moshe Landynski, who had been a Rosh Yeshivah in Radin; thus, whenever he visited his father-in-law in Radin, he would also go to see the Chofetz Chaim.) The Chofetz Chaim once told him the following story.

> There was a doctor who had an exclusive medicine that was able to cure children of a terrible disease. No one else had this medicine. Every day, children and their parents would line up outside his clinic to get this special medication. All of the children in his neighborhood were healed. The doctor began travel-

ing to other cities to heal the children there. Wherever he set up an office, long lines of patients and their families would form.

One night, as he was traveling, he was attacked and robbed by highwaymen. They took everything he had and ran to the riverbank to go through his bags. They hoped to take his valuables and toss the rest into the river. They did not find much, though, and threw everything into the water. The next morning the doctor went to his clinic, empty-handed. He was about to enter when he was approached by a hysterical man, pleading for some medication for his ill son.

The doctor looked more closely at the man and said, "Don't you recognize me?"

"No," the man answered, "have we met before?"

"Yes, we have," said the doctor. "You robbed me last night. What did you do with my things?"

"You had no money in your bags," stammered the man, "so I threw them into the river."

"Well, you fool, you tossed away the very medication you needed," said the doctor. "It was in your hands last night. Now I have nothing, and so do you."

The Chofetz Chaim explained that many times, we want the *rabbanim* or the teachers to guide our children properly. But if a family comes home from shul and the father criticizes the Rav or when the children come home from school and parents mock the teachers or ridicule the administration, they are undermining the credibility of their children's education. The child thinks he doesn't have to listen to the rebbi or the *morah*, because his parents told him the rebbi or *morah* is wrong.

If the parent takes away the Rav's credibility, the child is not going to listen to that Rav or to any other. If the parent takes away the credibility of the teacher, the child will feel that she is right and the teacher is wrong and will no longer listen to the teacher. When the teacher comes to advise the child, the child will reject the advice, even if it is correct.

"All these years you were not *frum*," Rav Plitnick told the father, "and you criticized *rabbanim* and *mechanchim*. Now no Rav can help you; she simply won't listen to someone who has no credibility in her eyes."

My daughter-in-law, Genendel, teaches third grade in the Yeshiva Ketana of Waterbury, Connecticut. She posted a sign in her classroom: Don't say to the teacher, "What you're saying makes no sense!" Say to the teacher, "I'm having trouble understanding what you're saying."

This can be deduced homiletically from the teaching of *Chazal*, לְעוֹלָם יְסַפֵּר אָדָם בְּלָשׁוֹן נְקִיָּה, *A person should always speak in a refined manner* (*Pesachim* 3a; see also *Yoreh Deah* 244).

Criticism and Love

Rav Shimon Schwab once told me that before a parent or anyone else criticizes someone, they should be sad, not angry. If you are sad that you must criticize another, you will talk differently than you will if you are angry. If you are angry, you will wipe away the other person and destroy him.

> **Rav Schwab told me that before a parent or anyone else criticizes someone, they should be sad, not angry.**

He then asked an interesting question, and provided a fascinating answer. In *Parashas Mishpatim* (*Shemos* 21:15-17), three verses follow one after another, but the middle one seems to have no connection to the others:

וּמַכֵּה אָבִיו וְאִמּוֹ מוֹת יוּמָת
One who strikes his father or mother shall be surely put to death.

וְגֹנֵב אִישׁ וּמְכָרוֹ וְנִמְצָא בְיָדוֹ מוֹת יוּמָת
One who kidnaps a man and sells him, and he was found to have been in his power, shall surely be put to death.

וּמְקַלֵּל אָבִיו וְאִמּוֹ מוֹת יוּמָת
One who curses his father or mother shall surely be put to death.

The first and third verses are about mistreating parents. How does the second verse, referring to kidnapping, connect to the other two?

Rav Schwab explains that this is a warning to parents not to treat their children like kidnapped hostages, constantly breathing down their necks, stifling their initiative, suppressing or ridiculing their youthful plans and aspirations. Parents who act like slave drivers might one day trigger an open rebellion, with disastrous results. (See *Selected Speeches*, p. 102.)

Hashem has blessed us with children. Let them grow. Build them, don't break them.

Hashem has blessed us with children. Let them grow. Build them, don't break them.

A study was conducted. Out of 20 comments made by parents to children, 19 were critical! That is incredible. "Why did you do that? Why didn't you do this? Why didn't you listen? How many times do I have to tell you …?"

Again, Rav Schwab brings out a beautiful point. In *Vayikra* (19:17) we are taught, הוֹכֵחַ תּוֹכִיחַ, *[at times] you must give mussar*. What does the next *pasuk* say? וְאָהַבְתָּ לְרֵעֲךָ כָּמוֹךָ, *love your fellow as yourself* (ibid. v. 18). What is the connection? The reason for giving *mussar* is to guide or inspire your fellow Jew. He may be doing something wrong, but if you want him to change his ways it can and will only be done through love.

The Shelah comments on *Mishlei* (9:8): אַל תּוֹכַח לֵץ פֶּן יִשְׂנָאֶךָּ הוֹכַח לְחָכָם וְיֶאֱהָבֶךָּ, *Do not rebuke a scoffer, lest he hate you; rebuke a wise man, and he will love you.* The Shelah, by adjusting the punctuation, says: אַל תּוֹכַח, *Don't give mussar* לֵץ by calling someone a scoffer. In other words, don't give *mussar,* by calling anyone a derogatory name, such as lazy, stupid, idiotic, etc. If you give that kind of *mussar* the person will surely resent you. Treat them as though they are fine, wise people: "You're such a *tzaddik*, so how could you do that?" They will appreciate your sensitivity and, hopefully, listen to you.

This happened with a father I know.

> This father had a son who was born with very curly hair, like steel wool. The parents had the *minhag* not to cut the boy's hair until he was 3 years old. Every day the boy rode his bike in the house, and every day his *yarmulke* flew off his head, and it drove his father

crazy. How could his son not pick up his *yarmulke*? Every night the father would yell at the boy when his son didn't pick up his *yarmulke* when it fell off. The father gave him Velcro and bobby pins, but nothing helped. One night the boy pedaled past his father's desk and his *yarmulke* flew off, but he kept on going. The father got so upset he said, "You're such a...!" and then he stopped himself. *Why am I going to yell at the boy*, the father thought. *Is it his fault that he has hair like that?*

Instead, he said to his young son, "You're such a *tzaddik*, how could you not wear a *yarmulke*?" From that night on, the boy never failed to pick up his *yarmulke* when it fell off his head. After all he was a *tzaddik*!

Cat and Mouse in the House

Rav Yitzchak Elchonon Spektor, the Rav in Kovno, once called in a person from his shul and asked him how he could have criticized others in the community. Even if it were true that they had done wrong, this man did not have the right to criticize them. The man replied, "Excuse me, but this past Shabbos you yourself criticized them for the same thing!"

Rav Yitzchak Elchonon answered, "There is a big difference between you and me, the same as the difference between a housewife and a cat. Neither the housewife nor the cat wants the mice in the house. However, the housewife would rather the mice never entered, but the cat wants the mice to come in so that it can catch and eat them. I would rather these people never committed the *aveirah* in the first place. You, on the other hand, can't wait for people to do wrong, so that you can criticize them!"

No Strings Attached

A young fellow went to Rav Chaim Ozer Grodzinsky, the *gadol hador* of Vilna, and asked for a *berachah* to be exempted from the draft. Rav Chaim Ozer asked him if he was *shomer Shabbos*. The boy could not lie and so he answered that he was not. Rav Chaim Ozer asked if the boy ever put on *tefillin*. Again the boy answered, sheepishly and with humility, no. Rav Chaim Ozer asked if he wore *tzitzis*. Deeply ashamed, the boy said no again. Rav Chaim Ozer said to him, "I give you a *berachah* that the Russian Army should be as disappointed in you as I am!"

Rav Chaim Ozer got his message across, but gave him a blessing as well.

A few weeks later, the boy returned to Rav Chaim Ozer to tell him that the Russian Army was indeed disappointed in him and had rejected him! Then he lifted his shirt to show the Rav that he was wearing *tzitzis*. He also told him that he was putting on *tefillin* and he was going to be *shomer Shabbos* for the rest of his life.

Rav Chaim Ozer had the opportunity to break him, but he built him up instead and he became a soldier in Hashem's army.

Open-and-Shut Case

In the 1950's, many stores were open on Shabbos in Yerushalayim. People tried to convince the owners to close, but they met with little success. One storekeeper, though, was adamant that he would remain open on Shabbos. Rav Aryeh Levin dressed for Shabbos early on one Friday afternoon, and went to that store and sat down a few minutes before candle-lighting time. The storekeeper knew who the Rav was, and he knew when Shabbos began. After a while he approached Rav Aryeh and asked him why he was there. Obviously, he was not planning to buy anything.

Rav Aryeh replied that he had come to see for himself how much business he did on Shabbos, and why it was so difficult for him to close his shop at that time. He had heard that he was very busy then, and now he saw that was true.

"I see," Rav Aryeh told the owner, "that it really is a very hard test for you, as you really do a wonderful business at this time. But, Shabbos is Shabbos."

The shopkeeper said, "Rebbe, you are the only one of my critics who came to see the difficulty of my situation. Only you cared enough to come and see how much money I stand to lose, how many customers I may alienate. But because you cared, I will close my store on Shabbos."

That was only the beginning. From that week on, this fellow kept his store closed on Shabbos. Why? Because Rav Aryeh Levin took the time to see the other man's point of view rather than just criticize him blindly.

Did You Make Your Friend a King?

Here is another level of *kavod*. The Vilna Gaon always wanted to go to *Eretz Yisrael*. He never made it, but while traveling toward the Holy Land he wrote a letter, the *Iggeres HaGra*. In part of it he addresses his mother: "Let there be peace between you and my wife. Get along well, because this is a very big *mitzvah* incumbent upon all people, as we find (*Reishis Chochmah*): 'When man is judged, he will be asked: Did you make your fellow feel like a king?'"

It is not enough to be socially proper and gracious. You have to make your friend feel like a king or a queen. That is what the Gaon is telling us. After 120 years you are going to be asked, "Did you make your friend feel like a king?" You see that you must make others feel important. It is more than just *kavod*; it is making someone feel very special.

The Gemara (*Eruvin* 13b) details the main differences between the schools of Hillel and Shammai. The Gemara then asks why we decide like Beis Hillel, if, after all, Beis Shammai is described as sharper. The Gemara answers: Because Hillel was easygoing and patient. Additionally, they always quoted what Beis Shammai said first before their own opinion. They always gave *kavod* to Beis Shammai.

Rav Chaim Shmulevitz (*Sichos Mussar: Vayeira* 5732) said that it is clear from this that giving respect to others, having *kavod habrios*, is not just a social grace, but a reason that Hillel had *halachos* determined according to his view.

When Rav Isser Zalman "Overslept"

Rav Isser Zalman Meltzer was known for his outstanding *ahavas Yisrael*. After his wife was *nifteress*, a *bachur* lived in the house with him. One night, he told the young man that he wanted to wake up early the next day in order to *daven vasikin*, instead of at the regular *minyan*. The *bachur* was very excited and promised to wake the Rav early the next morning. "No," said Rav Isser Zalman Meltzer, "I'll wake you up. I'm the one who wants to *daven* early."

The *bachur* did not sleep all night. He was so excited to *daven k'vasikin* with Rav Issar Zalman. By dawn he saw that it was time to get up for shul, but Rav Isser Zalman had not woken up. So, the *bachur* went back to sleep, and they got up at the regular time and went to their regular *minyan*.

On the way, Rav Isser Zalman told the *bachur*, "You may have thought that I forgot about my intention and overslept. It's not so. As I was lying in bed, it occurred to me that at our regular *minyan*, people come to me every day and wish me well, and I wish them a good day in return. Many of those people we *daven* with think I am somebody special, and it means something to them when I bless them. What right do I have to take away their pleasure, just because I want to start something new?"

What touching sensitivity.

The Gemara (*Bava Kamma* 83b) tells us that if someone embarrasses another, compensation is determined הַכֹּל לְפִי הַמְבַיֵּישׁ וְהַמִּתְבַּיֵּישׁ, *all in accordance [with the status of] the offender and the offended.*

If you embarrass someone, and someone else also embarrasses him, the payments may be totally different. If you are important in the eyes of that person, and you humiliate him or strike him in public, then you will have to pay more than if a simple, common man did the same thing. To the victim, the embarrassment is greater if it is caused by a greater person.

> The Maharal (*Yevamos* 62b) tells us that when you give *kavod* to another person, "*davar zeh hu etzem hachaim* — that is the essence of life."

Let us not forget that to others we may be important. The Maharal (*Yevamos* 62b) tells us that when you give *kavod* to another person, "*davar zeh hu etzem hachaim* — that is the essence of life."

We all want to be loved. We all want to be recognized and respected. If we want that, then we must remember that the next person wants it as well. And we should be giving it to them.

Coping with Life's Challenges

Sensitivity in Bikur Cholim

We are taught in the Torah that *bikur cholim* — visiting the sick — is one of the rare *mitzvos* that Hashem Himself performed when He visited Avraham Avinu the third day after he had his *bris milah* (see *Bereishis* 18:1).

The essence of *bikur cholim* is thinking what the *choleh*, the ill person, wants, and then doing it for him. That is what Hashem did here, Rabbi Mordechai Kamenetzky once pointed out to me. What did Avraham want more than anything? To do *chesed*. Therefore, Hashem helped him do just that: He sent Avraham guests to perform the *mitzvah* of *hachnasas orchim*. The Torah thus teaches us a great lesson about *bikur cholim* — think of what the *choleh* wants; then do it for him.

Some time ago, I underwent very difficult emergency gallbladder surgery. Although the Intensive Care Unit had one nurse for every two patients, I still felt afraid, isolated, and insecure. My wife Miriam and my daughter Elisheva Perlstein had been with me for Shabbos but had to leave Motza'ei Shabbos because of an impending snowstorm. Throughout Saturday night and early Sunday morning I was alone, notwithstanding the nurses who attended me. Then my daughter Faige walked in. She lives in Baltimore; in order for her to be with me at 10 a.m., she had left her home at 5 in the morning. All I wanted to do was look at her radiant smile, touch her hand, make some small talk, and know that she was there for me.

Every *choleh*, every ill or homebound person, feels as I did: a sense of fear, isolation, and insecurity.

That is the essence of *bikur cholim*. Each of us can do that. Every *choleh*, every ill or homebound person, feels as I did: a sense of fear, isolation, and insecurity. When you come to visit, especially if you are a close family member, you minimize that fear, eliminate that loneliness, and drive away that insecurity.

Yona Malina

In July 1996, I began a speaking tour in Switzerland. On my first evening there, a dear friend, Daniel Benjamin, approached and beseeched me to come with him to a hospital about 20 miles outside of Zurich, to visit a young man named Yona Malina. I began to explain that I was jetlagged and needed to rest in order to travel the next day and speak at numerous venues, but Danny insisted that I go with him.

It was one of the most moving experiences of my life.

Yona Malina was born in Switzerland. He was not religious, but he wanted to make *aliyah*. He wanted to be closer to Hashem and to his heritage, so he enrolled in Yeshivah Beis Meir and also studied at Hebrew University. One morning late in 1995, as he rode on the Number 26 bus, there was a terrible explosion. Four people on the bus were killed; 107 were injured. Yona Malina, tragically, was one of the most severely injured. He was paralyzed and could no longer speak or breathe on his own. He was brought back to Switzerland.

I asked Danny Benjamin what he thought I could possibly say to encourage this young man. You know something? When you do a *mitzvah* sincerely, Hashem somehow puts words in your mouth. Yona was lying in a huge hospital bed, a handsome 28-year-old fellow hooked up to all sorts of monitors with a respirator tube covering his mouth. He was able to acknowledge our presence only by blinking. I touched his cheek and said, "Yona, you represent all of us. They didn't mean to hurt you; they meant to hurt every Jew. And because you represent all of us, I will make sure that wherever I go in this world, I will talk about you and I will have children and adults connect to you, because you represent us all."

Before Danny and I left, I kissed him goodbye. When I returned to New York, I made labels with his name and address and gave out thousands of these labels to schoolchildren in various states in America and in the various countries to which I traveled. I told everybody about Yona Chaim ben Sarah. Yona's mother called me from Switzerland. "You don't know what this means," she told me. "Yona's wall is papered now with all these postcards and letters from children in Atlanta, Cleveland, Miami, Manchester, and Antwerp. We know where you are going all the time from these letters!"

Almost 10 years passed. Yona told his parents that he wanted to return to Israel, and they arranged it. I visited him again in Tel Hashomer Hospital. He still was paralyzed and unable to speak but he had a system of blinks that a computer interpreted and typed onto a monitor screen. He wrote: "People have not forgotten about me. Thank you, thank you." That was the last time that I saw him, because in May 2005, he passed away.

Bikur cholim is about making sure the person feels that he or she is not forgotten, that he/she is still part of society. Lying in a hospital bed or even at home alone, especially for people who have been active, is a terrible situation, because a person feels disconnected. But when you sit and talk with them and bring them something, it shows that you put in some thought about their pain before you came to visit.

Ashrei Maskil el Dal

David HaMelech writes, אַשְׁרֵי מַשְׂכִּיל אֶל דָּל, *Worthy and fortunate is the person who acts wisely with a person who is impoverished* (*Tehillim* 41:2). The commentators say that the verse does not refer only to one who is impoverished of money; it could be someone who is impoverished of health or happiness. You have to act wisely.

There is a beautiful story told about the great Sephardic Rabbi in Yerushalayim, Chacham Rabi Salomon Mustafi, who passed away in 1974. A colleague of his became bedridden and was homebound for months. Every Friday night after shul, Chacham Mustafi would visit this man. They would talk about the *parashah*, discuss some of the problems that the Chacham faced during the week, chat a bit, and then the Chacham would go home to make *Kiddush* and have the Friday-night *seudah* with his family. After a few weeks, someone asked Chacham Mustafi why he visited only on Friday-night; wasn't he inconveniencing his own family by coming home late on that special night?

The Chacham answered with brilliance. He explained that he remembered well that when the other rabbi was healthy, he would walk home Friday night accompanied by an entourage of the members of his shul and his students, and as he walked he would talk Torah with this one, give a blessing to that one, greet the little children, and so on. He didn't do that on the other nights of the week. So, the Chacham said, his friend's loneliness and pain was greatest on Friday night, and that was why he chose to visit him at that time.

That is "אַשְׁרֵי מַשְׂכִּיל אֶל דָּל," that is a person who is wise to the impoverished, who doesn't just do the *mitzvah* for the sake of doing the *mitzvah*; who is not only being there, but being there with *seichel*, with intelligence; being there when it counts.

We translate the words "*bikur cholim,*" loosely, as "visiting the sick," but the word "*bikur*" is from "*livakeir,*" which also means "to investigate, examine, look into" — that is the real meaning of *bikur cholim*. Not just sitting there, not just chatting, but seeing what a homebound or hospitalized person needs — to think of what to say and not to say, to think of how long to stay and whether to come at all.

A Chassid, Not a Chotei

Rav Moshe Chaim Luzzato writes in *Mesillas Yesharim* (Chapter 20), "What a person must understand is that you cannot judge piety at its first outward appearance. You must consider what the end result of your actions will be, for otherwise a person is not a *chassid*; he is not pious, but is a *chotei*, a sinner."

A *chassid* is someone who is kind and considerate, but at times when a person tries to do a *chesed*, it doesn't work out exactly as he planned it. Sometimes the outcome may actually be harmful. He may end up being a *chotei* instead of a *chassid*.

A woman once came to visit my wife's friend who was ill in a hospital in Arizona, where it is always hot. It was the middle of the summer. The woman said to the patient, who was connected to numerous tubes and monitors, "Oh, you're so lucky! You don't have to fight traffic, you have air-conditioning, and your meals are served on time." Suddenly the nurse on duty came running in, shouting, "What are you doing to my patient? Her readings are going crazy! Get out of here and stay out."

> At times when a person tries to do a *chesed*, it doesn't work out .... Sometimes the outcome may actually be harmful. He may end up being a *chotei* instead of a *chassid*.

Is that doing the *mitzvah* of *bikur cholim*? Is that what you say to someone in a hospital bed on a hot Arizona day? That patient would rather have been outside the hospital even if she had to fight the traffic and be without air-conditioning.

Some Guidelines

To help ensure that your visit leaves you a *chassid* and not a *chotei*, here are some guidelines to be followed when one is about to visit the ill.

The first is that not everyone is welcome at all times. The *Shulchan Aruch* (*Yoreh Deah* 335:1) tells us, "It is a *mitzvah* to visit the sick. However, only the closest relatives and closest friends may come immediately. The others, the *rechokim* (distant ones), must wait three days." When I had my operation, at first I didn't want to see any of my casual acquaintances. I only wanted relatives and close friends. I felt very vulnerable and did not want to be seen with all those tubes and IV lines. *Chazal* are teaching us that we can be there for our close friends and relatives. And after three or four days, we can be there for everyone else, too.

Before you visit a hospitalized person, ask the family if the patient wants visitors. Some people are embarrassed to be seen in bed, in a hospital gown, with tubes or bandages. Some people may be too weak to converse. Visitors may weaken patients rather than strengthen them.

The Gemara (*Yevamos* 79a) tells us that there are three signs for the Jewish nation: we are *rachmanim, baishonim, v'gomlei chasadim* — merciful, modest, and kind. That's the order, but it seems to me a puzzling order. *Rachmanus* and *gemilus chasadim* are things we do for other people, but *baishonim* (being modest) is how we behave. Why is that in the middle? *Chazal* must be trying to tell us something.

I believe the answer is that those to whom we show mercy and for whom we do good deeds are the *baishonim* that are being referred to. They have feelings and sensitivities. Become interested in what *they* need, not what *you* need! You are there to serve the *choleh*; the *choleh* is not to be viewed as an object with which you can do a *mitzvah*.

Keep your visit short. Know when to leave. The patient may be in pain; he may need to speak with the doctor without others hearing the details. He may need to have his bodily functions attended to, which certainly deserves privacy. There is no minimum limit to the *mitzvah*. If you made the effort and stayed a little while, unless you are very close to the person, you should go.

> **Don't ask too many questions about the illness or the treatment. It can be construed as prying. Perhaps the patient doesn't want to dwell on the illness.**

Don't ask too many questions about the illness or the treatment. It can be construed as prying. Perhaps the patient doesn't want to dwell on the illness. He/She might be in denial about it.

Don't read a patient's hospital chart. I have heard many complaints from recovered patients about this. Even if it is hanging right there, it is like reading someone else's mail. Don't do it.

Never tell a patient that his doctor isn't competent. If you feel you must say something about the doctor, say it to his family, but don't say anything directly to the patient. Some people visit and say to the patient, "That's your doctor? My aunt, may she rest in peace, used him too! And my cousin *alav hashalom* did too. And he was the doctor of my friend; I miss him to this day." What a thing to say to a *choleh*! Better not to come at all.

Don't stare at a patient who is disfigured or riddled with tubes, monitors, or bandages.

Be considerate of the patient's roommates. When a doctor or nurse enters the room, you should leave.

If you are there at the end of visiting hours and the nurse says it's time to go — go. If you don't, the nurse will have no choice but to come in again five minutes later and ask you nicely to leave. If this scenario repeats itself, she may be polite to you but you can rest assured that the nurses will be less polite to the next group of *frum* visitors, because they may expect the same discourteous behavior from them. So in addition to possibly tiring out the patient with an overly long visit, you've made a *chillul Hashem*. A *chotei* instead of a *chassid*.

I remember when I was in the hospital, a visitor was making me a bit tired and I said to him, "It's getting late and you really have a long ride home. Maybe you should be on your way?" I was trying to offer a gentle hint.

"Are you kidding?" he said. "Don't worry about me, I have nothing to do tonight; I can be here all night." He didn't get it.

Not Only the Choleh

It is not only the *choleh* to whom we must show consideration, but often to the doctors and hospital staff as well.

Rav Moshe Mordechai Chodosh, Rosh Yeshivah of Yeshivas Ohr Elchonon in Jerusalem, tells a story about his father, Rav Meir Chodosh, *zt'l*. When the elder Rav Chodosh was hospitalized with his final illness, a member of his family was always with him. Once a young doctor entered the room to take blood, and Rav Chodosh asked his family members to leave the room. This surprised them, for he was never left alone, but they complied.

When the doctor left, the family reentered the room and asked for an explanation. Rav Chodosh told them that he realized that the doctor was inexperienced and that he most likely would have trouble finding the vein even in a young patient, let alone an older patient where the veins are harder to access. If family members were in the room, watching closely and hearing their father cry out in pain while the doctor was trying to insert the needle properly, the doctor would be even more nervous and embarrassed. Rav Meir Chodosh wanted to spare the doctor that embarrassment.

The Shelah HaKadosh wrote, "The *mitzvah* of *bikur cholim* has to be a body and soul experience." What he meant was when you come to visit one who is ill, it is not enough even to *livakeir*, to investigate and bring good food and good cheer, but you pray for him/her, either in the hospital room or after your visit. As a matter of fact, the *Shulchan Aruch* (*Yoreh Deah* 335:4) tells us: "Anyone who visited the sick and did not ask for compassion from Hashem has not fulfilled the *mitzvah*."

You have to try to imagine the pain, the isolation, the insecurity of the *cholim*. You have to imagine their loneliness and their sudden sense of disconnection. And if you consider those feelings and then pray for those patients, you have done the *mitzvah* in its totality.

HILF

The mother of a woman in Brooklyn had been ill for over two years, requiring many hospital stays. The daughter would stay with her mother for hours, even while her mother slept. She wanted to be sure to be there in case, Heaven forbid, of a sudden emergency. After her mother passed away, this woman began to look for an organization that would provide volunteers who would sit with patients when family members could not be there, but who would notify the family when the patient was awake and needed them. She discovered "HILF" (Yiddish for "help"), which provides exactly that. They also cook for elderly people, especially Holocaust survivors, who can't do so themselves anymore.

This woman was so moved by this that she joined the organization. Every Tuesday morning she would cook for certain people, and by 3 p.m. the meals would be picked up and delivered by a volunteer driver. After a few months, HILF called her and asked if she would mind cooking one particular Wednesday for a woman who lived near her, because the usual volunteer would be unavailable then. The driver also would be out of town, and HILF asked if she wouldn't mind delivering the meal as well, since it was close to her home. Of course she was happy to do so. When she delivered the meal, she introduced herself as the HILF volunteer. The woman, old and frail, opened the door and invited the volunteer in. This woman brought in the meal and the two of them made small talk. Suddenly, the older lady asked the volunteer, "Do you mind if I look at you?"

The volunteer thought this was a strange question and felt a little uncomfortable, so she asked, "Why do you want to do that?"

The older lady replied, "Are you Rifka Goldberg's daughter?"

The volunteer was surprised because that was, indeed, her mother's name. "How did you know?" she asked.

"You look just like her," the lady answered. "Let me tell you a story. I was in the concentration camps with your mother. I remember her when she weighed only 80 pounds. One afternoon she came to me and asked me to share part of my bread, because she was sure she was going to die otherwise. Of course I gave her part of my bread and the next morning she said to me, 'I don't know if we will ever get out of here, but if we do, one day I will pay you back.' And today, she paid me back."

Can you imagine? That's what happens when you go visit the sick and the infirm. That's what happens when you reach out to others. You never know how you might make a connection. You never know the life, the strength, and the will to continue that you give to those people. Think of others ... and Hashem, Who taught us about *bikur cholim,* will think of you.[1]

Think About the Whole Family

Remember: When a member of the family is ill, it affects the entire household. The atmosphere of the home, if not the entire family structure, changes. The whole family must be considered when doing bikur cholim.

The worst thing you can say to a family is, "Call me if you need anything." That means nothing! If you want to be helpful, offer something specific. Offer rides to the doctor or hospital; offer babysitting. Offer to help the choleh's siblings with their homework. (Teachers may understand if homework isn't done, but the children

---

1. Rabbi Krohn and his son-in-law, Chananya Kramer of KOLROM Multi-Media, produced a free DVD about *bikur cholim.* To receive a copy, email Rabbi Krohn at krohnmohel@brisquest.com. Any schools or Bikur Cholim societies can order as many as they wish, free of charge.

might fall too far behind and not stay up with their class.) Offer to provide supper and ask about their favorite dishes. Be sure they are not allergic to any food before you prepare it for them.

A woman who was recently widowed told me that she was truly grateful to people who stayed overnight in the hospital with her husband. Families are mentally and physically exhausted from dealing with their loved one's illness and are often too embarrassed to ask people for help. Giving just one night is immensely appreciated.

Hashem should help that we always be givers and not receivers; that we be able to dissipate the fear, take away the isolation, and remove the insecurity of all those people who are ill in either mind or body. This, as we say each morning, will grant us reward in This World and in the Next. May it be a *zechus* for us, a *zechus* for our families, and may we all be united to see *Mashiach* in our times, when all will be healed and know of no pain in mind or in body.

Your Health Made E.A.S.Y.

*C*hazal teach that there was once a book called *Sefer HaRefuos* (*The Book of Remedies*). The Rambam writes (*Peirush HaMishnayos, Pesachim*, Chapter 4) that Shlomo HaMelech wrote this wondrous *sefer*. Everyone was able to read it and see what medicine they needed. Nevertheless, the Gemara (*Pesachim* 56a) tells us that King Chizkiyahu took this *sefer* out of circulation and hid it. Moreover, the *chachamim* agreed that it was good that he did! The question is why.

Rashi tells us that the reason is that once people had invested their faith in this *Sefer HaRefuos*, it lessened their faith in Hashem. When someone becomes ill, it is a message from Hashem. Hashem wants them to become a bit more introspective. When a person is weak and ill, he begins to wonder how much longer he will be in this world, what he has accomplished up to this point, and how he can improve himself and become closer to Hashem. According to Rashi, Chizkiyahu felt that people were not taking these things into account. That is why he took away the *Sefer HaRefuos*, and that is why the *chachamim* said that it was a wonderful thing that he did so.

However, the Rambam (ibid.) is adamantly against this reasoning. He argues that just because a person eats and feels satiated does not necessarily mean he will stop thanking Hashem. Even more so, if he has at his disposal a prescription from the *Sefer HaRefuos* that would heal him, he will thank Hashem! Therefore, the Rambam offers an entirely different reason.

He says that people were doing terrible things with those powerful drugs and medications. A person would slip something into someone else's food or drink and possibly harm or even kill him. The remedies were not used only for positive reasons. That is the reason that Chizkiyahu decided to hide it, and that is why the *chachamim* agreed with him.

Today, we do not have the *Sefer HaRefuos*. Today, we need doctors, hospitals, and rehabilitation facilities to help people heal and recover. We even need self-help health books and articles. I would like to offer my own "prescription" as to how we can, hopefully, improve and maintain our health. It's literally "easy" to remember. Just remember the word "E.A.S.Y.": "E" stands for **E**ating Properly. "A" stands for **A**ctivity. "S" stands for **S**tress Reduction. "Y" stands for **Y**early Checkups. This is how, *b'ezras Hashem*, one can *easily* gain his health and maintain it.

Eating Properly

The Gemara (*Berachos* 35a) presents an apparent contradiction between verses. One says, לַה׳ הָאָרֶץ וּמְלוֹאָהּ, *Hashem owns the whole earth and all that's in it*, and the other says, הַשָּׁמַיִם שָׁמַיִם לַה׳ וְהָאָרֶץ נָתַן לִבְנֵי אָדָם, *[Only] the heaven belongs to Hashem; the Earth belongs to man.* So which is it? Does the Earth belong to Hashem or to man?

The Gemara replies that there is no contradiction: כָּאן קוֹדֶם בְּרָכָה, כָּאן לְאַחַר בְּרָכָה, *One [verse] refers to before the blessing, and one [verse] refers to after the blessing.*

Most explain this to mean that before one recites a *berachah* on a food, for example, an apple, the apple (or any other food) belongs to Hashem; after we recite the *berachah*, the apple (or any other food) belongs to us. However, Rav Yosheh Ber Soloveitchik explains that the Gemara is saying the opposite. Before the *berachah*, it's a simple, earthy, materialistic apple. After the *berachah*, it becomes holy because we pronounced Hashem's name on it. Once we make a *berachah*, we have elevated that physical piece of food into something that is *ruchnius* (spiritual). Food is thus something potentially holy.

At the same time, we know that food can have a potentially devastating effect. We know the dangers of poor eating habits and of being severely overweight: terrible diseases, strokes, heart attacks.

Even if none of these result, food presents a tremendous test of self-control. Do you really have to eat all those potato chips? That extra frank-in-a-blanket (or as they are called in England, sausage rolls)? Four delicious pieces of seven-layer cake?

In order to control food and not let it control us, we have to make a commitment.

> **Do you really have to eat all those potato chips? That extra frank-in-a-blanket? Four pieces of seven-layer cake?**

Information about healthy eating habits abound. We know we have to eat healthy foods such as whole wheat bread, cereal with bran, and so forth. My friend who is a life coach tells me all the time, "Eat five fruits and vegetables a day, before you have a piece of cake." That's good advice, if for no other reason than that by the time you've eaten five fruits and vegetables, you won't have room for the cake.

We know that the best way to avoid nosh is by not bringing it into the house in the first place. Drink water instead of soda. Reward your children with fruit, not candy. We know all that. The question is commitment. We have to make the commitment to improve our eating habits. Join a group, enlist a friend, or hire a coach — but get help making a commitment to your health.

Activity

Now let's talk about the second part of E.A.S.Y.: Activity.

When Hashem rebuked Adam after he sinned, He said, "בְּזֵעַת אַפֶּיךָ תֹּאכַל לֶחֶם, *By the sweat of your brow you will eat bread*" (*Bereishis* 3:19). In other words, making a livelihood would be difficult and challenging. The *Kli Yakar* (ibid.) understands these words in a fascinating manner. He writes, "We have proof here to what the doctors say: before one eats, one should do [exercise] that warms up the body." Building up a sweat (בְּזֵעַת אַפֶּיךָ , *by the sweat of your brow*) is helpful before eating (תֹּאכַל לֶחֶם, *you will eat bread*) because that helps digestion.

The truth is that a person should walk at least 20 minutes a day. If you walk with your spouse, it is even better, because you can get to know each other all over again. It is boring to run on a treadmill for 30 minutes every night alone, but if you exercise with a partner, it becomes easier.

> I'm a big believer in sports. Young parents and young grandparents should be playing sports with their children. It's a good outlet and a good way to connect with your children and grandchildren.

I am a big believer in sports. If they can, young parents and grandparents should play sports with their children and grandchildren (not only Monopoly and Scrabble). It is a good outlet, a good way to connect with them — and a good way to exercise.

Stress Reduction

Let's talk about the "S" part of E.A.S.Y.: Stress Reduction.

Stress is not a modern malady. Every day, three times a day, we say in the eleventh *berachah* of *Shemoneh Esrei*, "וְהָסֵר מִמֶּנּוּ יָגוֹן וַאֲנָחָה, *[Hashem,] remove from us worry and sighing.*"

Studies show that excess stress can undermine the immune system and render a person susceptible to conditions such as frequent infections, cancer, and heart disease. Stress is not only mental; it affects the physical body. Recently, there was a study offering evidence that unhealthy food, lack of exercise, and inability to cope with stress can affect a person's well-being, including increasing the risk of developing heart disease, cancer, hypertension, diabetes, osteoporosis, and depression.

It is critical to learn how to manage and reduce stress.

How? One thing is to learn how to take care of yourself. Take 20 minutes a day and make it totally yours. Do a crossword puzzle, take up a hobby, listen to a lecture on a device, read a favorite book — and don't feel guilty about it. There is nothing wrong with taking 20 minutes a day for yourself.

Learning (in addition to the *mitzvah* of *limud haTorah*) is also a form of stress reduction. It puts you in an entirely different world, a totally different environment.

Another effective way to relieve stress — and this may seem too simple, but studies have shown it to be true — is having friends. A 10-year study on older people in Australia was recently completed. They found that older people with a large circle of friends were 22 percent less likely to die at a specific age than those who had fewer friends. The more friends you have, the more likely you will live longer. Friends create a support system. You feel that there is something worth living for if there is someone you can contact.

In the same study, they took statistics on 3,000 women across the country who had cancer. The mortality rate of women without close friends was four times that of those who had friends. Health and healing involves the mind, not just the body. People who have a large circle of friends tend to feel better about life. Therefore, part of stress reduction is to be involved with people. That may mean getting involved in organizational work, going out to lunch once a week, or spending an evening with friends once in a while. It is mentally and physically stimulating. This is so important for the elderly who tend to stay home alone and find it hard to get out. They or their family members should make sure that they don't atrophy at home alone.

Letting things go is another way to reduce stress. If you are seated at a table at a wedding and all of your friends are at another table, don't start complaining about the insensitive hostess. There are two ways to look at it. One: here's an opportunity to make new friends! Or two: when it's time for me to make a *simchah*, I will seat this hostess in the hallway.

Which attitude do you think will help you live longer?

If someone cuts into your lane at the grocery or on the highway, it's not the end of the world. If someone doesn't hold the door open for you, it's not the end of the world. If you don't get the *aliyah* you wanted, it's not the end of the world. If a person is *maavir al middosav* and is capable of looking the other way, he will live a much longer and less stressful life.

Learn to lighten up!

Another important thing is to have a Rav. A Rav is a person whom you can ask a question on almost any topic and get clarity from. My Rav is Rav Dovid Cohen of Brooklyn. When any serious *she'eilah* arises, I call him. Even my children's first reaction to a problematical issue is: "What does Rav David say?"

Every family has to have a Rav, Rebbe, or Rosh Yeshivah from whom they seek counsel. We all need direction and guidance. Fortunate is the one who has a sensitive, caring *talmid chacham* to shepherd him.

Another method of stress reduction is finding a support group. *Tzaras rabbim chatzi nechamah;* if you have a problem and there is a group that has that trouble, half the battle is won because you know that you are not alone. There are people out there dealing with your situation. There are support groups for widows, orphans, divorced people, for those who lost a child, for the unemployed, for those who are suffering from a specific illness — be it heart or lung maladies, diabetes, or mental health. Find the group that can help you. There are even support groups for people who have twins or triplets!

Finally, as far as stress reduction, we have to remember the Yerushalmi (*Kiddushin* 4:12): "A man will have to give an accounting for all the beautiful food that he didn't eat." In other words, enjoy life! Hashem wants you to enjoy life. If you can afford a little vacation, take it! Don't do anything that is forbidden, of course (see *Mesillas Yesharim*, Chapter 13, where this Yerushalmi is discussed), but enjoy life. You are allowed to.

Yearly Checkups

Now, let's get to the "Y" in E.A.S.Y.: Yearly Checkups.

Is there a reason a person should not have annual checkups to check his or her blood pressure, sugar levels, cholesterol levels, and the like?

Colonoscopies are imperative for anyone over the age of 50. A friend of mine called from out of town and was nervous about having a colonoscopy. He asked me if I had one.

"Sure," I told him, "and from the time they put you to sleep to the time you wake up about 20 minutes later, you don't realize anything even happened." He said that he would schedule it.

There is no excuse for being negligent about yearly checkups.

A few years ago, a dear friend of mine, Dr. Chaim Abittan, lost his father, Rabbi Asher H. Abittan. When I went to be *menachem avel*, he and his brothers told me that they wanted to do something *l'zecher nishmas* their late father. We tried to come up with ideas. A few months later, Chaim called and said, "Your sister-in-law gave me an idea."

"Which sister-in-law?" I asked.

"The one who passed away a number of years ago."

My sister-in-law, Mrs. Adel Krohn, passed away when she was in her early 50's. Dr. Chaim Abittan was one of her doctors. Dr. Abittan told me that he had just remembered that once, when entering my sister-in-law's room in the hospital, he noticed that as she was about to take a certain medication, she said a little *tefillah*. He asked her what she was saying. She replied, "There is a *halachah* that before one takes medication, one should say a certain '*yehi ratzon*.'"

Chaim had not known that, so at home later that evening, he looked it up and found it in the *Shulchan Aruch* (O.C. 234): '"If someone is about to have a medical procedure done, he should say, יְהִי רָצוֹן מִלְפָנֶיךָ ה' אֱלֹקַי שֶׁיְהֵא עֵסֶק זֶה לִי לִרְפוּאָה כִּי רוֹפֵא חִנָּם אָתָּה, *May it be Your will, Hashem, that this endeavor cure me for You are a free Healer.*'"

Meforshim explain that any time someone takes a pill, vitamin, injection, or undergoes a procedure, one should say this *yehi ratzon*. Dr. Abittan and I designed cards with the *yehi ratzon* written on them, and he made thousands of them, credit-card size, so that they are convenient and handy.[1]

Let me finish with a story.

In Minneapolis, there is a pediatric neurologist named Dr. Nesanel Breningstahl. He is world renowned in his field, especially in dealing with epilepsy in children. In 1987, Dr. Breningstahl went to a medical conference in *Eretz Yisrael*, the 17th annual Epileptic International Congress, which is held every year in a different country. The doctors in the field all know each other, so when Dr. Breningstahl saw a Yerushalmi *chassid* in the audience whom he had never seen before, he went over and introduced himself.

---

1. You can obtain these cards by writing me at krohnmohel@brisquest.com or writing Dr. Abittan at chaim@refuahcard.com (See also www.refuahcard.com)

It turned out that the man was not a doctor, but his daughter suffered from epileptic seizures, so he went to every conference he could in order to learn the latest developments in the field. Dr. Breningstahl got into a detailed discussion with the man on the topic, and realized that he was indeed well versed in treatments, medications, and the latest medical findings in the field.

They became close friends. The conference ended Friday morning, and Dr. Breningstahl planned to go home Motza'ei Shabbos on the 1 a.m. flight. He was going to stay in a hotel over Shabbos, but his new friend asked him to have the Shabbos meals at his home. The doctor accepted, and they arranged to meet at a certain shul in Yerushalayim on Friday night.

As they walked home together, the man told the doctor that he had five daughters, but only one experienced seizures. He told the doctor that he was positive that the doctor would not be able to figure out which daughter it was. When they got to his home, he saw all the children participating beautifully in the *divrei Torah* and the various topics of conversation that graced the table. Before the main dish was served, the man turned to the doctor and said softly, "Do you think you know which girl it is?" The doctor motioned to one of the girls. The father was astonished, because the doctor was correct!

"How did you know?" the father asked.

"I saw," Dr. Breningstahl said, "that when you were blessing each of your children, you spent the most time with her."

> **"I saw," Dr. Breningstahl said, "that when you were blessing each of your children, you spent the most time with her."**

Dr. Breningstahl figured that a caring parent who blesses his children Friday night might spend a few extra moments praying for this child and her condition. The father himself did not realize that he spent extra time with this child. It was a natural impulse.

Hashem should help each of us to be healthy every day of our lives. We should do our part with *hishtadlus* — it's really E.A.S.Y. Eat properly, be Active, reduce Stress, and have Yearly checkups. If you still find yourself or a loved one in the need of a *refuah* after all that, don't despair. Turn to the Healer of Healers, the One Who knows all remedies. He wants you to turn to Him. He is waiting for your call.

Family Values

In a discussion on *chinuch* and parenting, Rav Aharon Kotler once said that today *every* parent, rebbi, and *morah* has a dual responsibility. It is no longer enough for them to merely indelibly mark the value of Torah and family on their child's heart; today one must also eradicate and erase from their hearts the influence of the street (see *Mishnas Rav Aharon, Chelek* 3, page 171).

And we have to start by policing ourselves.

We at times read secular newspapers and magazines, we travel, we see ads, and we are exposed to a materialistic world. There are many who must use the Internet and at times are inadvertently exposed to inappropriate material. Often, by no choice of our own, we are compelled to mix with business associates who do not share our priorities or sensitivities. All these things affect us and eventually affect our children as well. Anyone who says otherwise is not being honest.

Therefore, we must be sure that we not only do as Shlomo HaMelech exhorts us in *Mishlei* 7:3, כָּתְבֵם עַל לוּחַ לִבֶּךָ, *Inscribe these [Torah] ideals on the palette of your heart,* but we must do some erasing as well.

Ideally, we should become people from whom nothing has to

be erased. Furthermore, we must always be cognizant that people observe us and learn from us, especially children and grandchildren. Therefore, our every action must be on a par with a high Torah standard. We may fool ourselves and think that others don't see our actions, but "the walls have eyes."

Think of this. Imagine one is in a car accident and afterward fills out his insurance claim but inflates the amount of the damage so that he doesn't have to pay the deductible. Children find out about these things. They may not say anything, but they know that the parent is dishonest. Eventually, there comes a time when they will use that lesson for their own benefit.

If a child goes to shul and sees his father or mother talking during *davening* or *Krias HaTorah* he/she absorbs that. Later, when parents complain that their children are running around the shul, or not paying attention to shul proceedings, they must ask themselves: Were they the role model in all this? How can any father who is part of a Kiddush Club in shul not expect that his son will someday imbibe alcohol as did his father? When parents come late to shul, it shows the child the value one puts on *tefillah b'tzibbur*. (Would he come that late to a business meeting?)

If a healthy parent parks the car in a handicapped space, it shows that "nobody counts in this world except me." And though the child may not say anything in protest at the time, he learns and absorbs these terrible attitudes.

Hence it's not only that we have to set positive examples for our children; we must make sure not to impart negative behavior by being poor role models.

Setting an Example

Here is a beautiful but positive, painful example.

Rav Mordechai (Mottel) Weinberg, the Rosh Yeshivah of Yeshivah Gedolah in Montreal, was in Camp Harim in the Catskills for the summer. Without warning, on the day that he had *yahrtzeit* for his mother, he suddenly had a heart attack. Rabbi Yoel Silverberg, who at the time was the head of Hatzolah in the mountains, went to the hospital with the Rosh Yeshivah and stayed with him the entire time.

R' Yoel told me he was in the emergency room and then in the examining room with Rav Muttel as Rebbetzin Esther Weinberg, who had been out of camp, was making her way to the hospital. Rav Muttel told R' Yoel that he had a pain in one shoulder. R' Yoel was standing on his other side and went around the bed to see how he could be of assistance. By the time he got to the other side, Rav Muttel had passed away. Yoel couldn't believe how quickly it happened. *One second ago Rav Muttel was talking!*

Now Yoel had to go out and tell the Rebbetzin.

By now the Rebbetzin was sitting with her daughter in the lobby. How do you tell a woman that her husband was just *niftar*?

He came out into the lobby and saw the Rebbetzin. He waited a moment and then said softly, "I'm so sorry to tell you, Rebbetzin, but the Rosh Yeshivah did not make it."

The Rebbetzin sat there quietly for about 15 seconds and then said, "Rabbi Silverberg, it must be so hard for you to have to tell me this."

Can you imagine? The first words from a woman who had just lost her husband expressed her concern about the difficulty the Hatzolah man experienced by having to tell her the bad news!

That night, as she was packing to return for the *levayah* in Montreal, she turned to some of her children and said, "Let's not forget to tip the waiters." That's what a woman has in mind at a time like this? Yes, indeed, great people have capacity for such greatness.

That is setting an example. That is thinking about other people. How can children — how could anyone — forget such incredible sensitivities?

Give Your Children Time

Years ago I spoke to the Rochester, New York, community during the *Aseres Yemei Teshuvah* on the issue of changing and repentance. I presented an interesting insight that I had mentioned in other lectures regarding parenting, but this time there was an incredible, unexpected reaction.

We all know the famous verse in *Mishlei* (22:6): חֲנֹךְ לַנַּעַר עַל פִּי דַרְכּוֹ, *Teach a child according to his way. Chanoch* is usually spelled חֲנוֹךְ. But here the *vav* is missing. (As we see, in this verse it is spelled חֲנֹךְ.)

Why would Shlomo HaMelech leave out a letter in a word that refers to teaching and education?

I suggested that perhaps he was teaching us a very important lesson. It is one thing to be *mechanech* a bright, quick-witted child. But if something is missing in the child — "the missing *vav*" — he won't grow unless someone puts in the extra time. Putting in the extra time and effort symbolizes what it means to be a *mechanech*.

In the speech I related an incident that happened to my father, Rabbi Avrohom Zelig Krohn, *a'h*. He was buying toys for us before Chanukah. He went into a store in Williamsburg and said to the fellow behind the counter, "I just don't know what the best thing is to give to my children."

The gentleman smiled and said, "The best thing to give your kids is time." So my father came home and gave us all time. (We wanted presents — just joking.) Yes, he gave us gifts as well but that lesson is one he imbued in us countless times.

"The best thing to give your kids is time."

After the talk we went to *daven Maariv*. Afterward, a high school boy approached me and said, "Rabbi Krohn, I really appreciated everything you said." I asked if there was anything in particular. He said, "Yes, I really loved the thought about חֲנֹךְ לַנַּעַר and the missing *vav*."

"Why is that?"

"Because I'm that child. When I was little, I didn't understand anything. My parents spent so much time with me, training me with patience, over and over. It's only because of their efforts that I was able to be accepted into this wonderful yeshivah."

As I mentioned, this took place during the *Aseres Yemei Teshuvah*. The boy said, "*Erev Yom Kippur*, I'm going to call my father and thank him again for all he did for me and the time he gave me."

Tears were rolling down my cheeks. Fortunate are those parents who have children who have *hakaras hatov*.

That's the second lesson: Give your children time. Every child needs undivided attention. The greatest *berachah* that Hashem bestows on us is our children. Let's nurture that gift, cultivate it, and help it blossom.

Making Time

I feel that *every* family should have a time for meals, and during that time there should be no phone calls or texting. Put a message on your answering machine: "We're eating a meal together at this time and are not taking calls during family time." It's so important. (The comments you will receive will be astounding and others will learn from you.)

Talk to your children. When you get home at night, let them know what you did. If there was something you learned, tell it to them. If you go out to do a *chesed*, let them know what you are doing. Tell them about the *mitzvos* you are involved with, so that they will know that is how you spend time.

If you want them to let you know what is going on in school, tell them about your life. Talk to them so they will talk to you.

My rebbe, Rav Dovid Cohen, always says, "If a father is so busy during the day and wants to learn, let him make a *seder* with his children: the boys and the girls."

What I did with each of my boys was that, before their bar mitzvahs, I learned a *masechta* with them. It took us two years, but a few nights a week I had a *seder* with that child. With the girls I learned *Neviim*, *Ezra,* or part of *Tehillim*.

The important thing is communication. Letting the child know you care, giving them time, explaining to them what is going on in your world and in the world in general.

My wife and I once went with the children to a school *Shabbaton* upstate, and Motza'ei Shabbos I had to go back to the city because I had to perform a *bris* on Sunday morning. All the other teachers and parents were staying until Sunday afternoon. I went outside in the snow and the windshield of my car was iced up. I looked at the other cars and they were iced up as well. I thought: *It will be so hard for the other teachers when they come out tomorrow. I'm going to scrape all the ice off the other cars, too* — and that's what I did. Then I went inside to say goodbye to my wife, and I noticed my daughter, Elisheva.

"Elisheva," I said, "I want to tell you something but don't tell anybody else. I just want you to know that I scraped the ice off of all the windshields of all the teachers' cars so that tomorrow they won't have to do it."

I didn't tell her for *kavod*. I wanted her to know that her father can sometimes do a good thing also, and that sometimes you do a *mitzvah* without needing any *s'char* or glory for it. I did it so that someday she, too, will do something noble for others. When you do something good, I feel it's obligatory to tell it to your children. It's not a matter of haughtiness; it's a matter of *chinuch*.

P'nimiyus

Another integral lesson was brought home to me by a *mechanech* who told me this story.

He had just started teaching his eighth-grade class. It was the beginning of the year, and the rebbi didn't know all the families yet, but he was invited to a bar mitzvah. After the *seudah*, he went over to the father, telling him it was a beautiful affair.

The father, who was exhausted from everything, said, "You can never imagine the effort it took us to reach this day."

The rebbi was a smart man and realized there was probably more to the story here, so he waited to see if the father wanted to say anything else. The father did:

> You see that my son is very short. When he was born, he barely weighed two pounds. The doctors prepared my wife and me to expect that he wasn't going to make it. Every day we went to the neonatal unit and were *mispallel*, hoping that somehow the child would survive.
>
> After five months, he was able to come home. After six months, he finally had a *bris*. As he grew older, the doctors told us that he would always be very short. We hoped they were wrong but they were right. In school, kids called him "Shorty" and other names. I used to tell him, "Look, many *gedolim* were short. Good things come in small packages!"
>
> In 1985, a new medication came out to stimulate growth. We went from doctor to doctor, seeing if we should give it to our child. We wanted to do what was

best for him. Some advised us to give it to him; others said not to because no one knew what kind of side effects it might have later. Back and forth; we didn't know what to do.

Finally, we went to Mt. Sinai Hospital, to one of the best endocrinologists alive, a non-Jewish woman. She took a whole battery of tests. Afterward, she expressed the same doubts about giving the medicine. Finally, I asked, "Please answer me as the mother of a child. If he were your son, would you give him this medication?"

The doctor sat there with her hand over her eyes, and when she took it away her eyes were filled with tears. "Rabbi," she said, "there's a great difference between me and you, between my people and yours. I come from a Scarsdale mentality. [Scarsdale is a wealthy suburb north of New York City.] Everything we do is superficial. Everything is about making a good impression. I would have no choice. I would have to give it to my child. But you come from a people where everything is internal; everything is character, personality, brains. You don't have to give it to your child."

> "I come from a Scarsdale mentality…. Everything we do is superficial. Everything is about making a good impression…. But you come from a people where everything is internal; everything is character, personality, brains."

The father told me he left there elated. The doctor showed him that a Jew is a person of *p'nimiyus*. That is what we have to teach our children, that *p'nimiyus* is what counts, not the *chitzoniyus*.

A Haven

One of the most important things is to make your home a happy place. *Chazal* teach, "A person should be careful never to instill excessive fear in his household" (*Gittin* 6b).

How many children are there who are afraid to come home? Monday morning, a child starts doing his homework. What do we say to him? "*Now* you're doing your homework? What happened to the whole week? On Sunday you couldn't do it? You needed to do research at the library! You didn't know the library is closed on Sunday? Why didn't you think about it on Thursday or Friday?"

Well let's ask ourselves, what do we look like on Erev Shabbos? How many times has Shabbos followed Friday? Since Hashem made the world! And yet whether Shabbos begins at 4 or 5 or 6 p.m., we're running around until the last minute. What happened? What's wrong with a child waiting to do his homework Monday morning? He's also leaving it until the last minute. Where did he see it? He saw it from the father who ran from the front door every Erev Shabbos straight to the shower. Every week it's the same thing. Why? Because we are not planning ahead. So how can we have complaints against our children?

How many times does the child take the milk from the table to the refrigerator, and we say, "Don't spill the milk!" Do you think he wants to spill the milk? And if he does spill the milk, is it the end of the world? Why should a parent say something to a child that is demeaning and uncalled for? Rav Mattisyahu Salomon says that often these children are not "dropouts," they are "push-outs."

How many times do children come home with a test with a 98 and the first question is: "What did you get wrong?" Why are we doing that? Why do we make our children feel bad or inferior? We should tell them, "98 — that's wonderful! Let me see everything you knew."

Our homes have to be places where children want to come; places where they are encouraged; where they feel that you are going to look for the good things they do. Look for the good your children have done and they, too, will look for the good in others and in themselves. If we focus on the negative, children will do the same and become bitter and critical.

The child looks for the home to be a haven, not a place of torment.

That's what we have to remember. The child looks for the home to be a haven, not a place of torment, *chas v'shalom*. Again, to quote Rav Mattisyahu Salomon: "Your home should be an *ir miklat*; a place of refuge and safety."

Seeing the Good, Bringing It Out

A number of years ago, Rav Shimon Goldstein, a rebbi at Yeshivas Chaim Berlin, was traveling with his Rosh Yeshivah, Rav Yitzchak Hutner, to a *bris* in the Bronx. The cab driver had a Jewish name, but he wasn't wearing a *yarmulke*. As they got into the car, the driver realized that his passenger was an esteemed rabbi, so he picked up a cap resting on the seat and put it on his head.

Rav Hutner noticed and said to Rabbi Goldstein in Hebrew, "Who knows how much *Olam Haba* this person gets for that little thing he just did!"

Rabbi Shimon Goldstein asked, "Rosh Yeshivah, is what he did really such a great thing?"

Rav Hutner answered him with a story. He told him that the Chiddushei HaRim used to go to the *mikveh* every day, escorted by his *gabbai*. After a while the *gabbai* noticed that every day the Rebbe went the long way around instead of taking the direct route. After a number of these trips, the *gabbai* asked the Rebbe why he did that.

"When we go around the long way," the Rebbe answered, "we pass the train station. In the station are these big fellows, the porters who help people with their packages. They are *Yidden*, but they don't know anything about *Yiddishkeit*. However, when they see me coming, they stop what they are doing and say, 'Oh, the Rebbe is coming!' and they bow and show me respect; they show *kavod haTorah*. They are going to get *Olam Haba* for that *kavod haTorah*. Therefore, I go out of the way to allow them the opportunity to get even more *Olam Haba*. The cabdriver put on his *yarmulke* because he saw us and realized we are *ehrliche Yidden*. He put on his *yarmulke* for *kavod haTorah*, and for that he will be rewarded in *Olam Haba*."

Just as the Chiddushei HaRim and Rav Yitzchak Hutner looked for the good in others, even the non-learned, so, too, must we look for the good in others. Let's start at home, with our spouses, our children, and, yes, ourselves. We will then be able to look for the good in others and make this world a happier place to be in.

Stress Management

very day we ask Hashem in the *Shemoneh Esrei,* הָשִׁיבָה שׁוֹפְטֵינוּ כְּבָרִאשׁוֹנָה וְיוֹעֲצֵינוּ כְּבַתְּחִלָּה, וְהָסֵר מִמֶּנּוּ יָגוֹן וַאֲנָחָה, *Restore for us the judges that we had in the earliest times, and give us again our advisers as we once had; and remove from us distress and sighing.*

Just the other day somebody called me and said, "I hear you're speaking about stress management. That's a modern problem."

"Not so," I said, "*Chazal* understood it long ago. The *Anshei Knesses Hagedolah* told us that every day we should *daven* to remove 'יָגוֹן וַאֲנָחָה, *distress and sighing,*' which the Vilna Gaon says is inner turmoil that comes from worry and depression. Stress management is something *Chazal* understood in their time."

Today many of us are overtired, overworked, and overwhelmed; perhaps because we are confronted by new challenges, our stress is intensified. But make no mistake, stress is an ancient problem. The question is, what can we do about it?

Stressful Implications

A recent study reported in the Science section of a world-renowned newspaper revealed the following:

> *Evidence shows that the foods people eat, how much they exercise, and how well they cope with stress can affect their health and well-being, including the risk of developing heart disease, cancer, hypertension, diabetes, osteoporosis, and depression.*

The study went on to say that excess stress can undermine the immune system and can render a person susceptible to conditions such as frequent infections and cancer.

When I read that, it gave me such a frightening insight. We may not even realize that when a person causes someone undue stress, he might bear responsibility for that person's health! If an employer causes an employee excess stress — if, for example, he insists that the employee rush unnecessarily to meet an artificial deadline and the worker has no choice but to comply — who knows if that employer is not *mischayev b'nafsho* (liable with his life)? If a mother-in-law makes a derogatory comment to her daughter about the son-in-law and creates a conflict between the young woman and her husband … if a husband doesn't call when he will be coming home two hours late … and similar situations — who knows what that person has on his or her record and conscience?

It's frightening. This only emphasizes the imperative that we must learn not only to cope with our own stress, but to make sure that we are not the cause of stress to others.

It's a Question of Perspective

I have a close friend, a psychologist named Byrech Lehrer, who told me that there is actually a progression; it begins with stress, continues into anger, and ends in an explosion. Stress … anger … explosion. Sometimes it is not an "explosion," during which the person lets out his anger or frustration, but an "implosion," such that the person suffers great internal anxiety. We must learn how to ensure that this terrible progression does not even begin.

In Kew Garden Hills there is a *beis medrash* near the home of an older man. Every Shabbos the children of the *mispallelim* (congregants) run across his lawn. One Shabbos someone approached the man and asked if this bothered him. The man answered, "I have been through the concentration camps. I have seen what they did to *heilige Yiddishe* children. When I see these children coming to shul and playing on my lawn, I am thrilled!"

> "I have been through the concentration camps. I have seen what they did to *heilige Yiddishe* children. When I see these children coming to shul and playing on my lawn, I am thrilled!"

Stress comes from viewing a situation through a very narrow focus. Children running across your well-trimmed grass can be stressful. When you focus on the whole picture though, and consider that these children are alive, no one is threatening them, they are coming to shul, and at times they play on your lawn, you can be happy.

I know a woman who is an immaculate housekeeper. You can go into her house at almost any time and everything looks perfect. She cannot go to sleep at night until the house is perfectly clean. Once I walked into her house on *Yom Tov* and could not believe it. Toys were out and strewn all over the place. Many grandchildren were visiting and the place looked like a playground. Was she upset? No! Not once did she complain about the mess. It was the greatest *berachah* she could imagine. She was very proud of it, and I was very proud of her. That woman is my wife.

Sometimes a person can see stress when there is no stress to be seen. I know a *kallah* whose grandmother bought candlesticks for her, as she did for all her granddaughters. But the mother-in-law of this *kallah* looked at the candlesticks and said the *kallah* could not use them because the petals on the flowers were facing the wrong way — and she insisted that the *kallah* take them to a silversmith to be "fixed." That's putting stress where there was none.

What we learn from these three incidents is that we must look at the whole picture. If we do, then often, instead of feeling stressed, we will find a positive element in that situation, and the progression of stress-anger-explosion will be prevented. It's a question of perspective.

Just Say "No"

Before Moshe Rabbeinu died, he blessed *Klal Yisrael*. Before Yaakov died, he blessed his children. Yitzchak as well, as he grew older, blessed his children. Yet, before Avraham died, he did not bless Yitzchak. As a matter of fact, the Torah tells us (*Bereishis* 25:11): וַיְהִי אַחֲרֵי מוֹת אַבְרָהָם וַיְבָרֶךְ אֱלֹקִים אֶת יִצְחָק בְּנוֹ, *After Avraham died, Hashem blessed Yitzchak, his son.* The *Midrash* (*Bereishis Rabbah* 61:6) asks why Avraham didn't bless his son; why did Hashem have to do it?

The *Midrash* answers with a parable. A gardener was taking care of his master's garden. Two trees were intertwined. One was a fruit tree that grew beautiful fruits. The other was a poisonous weed tree which had wrapped itself around the fruit tree. Now the gardener had a problem. If he watered the fruit tree, he would also be watering the poisonous tree. If he didn't water anything, the fruit tree would die. The gardener could not make up his mind. Finally, he decided to leave it up to his master.

Avraham was faced with the same dilemma. If he blessed Yitzchak, he would have to bless his other son, Yishmael, and the children of his wife Keturah (see *Bereishis* 25:1). If he didn't bless them, how could he bless Yitzchak? He didn't know what to do, so he left it to Hashem.

We too have to acknowledge that sometimes we can't solve *every* problem. One of the reasons that we feel stressed is because we are on a guilt trip, thinking that we have to do everything and we just can't fulfill that impossible task. *No one* can do it all.

This may come as a surprise, but we each must learn to say no. However, you must learn to say it politely (see below). You don't have to go to *every* wedding to which you are invited. You don't have to help *every* organization that calls you. If you overextend yourself you will find that the necessities of life are ignored and then, as Dr. Abba Goldman, a psychologist in Kew Gardens, says, "The necessities of life become emergencies [because you ignored them when they should have been tended to]."

Don't let the necessities of life become emergencies.

Many things in life are optional. If you do all of those *optional* things, the chances are that you will not have time to do the *necessary* things, such as spending quality time with your spouse or children. After a while you suddenly realize that you haven't spoken meaningfully to them in days. That could lead to a crisis and thus the necessities of life suddenly become emergencies.

Don't let necessities become emergencies. Learn to say no. My wife always says, "When you say yes to one thing you are saying no to another." Choose your priorities wisely and you will minimize your stress.

How to Say No

There is a sequence of three phrases that you should be aware of to help you say no respectfully: "I understand," "however," and "there-fore I suggest."

Say you have a daughter in high school and the class is planning a trip to Washington or Niagara Falls. The school calls and says, "Mrs. So-and-So, you're a very responsible person. We need you to be the chaperone for the class trip."

You know that you have to tend to your mother in the hospital that same day. Hence, you should say: "*I understand* that it is so impor-tant to have a responsible person travel with the girls. *However*, I have to be in the city that day because I am taking care of a sick parent. *Therefore, I suggest* that you call Mrs. Goldberg or Mrs. Silverberg, because they are each very capable and responsible and may be avail-able."

I understand … however … therefore I suggest …

Say someone calls you wanting to borrow money. You're afraid to lend it because you know the person doesn't have a good track record and hasn't paid back previous loans. You don't really have money to spare, but you also know that he or she really needs a car. Therefore, you should say, "*I understand* and realize that you need a car. I heard yours broke down a number of times. *However*, I am just not in a posi-tion right now to be able to help you out. *Therefore, I suggest* that you go to the local *gemach*."

Plan Ahead

How many times does it happen that you get stuck in traffic? Just as surely as the sun rises in the east, there will be traffic going to

Manhattan on a weekday morning. Traffic is very stressful. It drives people crazy (no pun intended). But it doesn't have to. If you plan your trip ahead there will be less stress.

Leave a little earlier, take a Torah CD into the car and listen to it or to a favorite music CD or tape. Certain frustrations are unavoidable. But, if you plan ahead, traffic doesn't have to be one of them.

How many parents start packing for their children's summer camp near the end of June? Doesn't everyone know that children are off to camp at the start of July? Why is packing done at the last minute? Whenever you see items in May or early June and realize that your children will need them in camp, buy them and put them into their suitcases that you set aside in advance.

People plan to go to *Eretz Yisrael* and then a week before they are supposed to leave they realize their passport has expired. They must then go to a specific passport office (usually a distance away) that can issue it in one day. Aside from the fact that it's time consuming, there is an extra fee involved! Plan ahead! Avoid the stress.

Is there any reason children can't be given baths on Thursday nights? They are not going to get *that* dirty on Friday. Is there any reason you can't pick up the clothes from the cleaners on Thursday afternoon? And shouldn't a husband prepare on Thursday or earlier in the week a *vort* he would like to say at the Shabbos table, rather than wait till Friday afternoon to do so?

Dr. Goldman tells his patients to allot an hour and a half for anything they think will take "only an hour." Always give time and a half to whatever you hope to accomplish. Usually people underestimate the time needed to finish a task.

Plan ahead. Organize. It will minimize your stress.

Talk It Out

Chazal (*Yoma* 75a) teach that there is another way to get rid of stress: talk it out (see *Mishlei* 12:25). It begins, דְּאָגָה בְלֶב אִישׁ יַשְׁחֶנָּה וְדָבָר טוֹב יְשַׂמְּחֶנָּה, *When there is worry in a man's heart, he should suppress it, let a good thing convert it to gladness.* It is imperative to have a good friend to talk to. Many of us have acquaintances, but not enough of us have good friends. A good friend is someone with whom you can share your successes and your failures, not being afraid that they will be jealous of your accomplishments or hold you in disdain for your shortcomings. If you find a good friend, you are very fortunate. And if that friend is your spouse, you are the luckiest.

> **If you find a good friend, you are very fortunate. And if that friend is your spouse, you are the luckiest.**

But even if your spouse is not the one to whom you feel you can open up in all situations, *Chazal* tell us to get a friend and talk it out, because one never knows where they can get advice.

In the same vein, help someone with stress. Become a friend who is a listener. The Hebrew word חָבֵר (friend) is from the word חִבּוּר (connection). There are many lonely, stressed people out there. Try to become a friend, and Hashem will be sure to send a friend to you when you need it.

> Reb Yisroel Klein was the *baal korei* of the Belzer Rebbe. When he was *niftar*, a man no one in his family recognized came to be *menachem avel*. He sat down and said to the children, "I am *frum* only because of your father."
>
> He then told them that at the end of the war, when he was 15, he was so hungry that he went around searching for food in garbage pails. Reb Yisroel, who was just a few years older, happened to see him and asked the younger man what he was looking for. He told him that he was starving. Reb Yisroel apologized, saying he didn't have any food either. The only thing he could give him, he said, was a hug.
>
> "I love you and Hashem loves you," he told the boy, and embraced him.
>
> Throughout the years, the man told the Klein family, whenever he encountered difficulties he remembered that embrace, and remembered that another Jew loved him and that Hashem loved him—and that helped him keep going and keep his *Yiddishkeit*.

Remember — look for a friend and be a friend.

Relax and Smile!

We have so many things on our minds, and we need to get so many things accomplished: religiously, financially, socially, in family situations, with health conditions, etc. But a person can't be working nonstop. Take time out *every* day to do something you enjoy; it's a necessity, not an option.

Read a book or magazine; do a puzzle or toss around a Frisbee with your child; exercise, take a walk in the park, sit in the car with your grandchild and go through a car wash. There is no reason for you not to take 15 to 20 minutes a day to do something that relaxes you.

And when you need a bigger break, when you need a vacation, take *one you can afford*!

Enjoy life — and give yourself permission to do so. The *Yerushalmi* (*Kiddushin* 4:12) tells us that we will have to give a final accounting in Heaven as to why we didn't partake in beautiful foods that we saw. However, we can't do anything that will lead to sin. The *Mesillas Yesharim* (Chapter 13) gives us the guidelines. Learning to enjoy life within the parameters of *halachah* is a sure way to reduce stress.

Enjoy life — and give yourself permission to do so.

It's no shame and it's not forbidden to tell a good joke or to be humorous. Before Rabbah (*Shabbos* 30b) gave a *shiur*, he would say something humorous. Rashi explains that he did that because the resulting joy and *simchah* would stimulate the minds of his *talmidim* for the more serious discussion that would follow.

In summary, realize that a great deal of stress is avoidable through better planning. But even stress that is unavoidable can be better dealt with in these ways: be a forgiving person, be willing to look away if someone wrongs you, become organized and plan ahead. Attain a friend you feel free to talk to, at the same time make sure you are a true friend and listener to others, and finally … relax and smile. It will make you happier and healthier — and make the world around you a better place.

Overcoming Struggles
and Failure

Some time ago, a dear friend, Yitzchak Saftlas of Bottom Line Design, held a seminar on fund-raising. One participant, Jonathan Gassman, of the Gassman Financial Group, went up to the large whiteboard in front of the room and wrote on it in big letters: $(SW)^3/N$.

"This," he said, "is what fund-raising is all about: Some Will, Some Won't, So What? Next!"

I think this slogan applies to more than just fund-raising. I think it's a great attitude in life. It's a way of saying, "Don't be discouraged." You want to have friends? Some people will become your friends, some won't. So what? Move on. Trying to get a job? Some companies will give you an interview, some won't. So what? Next!

$(SW)^3/N$ — It's a way of life.

Next Chapter ...

When someone finishes a *masechta*, he makes a *siyum* and says a special *Kaddish*. The beginning of that *Kaddish* is a bit longer than the usual one. What's incredible, and puzzling to me, is that this *Kaddish* said at a *siyum* is also said at a funeral. Right after the burial, the mourners stand and say this longer *Kaddish*. What is the connection between a *levayah* and finishing a *masechta* in *Shas*?

A former classmate of mine in Torah Vodaas, Rav Yaakov Hopfer, today of Baltimore, spoke at a funeral. He said, "Life is like a *masechta*." He explained that just as a *masechta* has numerous chapters, some longer, some shorter, some more difficult, some more simple, so too is man's life. Some chapters are long, some are short, some are hard and worrisome, others are easy and relatively worry free.

It's a wonderful insight because it is so true.

For example Masechta Berachos has nine chapters, *Masechta Shabbos* has twenty-four, *Masechta Bava Kamma* has ten. In every *masechta* there are chapters that are longer and chapters that are shorter; chapters that are very difficult and chapters that are simpler. That's what life is like.

In a person's life there are many chapters: the chapter of childhood, the chapter of adolescence, the chapter of seeking an education (be it religious or secular), the chapter of *shidduchim*, the chapter of earning a living, the chapter of marriage, the chapter of child-rearing, the chapter of retirement, and sometimes the chapter of remarriage. For every person life is different, some of the aforementioned segments are longer or shorter, harder, or easier. One of the priorities in life is not to become discouraged. Some chapters will work out, some won't work out — so what? … next! Life is a like a *masechta* and thus they warrant the same *Kaddish*.

(SW)³/N teaches us not to be burdened by past failures or disappointments. However, the *yetzer hara* tells us the opposite. The word עָבַר means *past*. Interestingly, the word עֲבֵרָה, *sin*, comes from the same root. The connection? It's to show how at times the *yetzer hara* operates. It says, "Look, you've done so many bad things in the past, how can you go and do *mitzvos* now? You're suddenly a *tzaddik*? Don't waste your time on starting *mitzvos* now."

> **The *yetzer hara* convinces people who are thinking about their past to give up on their future.**

The *yetzer hara* convinces people who are thinking about their past to give up on their future. It works on them to keep them from elevating themselves. Success in life means knowing that although you may have failed in one chapter, you can still move on to the next.

We must have the attitude that we are not failures. We are wonderful people who may have made a mistake, but that is not the end of our lives. If a business fails, if a vacation fails, or even if, Heaven forbid, a marriage fails, *you* are not a failure. Each of us is great. Each of us can build. And each of us has potential. The *Tzidkas HaTzaddik* writes, כְּשֵׁם שֶׁצָּרִיךְ אָדָם לְהַאֲמִין בַּה׳ יִתְבָּרַךְ כָּךְ צָרִיךְ אַחַר כָּךְ לְהַאֲמִין בְּעַצְמוֹ, *Just as you've got to believe in Hashem, you've got to believe in yourself.*

Stories About Gedolim

Rav Yitzchak Hutner wrote a very special letter (*Pachad Yitzchak*, Letter 128) to a young man who felt like a failure. This *talmid* had written him how so many people all around him are growing and *shtieging*, but he is not making progress. He reads books about *gedolim* to inspire himself, but he only feels worse because it makes him realize how far he is from the ideal. Rav Hutner wrote back:

> *My dear talmid, you make a great mistake that many people make. Don't look at gedolim in their final stages. All of us know that gedolim are great, but most of them were not born that way. They made themselves that way. There were many battles they had to fight. There were many confrontations they had to go through. They battled and battled, and won.*

When you read a story of a *tzaddik*, it should inspire you not because of what they are doing now, but because it shows that they went through confrontations. Furthermore, they may have lost some battles but they won the war. Remember what it says in *Mishlei* (24:16): כִּי שֶׁבַע יִפּוֹל צַדִּיק וָקָם, *Though the righteous one may fall seven times, he will arise.*

All of us have failed in one area or another. Take *middos*. We have given into *kaas* (anger), *gaavah* (pride), *sheker* (falsehood); we have at times shown lack of *chesed*, lack of concern. We are all human. It is normal. Expect failure at times. It is going to happen. But we can make it temporary.

Struggles are part of life. Let us observe how others have dealt with them and let's consider how we can be of help.

The Emotional Wheelchair

I was asked to speak in a very wealthy community. Each house out-did the next. However, the economy had taken a nosedive and many people lost a great deal of money. Now many of them could no longer afford what they were once able to afford. They asked me to speak about the ups and downs in life.

I considered carefully what I would tell them. I decided to start with a story that happened to Mrs. Chumi Bodek of Brooklyn, a noted lecturer, author, and community activist. She has a son, Yoel Yitzchak, who was stricken with a life-threatening illness at the age of 1 year. No one thought he would live, but he underwent many painful operations and survived them all.

> One freezing day, Mrs. Bodek had to take Yoel Yitzchak to the rehab unit. He was in a wheelchair and she had to take him by bus. Some of the buses are outfitted with a lift (i.e., before entering the bus, one can slide the wheelchair onto a platform and it lifts the wheelchair and the handicapped person up to the bus's floor level). Many buses, though, do not have the lift. The first few that came to her stop were not so equipped. It was freezing and little Yoel Yitzchak was crying. His mother decided that she would take him on the next bus no matter what, lift or no lift.
>
> Sure enough, the next bus did not have a lift. Nevertheless, she tried to raise his wheelchair up the steps. The bus driver yelled, "You can't take him on this bus, lady. The bus doesn't have a lift. You'll have to wait for the next one."
>
> Two passengers jumped up and shouted at the driver, "Are you crazy? That little boy is freezing. Look at him."

Intimidated, the bus driver decided he had no choice and stopped arguing. Someone helped Chumi wrestle the wheelchair onto the bus. As she was walking down the aisle, a woman said to her, "Lady, there's nothing wrong with your son. It is the bus driver — he has a handicapped mind!"

It is a powerful story and I tell it often. Usually, after that story, I tell the audience about the explanation of Rav Levi Yitzchak Berditchiver on the meaning of וְאָהַבְתָּ לְרֵעֲךָ כָּמוֹךָ, *You shall love your neighbor as yourself* (*Vayikra* 19:18). How can people love anyone else the way they love themselves? The answer is recognizing that we are not perfect. Just as you are not perfect and yet you love yourself, love your friend even though he is not perfect. This is what I planned to say in that community. Love and regard everybody in the community. Do not look down on someone who does not have money anymore, cannot pay tuition, or has to move to another house that cost less. Simply put: Do not have a handicapped mind.

When I came to speak, I entered from the back doorway and walked down the aisle. I was holding the notes in my hand when suddenly I saw a girl in a wheelchair. My heart went out to her. I could only see her from the back, but she seemed to be about 13. It was a freezing night, so I went over to her and said, "I just want to thank you for coming tonight, because I'm sure it was so difficult for you to get here in this weather."

She turned to look at me and my heart fell; she had a terrible case of cerebral palsy. Her hands and head started moving without control. She started talking, but I could not understand. Her sister sitting next to her tried to translate for me. "My sister is so excited that you came over to her tonight," she said.

I thought I would cry.

I went and sat down in the front row. Two minutes later someone handed me a letter from that handicapped girl that she had her sister write. She didn't think she'd even have the nerve to give it to me, but now that I had gone over and acknowledged her, she had the letter given to me.

Here is what she wrote:

Dear Rabbi Krohn,

Let me introduce myself. My name is Rivka Baila Rosenbaum. I'm 20 years old. Unfortunately, I'm confined to a wheelchair. Until just about a year ago, everyone in my family thought I was dumb. Finally, after 19 years of misery the psychologist let it be known that I was an intelligent young lady. I'm deeply grateful to you, Rabbi Krohn, for providing me with tapes and books. My favorite story is about Chumi Bodek's son and the bus driver with the handicapped mind. Perhaps you can further strengthen this important point with my enclosed letter.

People in wheelchairs are still people and should be treated that way. Those of us who cannot speak know so much more because we spend our time listening. If you have nothing nice to say, go elsewhere.

Then the sister gave me a letter she had written to the 11th grade Bais Yaakov class in that neighborhood:

My name is Rivka Baila. Most of you smile at me when you see me. Some of you ignore me when you stare and think I don't see you. Don't think I don't see you staring at me like I'm nuts. Hashem didn't give me the ability to do all the things that you can, but is that a valid reason for you to stare? Why don't you thank Hashem for being able to do all the things you do instead of pitying me? I saw you perform in the play. How I'd love to sing and dance like you! I'm not complaining. I just want you to understand me.

There are people living in an emotional wheelchair. They are in it because they do not have a job or because they have tried everything they can and they are just not successful in *parnassah*.

There are people living in an emotional wheelchair. They are in it because they do not have a job or because they have tried everything they can and they are just not successful in *parnassah*. We have to know that people stuck in an emotional wheelchair cannot easily get out of it; they're in a rut. We have to have *rachmanus* (pity) on them. We should try to help them. But if we cannot do that, then the least we can do is not look down on them. If find ourselves looking down at them, we have to ask ourselves: *Who really is the one with the handicap?*

Hearing the Music

Having genuine *rachmanus* on Jews that are struggling is a remarkable virtue. However if one can go from beyond having *rachmanus* to actually improving someone else's situation, that is noteworthy and praiseworthy in the highest degree.

One person who recently did just that in a big way was R' Duvi Honig of Lakewood, New Jersey. He was inspired by the following Gemara (*Berachos* 3b):

> At midnight, the wind would blow through the strings of a harp, and David HaMelech would arise and learn throughout the night. In the morning, the sages of Israel would come to him and say, "Our master, our king, *Klal Yisrael* needs *parnassah*! What should we do? They are wonderful, capable people, but what can we do?"
>
> David HaMelech answered, לְכוּ וְהִתְפַּרְנְסוּ זֶה מִזֶּה, *Go out and support one another.*

Reb Duvi in Lakewood studied David HaMelech's answer and then became an imaginative visionary. We all saw the same problem that he did. In notable Jewish communities, there were people with large families, people who needed jobs. People with good minds who felt that they lack direction. And when the head of the household feels a lack of direction, the entire household suffers. These husbands did not know what to do. They had to put bread on the table and pay off debts. Both the husband and wife needed some self-esteem. We all saw the problem, but no one was really doing anything about it.

Then Duvi Honig came along. He heard the music. What music did he hear? That of another man named David: David HaMelech. Duvi understood David HaMelech's answer: לְכוּ וְהִתְפַּרְנְסוּ זֶה מִזֶּה, *Go out and support one another.*

Overcoming Struggles and Failure | 167 |

Duvi saw young men having a difficult time making the transition from *kollel* to the workplace, so he created a "transition *kollel*." He said to these men, "You are all bright and capable. Come learn at my *kollel*, and once a week I'll have someone teach you how to write a resumé. During the following week, someone will come and teach you how to land a job appropriate to your strengths."

These men were brilliant. If they could understand a *Ketzos* they could understand a contract. If they could understand *Mesillas Yesharim* and *Sichos Mussar*, they could understand people and manage an office. People started joining his *kollel*. Every Tuesday night Duvi arranges a different counselor, office manager, or other professional to come and teach these men, and it opens doors for them.

What is so beautiful about Duvi's Learn & Network Kollel is that it has people who were never employed, people who have become employed, and people who are underemployed. And everyone feels that he has a chance, because somebody cares. As Duvi saw the incredible response, he created the Parnossah Expo held in the Meadowlands Exposition Center, which thousands of people attended. Employers and future employees met for the first time as merchants, lawyers, insurance brokers, and others came and met their "*basherter*" boss or worker. Hundreds found employment. Another such Expo is planned to take place in the near future.

Dark Clouds

A friend had a wonderful business, an advertising agency. A few years ago, one of his main clients decided to switch to another agency. My friend was devastated. Not only did he lose a major source of income, but when other clients learned of the move, they also left him. His business was falling apart. He realized that to keep from losing everything, he would have to do something different, something special.

He thought of a fabulous idea, put it into action, and revitalized his business beyond its original success. One year after this turnaround, he made a *seudas hodaah* to which he invited many of his friends. When he spoke at this gathering, he repeated something Rav Don Segal (the former Mashgiach of Mir Yeshivah in Brooklyn) once said. It says in *Tehillim* (147:8), הַמְכַסֶּה שָׁמַיִם בְּעָבִים הַמֵּכִין לָאָרֶץ מָטָר הַמַּצְמִיחַ הָרִים

חָצִיר, *[Hashem] covered the heavens with clouds, prepared rain for the earth, and made the mountains sprout grass.* Rav Segal says that the simple explanation is that before it rains there are clouds, and the rain makes the grass grow. But there is a deeper meaning. Sometimes Hashem makes dark clouds gather in a person's life. Difficult problems — dark clouds — bring about the rain that causes the grass to grow.

> **Sometimes *Hashem* makes dark clouds gather in a person's life. Difficult problems — dark clouds — bring about the rain that causes the grass to grow.**

My friend acknowledged that there was no way he would have thought of the new, greatly successful business if he hadn't suffered the loss of the old. Only desperation motivated him to think differently. The dark clouds prepared him for the rains that brought special blessing.

Only Hashem knows the reason that we experience the suffering we do. But it may very well be that it is the preparation for the blessing that's on its way.

Rabbi Akiva: Start Again Anew

Rav Dovid Orlofsky is a fantastic *mechanech* who has influenced thousands of *talmidim* and *talmidos*. He told me a tremendous insight into the story of Rabbi Akiva and his students (*Yevamos* 62b and *Midrash Bereishis Rabbah* 61:3).

Rabbi Akiva had 12,000 pairs of *talmidim*, 24,000 students. They extended from Akko in the north all the way down to a town called Antiflus in the south. They all died during a 33-day period between Pesach and Shavuos. If you divide 24,000 by 33, you get an average of 700 *talmidim* dying every day! Can you imagine?!

Someone would run to Rabbi Akiva and say, "A young *talmid chacham* in Yerushalayim, who just got married, died! Come eulogize him."

The next day they called him to come up to Akko, where a young *talmid*, a father of young children, had died. The next day they called him down to Ashkelon, where a young genius, an only child, had passed away.

Rabbi Akiva had to hear this 700 times *every* day. Can you imagine the toll it takes on a person to run up and down *Eretz Yisrael* for 33 days, saying eulogies, comforting mourners, trying to give *chizuk*, etc.? What would most people do? They would say, "*Ribono shel Olam*, You obviously don't like the Torah that I'm teaching. I'll forget about it. I'll stop teaching Torah."

However, that is not what Rabbi Akiva did. He did not allow himself to be broken. He started all over again. The *Midrash* says that he found seven new *talmidim*. It is from these *talmidim* that Rabbi Akiva started over again and from whom we have the legacy of Torah.

A Jew can never be broken, no matter what the situation is. No matter what has happened in our lives until now — no matter what devastation, desolation, or destruction we have been through — we can always start anew. It is never too late. That is what Rabbi Akiva teaches us.

"It's Not Me, It's My Wheels"

I travel quite often. Like most people I travel with a little wheeled suitcase that will fit in the overhead compartment of an airplane. The first time I used one, the wheels did not turn smoothly, and when I pulled it they made so much noise that many in the airport turned to see where the noise was coming from. My wife later asked if I was embarrassed by the negative attention. "No," I said, "it's the wheels that were making the noise, not me. I'm not my wheels."

We are all wonderful, special people. Every person has to be able to say in his heart of hearts, *I am not a failure. I made a mistake or failed at a project, but that is not a reflection of who I am. It is not me.*

The problem with so many of us is that if we make a mistake or fail at something, we take it as a reflection of who we are. We all make mistakes. When you find a mistake getting you down, remember: $(SW)^3/N$. Some Will, Some Won't, So What? Next!

It's All in the Name — Part 1

In 1976, a watershed event occurred that would have a major impact on *every* English-speaking Orthodox Jew in the world: the first ArtScroll *sefer*/book was published — *Megillas Esther*. It was published *l'zecher nishmas* R' Meir Fogel, *z"l,* a young married man who had no children. His dear friend, *y"lc,* Rabbi Meir Zlotowitz, collaborated with Rabbis Nosson Scherman and Sheah Brander to put together a *sefer* on *Megillas Esther*, which literally overwhelmed *everyone* who read it.

The lucid, informative commentary was based only on traditional sources, the graphic layout was original and captivating, and the overview gave a broad insight into the spiritual and historic lessons that one could glean from the Purim story. Thousands and thousands of these *sefarim* were bought almost immediately. Thus began a major phenomenon in the Jewish publishing world.

Genesis of My Writing on Names

I always enjoyed writing and now I approached Rabbi Zlotowitz to ask if I could write on a topic that he would be willing to publish:

Koheles? No, they would be doing the five *megillos* themselves. I suggested perhaps *Mishlei* and actually started writing a commentary on it, but it was too overwhelming. Every *pasuk* seemed to be a book by itself. Interestingly, ArtScroll finished the entire *Shas* before someone was able to complete a commentary on *Mishlei*.

Eventually, I asked Rabbis Zlotowitz and Scherman if I could write a book on *bris milah*, because as a fifth-generation *mohel* I felt equipped to write a *sefer* that would be all inclusive: the *hashkafah* of the *mitzvah*, the *Midrashim*, the practical aspects, the *minhagim* both Sephardic and Ashkenazic, the meaning of the ceremony, honors, and various *tefillos*, etc. They asked me to present an outline and it was at that time that I realized that the *sefer* could include essays that would delve deeper into various aspects of *milah*. One of those essays would be on Jewish names, a topic that always fascinated me.

I worked for two and a half years on the *sefer*, together with my mother, who gave me my love for writing. The essay on names became my favorite part of the book. One night an extraordinary insight came to me by "accident." Of course there are no "accidents" in life; it was a wondrous *hashgachah pratis* that gave me the most important insight I ever gained on names. To appreciate what happened, one must understand that I was writing the *sefer* at the end of the 1980s, before I had a computer.

I wanted to quote from the words of the Rebbe Reb Elimelech who speaks in *Parashas Bamidbar* how the *neshamah* of a child is connected to the *neshamah* of the person for whom he/she is named. Wishing to write the Hebrew word *neshamah*, I pulled the piece of paper out of the typewriter and wrote the word by hand on the manuscript. As I wrote the word, my jaw dropped. The two middle letters of the word *neshamah* (שׁ and מ) spell *sheim*, "name." In the word *neshamah* itself there was a hint that the name plays an integral role in the essence of the *neshamah*. I get the chills even now when I say it.

> In the word *neshamah* itself there is a hint that the name plays an integral role in the essence of the *neshamah*.

It made me think further. What then do the ו and ה outside of those middle letters of שׁ and מ represent? Suddenly, it struck me — and later someone showed it to me in the *Zohar* — נ and ה stand for "*ner Hashem*." "נֵר ה' נִשְׁמַת אָדָם" is the famous *pasuk* in *Mishlei* (20:27): *A man's soul is the lamp of Hashem.* The "spark of Hashem" is the essence of our *neshamah*.

Let us now observe what the Torah says about names.

Adam Gave Names

Name-giving started in Gan Eden. In fact, it's one of the first things Adam HaRishon did. The *pasuk* tells us (*Bereishis* 2:19) that Hashem brought all the animals to Adam *lir'os mah yikra lo*, "to see what he would call them." The names Adam gave were not just meaningless labels but representations that defined the animal. The *Midrash* provides two examples: a lion and a donkey. The lion is called *aryeh*, spelled א, ר, י, and ה. We know that י and ה together form Hashem's Name. Just as Hashem is the King of the world, the lion is the king of the jungle.

חֲמוֹר, "donkey," is one of the simplest animals. Why is it called *chamor*? Because that word is related to the word חֹמֶר, which means "matter." The donkey is simple; it's just flesh and bones. It's also called *chamor* because it carries a *chomer s'orim*, which is a measure of weight. A *chamor* carries a *chomer*, "a measure of" wheat or barley. That's why it's called a *chamor*.

It's not only animals whose names in *lashon kodesh* ("the Holy Tongue") define what they are. When I was working on a DVD about the amazing human body,[1] I realized that the Hebrew names for the parts of the body are significant, as they have a double and triple meaning. The word for skin is *ohr* — ע, ו, ר. What other word can you make from it? עָ, וֵ, ר — *Eevair*, "blind." Why did Hashem make the word for *skin* the same as the word for *blind*? Rav Samson Raphael Hirsch says it's because the blind person sees with his skin. A blind person has to feel something to "see" what it is, so it's his skin that takes the place of the eyes. Rabbi Dr. Akiva Tatz adds that the skin blinds us to what is going on in our body. We cannot see the

---

1. By the way the DVD, *Designer Perfect, The Miraculous Workings of the Human Body,* is available free; write krohnmohel@brisquest.com.

functions of the heart, colon, lungs, kidneys, etc. because the skin blocks our view.

"Liver" in *lashon kodesh* is כָּבֵד. What else does the word כָּבֵד mean? "Heavy." What's the heaviest organ in the body? Not the lungs, heart, or spleen, but the כָּבֵד. It's called כָּבֵד in *lashon kodesh* because it's the heaviest organ in the body.

עַיִן — eye. Did you ever notice that your eyes are always wet? The עַיִן is a *ma'ayan*, a "wellspring."

אֹזֶן — ear. Losing one's balance can be caused by something that has gone awry in the cochlea, the auditory portion of the inner ear. The word אֹזֶן is similar to *moznayim*, "scales or balance." The ear is called אֹזֶן because of what's going on in the inner ear to balance you.

Teeth are called שִׁנַּיִם. One dentist said it's because you get *two* sets: one set as a child; then a second set as the child matures. Also there are top and bottom sets of teeth. Another dentist told me that שִׁנַּיִם comes from the word *shinui,* which means "to change." Teeth grind and change food into a different form so that you can swallow it.

Dr. Irving Lebovics in Los Angeles told me something amazing. The Gemara *(Pesachim* 63a) says, *"Piv v'libo shoveen* — Your mouth and your heart must be the same." The simple meaning is that you can't be a pretender. You should only verbalize with your mouth what you believe in your heart. The word *lev* (heart) is equal in *gematria* (numerical value) to 32. How many teeth do you have? 32. *Piv v'libo shoveen* — your mouth and your heart are the same.

He also mentioned that according to the latest findings, people who have gum problems are more apt to have cardiac problems. Isn't that amazing? The health of your gums in your mouth corresponds to the health of your heart. That is also hidden in the words of *Chazal* stating that the mouth and the heart are equal.

יָד — hand. יָד has the *gematria* of 14. Each hand has 14 joints. Count them. Thus, יָד is 14.

The names of our body parts reveal some of the wisdom of *lashon kodesh;* the *lashon kodesh* name is more than a label: it defines and describes the part. Here is one more example. The nose in Hebrew is אַף. The word אַף in Hebrew means anger, and it is with the snorting or twisting of the nose that one displays his anger.

Every Name With Ruach Hakodesh

Let's return to the idea of naming at a *bris*.

At Avraham Avinu's *bris*, Hashem changed his name from Avrom to Avraham by adding the letter ה. Likewise, at the same time Hashem changed Sarai's name by adding the letter ה. (See *Bereishis* 17:5 and 17:15.) Why a ה?

I believe the answer is that *Chazal* (*Menachos* 29b) tell us that the world was built with the letter ה. What does that mean? If you look at a ה, you'll see that it has a bottomless floor, as if a person could fall through it; there is no end to the depths that a person could fall if he does *aveiros*. However, at the same time, a person has to know the door (the little opening on the upper left side of the ה) is always open for *teshuvah*. Thus ה represents *teshuvah*. That's why the *berachah* of *teshuvah* in *Shemoneh Esrei* (*Hashiveinu*) begins with a ה and ends with a ה (*harotzeh b'tshuvah*). It is also why this is the fifth *berachah* in the *Shemoneh Esrei* — ה is five in *gematria*. (Interestingly, the *Tur Shulchan Aruch O.C.* 115 writes that the two הs at the beginning and the end of the *berachah*, equaling 10, represent the 10 days of *Aseres Yemei Teshuvah,* which are the most ideal time to repent.)

Avraham is the father of all the *baalei teshuvah*. Sarah is the mother of all those women who became *baalos teshuvah.* That's why, I believe, they both received the letter ה. Thus we see how significant even one letter is in a name.

When a baby is born, everyone begins wondering what name the child will be given. It is written in *sefarim*, in the name of the *Arizal*, that every name bestowed has an element of *ruach hakodesh*. When your parents chose your name, they may have thought about a relative, *tzaddik,* or dear friend whose name they wished to use, but in reality there are many relatives, *tzaddikim,* and dear friends to choose from. Why did they choose the particular name they did?

The answer is that your parents were given a certain degree of *ruach hakodesh* to come up with a name that fits you. Your name defines your personality. Your name connects with the person you were named after. People are guided in giving names by Heavenly wisdom even though they don't realize it.

The Happiest Boy

Let me tell you the story about an out-of-town rebbi whose wife was expecting. During a routine blood test, one of the doctors became concerned and asked the young woman to bring her husband to the office so he could talk to both of them. The woman suspected something was wrong, and indeed, the doctor told them that a blood test showed that the child could very well be born with a frightful congenital disorder, spina bifida. Spina bifida, literally "split spine," means that the bones of the spine do not completely form and fuse together. Furthermore, the child might have water on the brain and need numerous operations and, in the worst-case scenario, be in a wheelchair his entire life.

The parents were devastated. They were hoping against hope that it wasn't true, but every test showed that it was. And when the baby was born he indeed had spina bifida.

The parents were devastated. They were hoping against hope that it wasn't true, but every test showed that it was. And when the baby was born he had spina bifida.

Who knew what their child's future was going to be? How could he live a normal life? Obviously, they couldn't have a *bris* right away; the child needed an operation. But they knew they had to name this child eventually.

This father told me that he had heard that when a disabled child is born, the Steipler, Rabbi Yaakov Yisroel Kanievsky, said you should name the child Baruch, because it means blessing. He was uncomfortable with that, however, because he already had a daughter named Brachah; he didn't want two siblings, brother and sister, to have such similar names. He went to his Rosh Yeshivah, Rav Shmuel Kamenetzky, and told him the dilemma.

Meanwhile, weeks went by and the baby still had not had the *bris*. Now it was Friday afternoon. The father came to shul early. It was *Parashas Shelach*. He was sitting in a corner, distraught. He decided to open up a *Chumash*. The first *sefer* that he saw on the shelf was by Rabbi Samson Raphael Hirsch. At the beginning of *Parashas Shelach*, Rav Hirsch asks this question: If Moshe Rabbeinu thought that there could be a problem with the *meraglim*, the spies, why didn't he change the names of all of them? Why did he only change

Yehoshua's name? If he had any inkling that the *meraglim* were going to falter, shouldn't he have changed each spy's name?

Rav Hirsch answers that Moshe's intent was that Yehoshua should be a role model for the other *meraglim*; they would be so inspired by his honesty and integrity that they would not fall into the trap of speaking against *Eretz Yisrael* but would follow his lead.

This father read this and decided that his son was going to become the poster boy for what a disabled child could accomplish in the world. Every child who is disabled will be able to look at his son and say, "You see how happy he is? I'm going to be like him." Like Yehoshua, he would be a leader. And the rebbi decided on the spot that he was going to name his son Yehoshua.

He came home and told his wife what he had seen in Rav Samson Raphael Hirsch's *sefer*. She agreed that they would use the name Yehoshua.

Two nights before the *bris*, this rebbi's father called him on the phone and said, "Tell me, does your wife have a *chiyuv* (obligation) to name after anyone?"

"Dad, what do you mean?"

"Does she have an obligation to use any particular name?"

"No."

"Well, you have to name the child after Uncle Bernie."

"Uncle Bernie?"

"He died just a few months ago. He was a wonderful person. You should name the baby after him."

Yes, Uncle Bernie was a nice guy, but the rebbi didn't want to name his child after him! Nevertheless, for the sake of *kibud av* he asked his father, "What was Uncle Bernie's name?"

"Yehoshua Baruch."

This story took place many years ago. This baby, Yehoshua Baruch, grew up and just graduated high school. He is the happiest child you can imagine. He races his friends down the block; they're riding on bikes and he in his wheelchair. He has traveled to *Eretz Yisrael*. On Purim everybody comes to his house. He is the general and they are his soldiers. You have to see that home — it's not to be believed.

He is the poster boy and role model for a disabled child. That's the *ruach hakodesh* that prompted the name Yehoshua Baruch.

A Crown for a Name

A woman I know was about to have a baby and knew the child was a girl. She and her husband had already decided that they were going to name the baby Sarah Malkah — and then the mother came up with a new idea.

"I don't know why," she told me. "All I know is that when we were on the way to the hospital I said to my husband, 'I want to add another name, a modern name. Sarah and Malkah are both very nice names but they're traditional names. I want something more modern as well.'"

"What do you want?"

"Atarah." (Atarah means "crown.")

"Fine," the husband said, "if that's what you really want."

"Yes, that's what I want. I don't know why, but that's what I want."

A few hours later she had the baby. Thursday morning her father, the little girl's grandfather, called and asked, "What did you name the child?"

"Atarah Sarah Malkah."

Her father was stone silent.

"Is everything okay?" she said.

"Why did you name her Atarah Sarah Malkah?" her father asked.

"I just felt that I wanted a modern name. I hope you're not angry."

"You don't understand," he said. "Last night, my Tante Kreindel [Kreindel means "crown" in Yiddish], who lost her life in the Holocaust, came to me in a dream and said, 'Hershele, *fergess mir nit* (don't forget about me). Nobody has named a child after me.'"

This young mother had no idea why she suddenly got an urge at the last minute to name her daughter Atarah, but now the woman in the family who felt forgotten suddenly had a name! It happened because *every* name comes with *ruach hakodesh,* whether the parents realize it or not. The name you carry, dear reader, was also bestowed with *ruach hakodesh.*

Lashon kodesh is not necessarily modern-day Hebrew, as we know it. *Lashon kodesh* is a holy language. It captures the essence

> **Lashon kodesh ("the Holy Tongue") is not necessarily Hebrew, as we know it .... Your lashon kodesh name is the definition of who you are ... your name is a book. It's a whole story.**

of the person. Your *lashon kodesh* name is the definition of who you are. The word for "name," *sheim*, has the *gematria* of 340. The word for "book," *sefer*, is also numerical equal to 340 — because your name is a book. It's a whole story about you!

In Part 2, we will discuss more details and insights about giving names to children.

It's All in the Name — Part 2

Chazal (*Vayikra Rabbah* 32:4) teach that *Klal Yisrael* was redeemed from Egypt for four reasons. The first reason was *shelo shinu es sh'mum*: because they didn't change their names. They kept their Jewish identity by using their sacred Hebrew names. It is something to remember as we wait and try to bring about the ultimate Redemption.

One has to be so careful in naming a child, because names have an influence. We are guided by *Chazal* who teach (*Berachos* 7b), "*Sh'ma gorim* — A name has an influence." The Gemara (ibid.) relates that Rav Meir and a group of *Tannaim* were traveling on a Friday afternoon and came to an inn. They asked the innkeeper his name, and then everyone except Rav Meir gave him their money. Then, on Motza'ei Shabbos the innkeeper denied he ever took money from anyone. They all lost their money except Rav Meir.

"Why didn't you give him the money?" the *Tannaim* asked him. "How did you know he was untrustworthy?"

"Because of his name," replied Rav Meir. "He told us his name was *Kidor*, and the *pasuk* says, כִּי דוֹר תַּהְפֻּכֹת הֵמָּה, *These are a generation of rebellious people* (*Devarim* 32:20). To Rav Meir, the innkeeper's name indicated his suspect personality.

It is for this reason that Jews have always been careful to name children after the righteous and people who lived wonderful lives of *mazal* and blessing. That's why no observant people name their children after the Biblical characters of Esav or Korach. (See *Tosafos Yeshanim Yoma* 38b, as to why the name Yishmael could be used.)

Chanah called her son Shmuel. Why? The *pasuk* (*I Shmuel* 1:20) tells us, "Because I *asked* (שְׁאִלְתִּיו) for him from Hashem." The Chasam Sofer (Responsa, *Even HaEzer* II, 22) asks: The obvious name should have been Shaul (which comes from the same word Chanah used, meaning "to ask"). Why did she use Shmuel instead?

He answers that the name Shaul is found in *Bereishis* referring to a *rasha,* an Edomite king (*Bereishis* 36:37). Therefore, he writes, Chanah did not name her son Shaul, because that was the name of an evil person.

Why did Shaul's parents name him Shaul? It's not clear, but the Chasam Sofer writes that he is sure that was the reason that Shaul had a bitter end. He died in a terrible way, because he carried the name of a *rasha.* (Today, though, one can use the name Shaul because over the years many righteous people have carried that name).

Strange-But-True-Name Stories

Name-giving is serious business, and in my years as a *mohel* I've heard some pretty interesting name-giving stories. I am sure that every *mohel* can tell you these types of stories; here are some of mine.

Did I hear her right? I thought, No, it's impossible. Non-religious people don't call their children by Jewish names. And why would she call her dog Shlomo? I must have heard it wrong.

I once traveled to Glen Cove, Long Island to perform a *bris.* When I knocked on the door, I heard a dog barking on the other side. Suddenly I heard a woman's piercing voice from inside the house: "Shlomo, get down!"

Did I hear her right? I thought, *No, it's impossible. Non-religious people don't call their children by Jewish names. And why would she call her dog Shlomo? I must have heard it wrong.*

I went inside and as I prepared the *bris,* the dog rubbed up against my knee. I said to the woman, "Could you maybe take the dog outside? This isn't the way you want a *mohel* to do a *bris.*"

"Shlomo, get out," the woman said.

Now I knew I hadn't heard it wrong. The dog's name was Shlomo! I couldn't believe it. After I finished the *bris* I said to her, "Excuse me, I hope you don't mind my asking, but you didn't even have a Hebrew name for your child. How did your dog get a name like Shlomo?"

"Rabbi," she replied, "you can see we're not religious."

"Yes, I can see that," I said.

"Well, my husband and I went to Kent State University. And the first Jewish experience we ever had was when Shlomo Carlebach came and gave a concert. We were very moved and so in his honor we named our dog after him."

On the subject of unusual names (this story deals with an English name), a fellow once said to me, "Rabbi, I'm going to name my baby Justin, but I'm going to give him a second name that you've never heard of."

"I've been a *mohel* 25 years already [now it's more than 40, *Baruch Hashem*]," I answered, "so I doubt there's a name that you can think of that I haven't heard before."

It turns out that he was right. He gave his son the middle name "Time," making his son's name Justin Time. True story!

—————⟫●⟪—————

My father, was also a *mohel*, and I'm proud to say that my son and my son-in-law are now *mohelim* as well. My father once said to a new father who was non-observant, "What is your Hebrew name?" The man didn't know.

My father then said, "When we announce your son's Hebrew name [which in that case was Hillel], we'll proclaim him to be Hillel son of … your Hebrew name. Would your father know your Hebrew name?" The man didn't think his father would know it, and tragically, he was correct. The father had no idea what he had named his son years ago at his *bris.*

"Well, was your grandfather religious?" my father asked.

"Yeah," he answered, "he was very religious."

"Then," my father asked, "what did your grandfather call you?" My father figured that maybe the grandfather used the lad's Hebrew name. My father was flabbergasted by the answer.

"He called me *meshuganeh!*"

Naming Conflicts

Choosing a name can sometimes be a source of family conflict. I was once called by young parents to come to their home a few days before the *bris,* presumably to check if the baby was jaundiced, which could be a cause for delaying the *bris.* As soon as I entered the home, I realized immediately that it was not the reason they wanted me to come. There was a discussion — a bit heated, I might add — between the husband and the wife about whom their child should be named for.

The father had a *zaidy,* who had passed away but to whom he was very close, named Yaakov. The mother's father, who was still alive, had a middle name, Yaakov. No one knew him as Yaakov; they called him Jack. However, the mother did not want to name her baby Yaakov since that was her father's name.

It was during *Sefirah* and I suggested a compromise. "Who, during the *Sefirah,* do we talk about more than anyone else? Rabbi Akiva! Name the boy Akiva. It also has the *osiyos* (letters) of Yaakov in it." And that's what they named him: Akiva. (The letters ק, ע, י, and ב all appear in both יַעֲקֹב and עֲקִיבָא.)

Indeed, that is what is done when one needs to transpose a female name to a male name or vice versa. One uses as many of the Hebrew letters of the original name as possible. Examples would be Melech from Malkah, Rachel from Raphael, Chayah from Chaim, Chananyah from Chanah, Dov from Devorah, and Elisheva from Eliezer.

Here's a question that many people want answered: Who has the right to the first name? Before getting to the answer, I would like to state emphatically that grandparents should *never* interfere when it comes to giving names. Families have been ripped apart for months and years when grandparents mix in. My opinion? If the couple is old enough to have a baby, they are old enough to name the baby! And another thing: If you are a grandparent and want to name a baby, have another one. But that's it. I'll give you my business card if you need it.

I've told this story about interfering many times. The night before a *bris,* the father called and said, "Rabbi, I don't know who to make *sandek* for my baby at tomorrow's *bris.*"

"What are the choices?" I asked.

"It's either my father or my father-in-law."

"Has your father *ever* been *sandek* before?"

"Yeah, he has many grandchildren; he's been *sandek* many times."

"What about your father-in-law?"

"It's his first grandchild. My wife is the first of her siblings to have a child."

"Wouldn't you think it's obvious that your father-in-law should be *sandek*?" I asked.

"That's what I thought," he said, "but today my father called me and said the baby came to him in a dream and told him he wants *him* to be *sandek.*"

I said to the young father, "Ask him what language the baby spoke."

Can you imagine the nerve? Even if he had the dream, to go and put pressure on a young couple like that! It's inexcusable.

In Sephardic custom, the husband has the right to the name of the first child, be it a boy or a girl. For Ashkenazim, the usual custom is that the wife has the right to the first name, and there are two reasons given in *sefarim.* One reason is that for the first child, the labor is usually more difficult. In deference to everything that she has gone through, she has the right to the name. Another reason given is that many times the parents of the mother are still supporting the couple. Hence that side of the family is entitled to the name (*Zocher HaBris* 24:19).

Naming for One Who Passed Away Young

If a person passes away young (under the age of 60), may one name a child after him/her?

Rav Moshe Feinstein (*Igros Moshe, Yoreh Deah* 2:122) *paskens* that if a person died a natural death (including from illness) and left children, it is not considered *raiah mazlei* (bad fortune) and one can name a child with that person's name. Rav Moshe notes that both the *navi* Shmuel and Shlomo HaMelech died at the young age of 52, and their names have always been used. If a person died in an unnatural way, then Rav Moshe suggests that a name be added.

One of the reasons we are hesitant to name after the young is that it might be a bad omen for the child. Rabbi Dovid Cohen of Brooklyn points out that if one names a child after a parent who passed away young, and the other parent is still alive, one is fulfilling the mitzvah of *kibud av v'eim* because the living parent is overjoyed that the departed spouse is being remembered. That, he says, is the greatest *segulah,* because it is a *mitzvah d'Oraisa.* Rav Yaakov Kamenetzky held that the age of 60 is the demarcation between young and old and thus if one died before 60 years of age the person's exact name should not be used alone. Either another name should be added or a slight change in the name should be made. Of course, one's Rav should be consulted in these matters before making a final decision.

Two Names, Anything Gained?

Many people today have two names. In the Torah, only Tuval-Kayin has two names. In the Gemara, very few people have two names. Does giving two names really count as naming the baby after two people? For example, if you want to name after an aunt named Rivkah and an aunt named Leah, and you give the baby the name Rivkah Leah, is it considered naming after both, or is it naming after none? Rivkah Leah is a new name. It's not Rivkah and it's not Leah.

Many people today have two names .... Does giving two names really count as naming the baby after two people?

I can't stress enough the importance of asking your Rav in all these types of situations. There are many different circumstances and views. The Chazon Ish was against using two names from two different people (see *Pe'er Hador* IV, p. 200).

Rav Yaakov Kamenetzky told me personally that if parents give a child two names, they should call the child by both names.[1]

Rav Yaakov also said that one should not give a child a name if that child will be embarrassed by that name. He said this can be so particularly with certain Yiddish names for girls that either have a negative meaning or an unusual sound. One should ask a Rav before giving a name that is unusual.

> **Rav Yaakov said one should not give a child a name if that child will be embarrassed by that name. One should ask a Rav before giving a name that is unusual.**

Pressure? What Pressure?

What happens if there is pressure to name a child after a certain family member, and the family member was either not a nice person or not observant?

Rav Moshe (and many others) says that when the child is being named, the parents should have in mind a righteous man or woman who had that same name. It is then considered that the child was named for that great person.

Let me tell you an incredible thing that Rav Moshe writes in *Igros Moshe* (*Orach Chaim* 4:66): "If you don't have a specific reason to give a name, pick one of the *neviim* or one of the *tzaddikim* that people in this generation know as a *tzaddik*, even if he is living."

It is fascinating that Rav Moshe adds, "even if he is living." Ashkenazim generally never name a child after the living, but Rav Moshe says that if you have no other name, pick a name of a *tzaddik* even if he is presently alive.

Listen to this story. There was a young fellow in a Brooklyn *kollel* who had a son and was being pressured by his parents to name the newborn after his late grandfather, who, unfortunately, was not a nice person. He saw no way out. However, because the name he had to use was Naftali, he had in mind the great *gaon*, Rav Naftali Tropp, Rosh Yeshivah of the Chofetz Chaim's yeshivah in Radin.

---

1. For a detailed explanation of Yiddish names coupled with Hebrew names such as Aryeh Leib, Tzvi Hirsch, and Zev Wolf, to name a few, see ArtScroll's *Bris Milah* p. 47.

After the *bris*, the grandmother ran over to him and said, "My darling, you did such a beautiful thing, naming the baby after Zaidy. I want to give you $500." She then handed him a check.

Now, he specifically had in mind that the name was *not* after his grandfather, so he went to his Rav to ask a *sh'ailah*. Could he cash the check? His Rav said that he could not. Two months later his grandmother called him and said, "I was going through my books and I see you didn't cash my check."

"Bubby," he replied, "I don't want you to give me money just for using the name."

"No," she said, "I was going to give it to you anyway."

The young man went right to the Rav, who looked into the matter and told him, "If she said she was going to give it to you anyway, you can cash it." He did so the next morning.

Keeping the Important Things in Focus

One Purim I was called to do the *bris* for twin boys. You can't imagine how *leibedik* a *bris* is on Purim. It's a double *simchah*: Purim is a *simchah* and a *bris* is a *simchah*. And when there are twins it is a quadruple *simchah*! Everyone was sky-high with joy in shul and it was filled to capacity.

Prior to the *bris*, I went into the room where the mother and nurse were in order to check the babies. Meanwhile, the two grandfathers were, discussing which child they would each be *sandek* for. Each grandfather wanted to be the *sandek* for the baby who was going to be named for his side of the family which is, of course, understandable.

Finally, the big moment came. The first *sandek* sat down and they brought in the baby. When *brissen* are to be performed on twins, the older boy's *bris* is done first (see *Pischei Teshuvah, Yoreh Deah* 265:9). I opened up the diaper and realized it was the younger baby. I turned to the father and told him.

"How do you know?" he asked.

"A *mohel* knows," I replied.

We asked the Rav what to do because now the younger boy was on the lap of the grandfather who wanted to be *sandek* for the older boy. The Rav said that once a child is there, אֵין מַעֲבִירִין עַל הַמִּצְוֹת,

You do not bypass the opportunity to do a mitzvah (Pesachim 64b). Thus, at this point, Zaidy A was holding Baby B. But the Rav said we couldn't move Baby B because he was ready to have the *bris* performed.

At that moment, the father lost it. He was so upset at his wife and the nurse for sending the wrong baby with the *kvatter* that he began shouting at both of them at the other end of the shul. "Why did you send in the wrong baby?"

Suddenly, everybody was quiet. There was tension in the air. At that moment, Hashem put something in my head, and I called out. "Wait a minute. This had to happen this way. It's Purim and everything is *venehapechu*; the opposite of what should really be."

Everybody laughed and I did both *brissen*.

Afterward, a *talmid chacham* said, "Do you know why it happened? To show the grandfathers that you don't have to be the *sandek* only of a grandchild named from your side. You have to love every child and every grandchild — whether it's named from your side or not."

I thought that was a very special insight. We must always remember what really matters.

Time Management

I f you look in *Webster's Dictionary*, the meaning of the word "manage" is "to have under control, to direct, or to use in a manner desired." One of our most important commodities — and probably the most mismanaged — is time.

Time management is a very important topic, because when our time is managed properly, it enhances our lives. When mismanaged, it can make our lives miserable.

Shevet Yissaschar was considered the brightest of the *Bnei Yisrael*. It says about them (*I Divrei HaYamim* 12:31): וּמִבְּנֵי יִשָּׂשׁכָר יוֹדְעֵי בִינָה לָעִתִּים, *And the sons of Yissaschar understood time*. It defines them and is a great compliment. *Yod'ei binah la'itim*; they knew how to take advantage of time and when to give timely advice. If we want to be smart and make the most of our lives, we have to become people who are *yod'ei binah la'itim*, who understand how to manage time.

In each of her schools, Sarah Schenirer posted this *pasuk* from *Tehillim* (90:12): לִמְנוֹת יָמֵינוּ כֵּן הוֹדַע, *Teach us how to count our days*.

She used to say, "Count your days, count your hours; know that every minute and every second count. You cannot retain it, you cannot save it. Once it is used you can only store it away in a treasure chest, so that one day you can recount it."

When she left a school she was visiting, students would ask her to stay a bit longer, but she would answer, "If I come one minute late and miss the train, I have lost it all. I won't get to the next city. Every minute counts."

We see that in the Olympics, a difference between winning a gold medal or a silver medal can be one one-hundredth of a second. Gold is glory. Silver is second fiddle. All the endorsements on the Wheaties boxes only showcase the gold medal winners; only in the merit of that 1/100th of a second.

That helps us understand what time is all about.

Our watches and clocks are deceptive, because the seconds roll into minutes, and minutes into hours, hours into days, days into weeks, weeks into months, and months into years. It seems as if it is a natural transition. But it's not like that. Our watch is not telling us the truth. We live in compartments. We live different segments of time, each with different opportunities, different challenges, and different responsibilities.

That's what we have to learn: to be *yod'ei binah*, to make the most of every compartment of life that we are currently in.

Delegate

Why is time management so difficult? Because of all the demands on our time! Your spouse wants attention, your children want attention, your friends want attention, your relatives want attention, your business associates want attention, every organization wants your attention — and you also want attention. Everyone wants some of your attention.

How are you going to manage it all?

The first thing to remember is (*Pirkei Avos* 2:7): לֹא עָלֶיךָ הַמְּלָאכָה לִגְמוֹר, *It's not upon you to finish the labor.* You are not a failure if you are not a supermom or superdad. You are not a failure if you can't do it all. Everybody has to know that. We walk around with guilt because we think the person next door does everything.

You think the other person is a supermom. Not true. You only just see what is happening on the outside. But nobody can really do it all.

Even Moshe Rabbeinu couldn't do it all. People were coming to him day and night. Then Yisro asked him, "What are you doing? You can't do it all!" (see *Shemos* 18:13-23).

Moshe answered, "They all want to know about Hashem. I have to help them."

"This is not a good thing," his father-in-law answered. "There is no way you yourself can do it all. You will become exhausted, the people will become exhausted; nobody can do it alone. Appoint officers over thousands, officers over hundreds: set up a system!"

What do we learn from that? You have to delegate.

Your Family, Your Team

Do you know what the word "TEAM" stands for? Together Everyone Accomplishes More.

You as the parent must show the family that you are all a team; that you are all doing it *together*. Each family member has a responsibility.

I have heard that there are parents who come up on visiting day to camp with a nanny and a maid, and tell them to spread out the blanket and make a picnic because their little princess can't do that. Anyone whose children do not do anything around the house is following a recipe for disaster. We are spoiling our children by not getting them involved in household chores and responsibilities.

In our home, when the children were small, my wife and I assigned jobs to all of them, and these jobs were posted on the refrigerator: one would wash the dishes, another would dry them, a third one set the table, a fourth cleared the table, and another one swept the floor. Even the boys. The mother can't do everything. She didn't eat all the food, so she doesn't have to clean up all the food. Every boy and every girl has to help.

That's delegating. When you delegate, the mother is not dropping from exhaustion at night. It's a team effort. When a child wakes up, he makes the bed. When a child comes home, he hangs up his coat. No mother should hang up a coat for anyone, including her husband.

In our home, we had two sets of hooks. The little children hung their coats on the low hooks. The older ones used the taller hooks. Everyone had to put away their hats and their boots.

And what is wrong if you send a child shopping?

Laundry? A mother has to pick up laundry from the floor? Are you kidding? Every child should take his own laundry and put it in the hamper. A mother is not a slave. She is not a servant or a waitress.

Don't spoil your children! Part of time management is that it is a team effort. A house is a team effort. There is no reason for the mother to be so exhausted. Of course, the mother is usually the one who is primarily in charge of making suppers and doing the laundry, but every child has to help. In our house, on Motz'aei Shabbos, when it is their turn, the boys also vacuum.

Wives, make sure that your husbands read this article, too. Husbands have to be involved in the care of a house and the raising of children. Doing homework is part of time management. My mother claims she went through high school seven times. Of course, my father helped us, too. And when I did the homework with my children, my wife and I divided it.

I once asked Rav Shlomo Wolbe, *zt'l*, what message I should be telling parents. He gave me a phenomenal answer: "Tell them to give their children two things: love and time."

My son was there and he asked, "Rebbe, how much time?"

"As much as they need."

That's time management.

The Joys of Slumberland

There is another item that is important for proper time management: sleep.

How many people wake up exhausted in the morning? Everybody complains about not getting enough sleep.

A big part of time management is getting to sleep at a reasonable hour.

A big part of time management is getting to sleep at a reasonable hour. (Maybe I should read this article to myself after it's printed.) We really cannot be productive without sleep. Sleep is an investment in productivity and good mood. When we're tired, we're moody and grouchy. We say things we really don't want to say, and often we regret having said them.

If you go to sleep on time, you will be a more refreshed and cheerful person tomorrow.

I have often wondered why Hashem makes us sleep. To me — until I found the following answer — it seemed like the greatest waste of time. Think about this for a minute. Imagine someone who sleeps five hours a night. That means he sleeps 35 hours a week. Multiply 35 hours times 52 weeks. It comes to 1,820 hours a year! That's 75 days! Can you imagine? He is sleeping 75 days out of the year! And that's a person who sleeps only five hours a night!

Next, if you multiply 75 days times 50 years (from age 20 to 70), you end up sleeping 3,750 days! That's 10 years! Explain it to me! What I could do with an extra 10 years! What could we all do with an extra 35 hours a week?

Why did Hashem make us sleep? This always bothered me until I asked my rebbi, Rav Dovid Cohen. He told me that the Gemara (*Berachos* 57b) says there are five things that are one-sixtieth of something else. For example, fire is one-sixtieth as hot as *Gehinnom*. Honey is one-sixtieth as sweet as the manna. The joy of Shabbos is one-sixtieth the joy of *Olam Haba*. And sleep? It is one-sixtieth of death.

Rav Dovid said that a person has to realize that he is not going to live forever. However, if a person never slept, never had that feeling of being "out of it," he would never believe that it will happen to him. Therefore, Hashem makes us sleep so we realize "a taste" of death, and that nobody lives forever. If so, we had better accomplish what we are meant to accomplish now, because we are not sticking around here forever.

Taking it one step further, I believe it has to do with time management. I believe that if we never went to sleep, we would never get out of a rut. A person becomes locked into a bad routine. He is doing things he knows he shouldn't do but he can't get out of it. How can he stop? He goes to bed and wakes up a new person. It is the same with someone who is in a bad mood. After a restful sleep he wakes up refreshed.

That's one of the great purposes of sleep. It creates the opportunity for new beginnings. Time management means understanding that tomorrow I start a new day. Whatever I did yesterday is not as significant as what I can accomplish tomorrow. I wasted time? Now is a brand-new beginning. I'm not going to waste time anymore.

Just Say No

Here's another thing that I believe is very important in time management. You must learn to say no.

Many of us are very good people and we feel that we are bad people if we say no. My wife always says, "When you say yes to one thing, you are saying no to another." You cannot be every place. You have to be in control of your life. You cannot have others control you. (Learn how to say "no" in "Stress Management," page 153.)

Rav Avraham Pam writes in his *sefer Atarah LaMelech* that sometimes you want to take your friend to the airport, but your wife has supper on the table. You have to say no. Pay for a cab for your friend, but you belong at home with your wife and children at the supper table.

Learn to say no. It doesn't make you a bad person. As much as possible, try to accommodate others, but there comes a point where every person has to realize there is a limit. Otherwise, without that limit, not only will you be frustrated and angry, but you will take it out on others in your house, and in the end you will suffer.

The Greatest Time Manager

Who is the greatest time manager of all?

Every night, when we *daven* Maariv, we say, בְּחָכְמָה פּוֹתֵחַ שְׁעָרִים, *With wisdom [Hashem] opens gates [of day and night]*, וּבִתְבוּנָה מְשַׁנֶּה עִתִּים, *and with His understanding He alters the periods of time.* Day and night, night and day — Hashem is the ultimate time manager.

In *Ashrei,* we say, עֵינֵי כֹל אֵלֶיךָ יְשַׂבֵּרוּ, וְאַתָּה נוֹתֵן לָהֶם אֶת אָכְלָם בְּעִתּוֹ, *The eyes of all look to You in hope, and You give them their food in its proper time.* The Radak explains that some animals eat grass, some eat seeds, and some eat other animals. Yet, Hashem orchestrates circumstances so that every animal receives its food right on time. Hashem is the "Conductor"[1] who manages a super-complex time schedule.

> When you think about it, every *hashgachah pratis* story is about time management.

When you think about it, every *hashgachah pratis* story is about time management. It strikes us as amazing because this person was in this place at just the right time. The bus came … he missed the plane ….

---

1. See *Perspectives of the Maggid*, page 259, for the story about the famous orchestra conductor, Arturo Toscanini, and how that story relates to the Conductor of the World.

It's all about Hashem's time management. Here's a story that illustrates this thought.

Rabbi Shmuel Amon is a Rav in Eatontown, New Jersey. Every year, before Rosh Hashanah, he and his wife go to the *kever* of his mother-in-law and are *mispallel* there. They would always go on a Sunday, because that was the most convenient time. However, one year they were very busy and they knew the cemetery would be so crowded on a Sunday that it was better to go on a different day. They decided to go on Tuesday that year.

Sure enough, they were able to drive right up to where they needed to go. Rabbi Amon and his wife got out and started to say *Tehillim*. Suddenly, off in the distance, he noticed a group accompanying a coffin. He could tell they were not religious, and they, on the other hand, could see from his suit and black hat that he was. They motioned for him to come over to them. His first thought was that they needed a *minyan* or they needed help saying *Kaddish*.

Sure enough, that was the situation. They had only nine men and they didn't know how to say *Kaddish*. He was very happy to help.

After *Kaddish*, the men start walking away.

"Wait! Where are you going?" Rabbi Amon asked. "He's not buried yet."

"The workers will finish," they said.

"Who is the *niftar*?"

"Our father."

Rabbi Amon was shocked. "Listen, you really have to bury your father. That would be truly showing him honor."

"That's what the workers are there for," one of them said.

"And we already said *Kaddish*," chimed in another. And they left.

The rabbi was dumbstruck. He was the only one who stayed behind. It was a lack of honor to leave this man alone with only the non-Jewish workers to bury him. Indeed, Rabbi Amon realized he was faced with a *meis mitzvah*. He went over to the workers and asked if they minded if he finished the job. They said they didn't mind.

The rabbi took the shovel and began shoveling … and shoveling. He worked diligently until the whole coffin was covered with dirt. He was exhausted but he also felt elevated.

He then began to wonder: *Who is this man to have merited kevu-ras Yisrael* (a proper Jewish burial)?

Rabbi Amon went to the cemetery office and asked about the man. He was told the man's name. The rabbi went home and started making inquiries.

He found out that the man had come to America in the 1960s. At that time, a large number of Syrian Jews came to America. An entire group moved to Seattle, Washington, thinking they would be able to find jobs there.

They sent their children to the day school. The principal, Rabbi Shlomo Maimon, knew that these children would not continue on to a Jewish high school, so instead of dividing the elementary school into eight grades, he made it nine grades. In this way, he would keep them in yeshivah for another year.

Shmuel Amon was one of the boys in that grade. After ninth grade, Rabbi Maimon brought over a boy from Ner Yisrael in Baltimore who had lived in Seattle to talk to the students about Ner Yisrael. This boy was so extraordinary that six out of the seven ninth graders decided to go to Ner Yisrael. Can you imagine the power of that child? Who was it? Rabbi Yissachar Frand. Even as a high school boy, he had such *koach* (strength).

When those Syrian boys came to Ner Yisrael, the executive director, Rabbi Naftali Neuberger, had to raise money for their tuition. He called the Syrian community in Brooklyn for help. Who was in charge of raising funds for these boys? This man whom Shmuel had just buried! In those days this man was very wealthy — and he had paid Shmuel Amon's tuition. Later, when he became poor, everyone forgot about him — including his children.

But Hashem did not forget. The ultimate Time Manager knew that when the time came to bury this man, He would make Shmuel Amon busy on Sunday so that he would go to the cemetery on Tuesday to bury his unknown benefactor.

That's time management.

When Tragedy Strikes

A horrific tragedy took place within the community of Boca Raton, Florida, in April 2013. A 12-year-old girl, Shoshie Stern, was killed in a traffic accident. At an emotional communal gathering, one of the rabbis, Rabbi Ephraim Goldberg, summed up everyone's feelings:

> We reel from this tragedy. It feels like it was just moments ago, hours ago, that we received a phone call or text message informing us that a 12-year-old girl — a precious neshamah — has been lost. The pain is still so acute, the grief is so overwhelming — and it could not have happened to a more special family.
>
> As those who spent time in the shivah home have come to realize, Rabbi Michael Stern and his Rebbetzin, Denise, are incredibly special people. Tonight, at their home, they spoke to two people from our community who saw the entire horrific event unfold. I heard Rabbi Mike turn to Denise and say, "We need to be here for those who wit-

*nessed it. They really went through a very diffi-
cult thing. We have to lift their spirits; we have to
give them comfort, because they are really going
through a horrible time."*

Can you imagine! What extraordinary people —
to think of others even as they are going through this
themselves.

*Nothing is coincidental. I had been called to perform a bris in
Boca Raton. Sadly, the bris turned out to be during the shivah for
Shoshie Stern. I was asked to address the community the night
before the bris. A large crowd gathered in one of the community
shuls. The following is adapted from what I said then.*

We have come together in a week of anguish and in a week of
heartbreak. What happened this past week will affect all of you forever. As a New Yorker, I can tell you that years ago, 9/11 affected us,
and it still affects us to this day. Similarly, all those who live in Boston
will be affected forever by what happened at the Marathon. And all of
you here in Boca Raton will be affected forever by the sudden terrible,
tragic loss of that special girl, Shoshie Stern.

In Boca, the sun has set prematurely, and it has cast a pall of darkness on the entire community. The shadows of this darkness spread
across Jewish communities throughout the world. So many of us who
do not live in Boca feel your pain and share your grief, because whom-
ever we speak to tells us about the greatness of Shoshie's parents,
Rabbi and Mrs. Stern.

As I was being driven here from the airport, Rabbi Yaakov Astor, a
friend who knows the Sterns called me and said, "Rabbi Stern was my
closest friend growing up. He is the embodiment of Avraham Avinu.
He has an organization called Rabbi Without Walls, which does just
what it says: He does not wait for unaffiliated Jews to come to him.
He goes out to people and is *mekarev* them."

I want to tell you a very painful lesson I learned as a young man.

My father passed away when I was only 21. I am the
eldest of seven children. I had known for a while that

he was ill. One day, my father was taken to the hospital in Washington Heights. He had been a *talmid* of Rav Shimon Schwab when Rav Schwab gave *shiurim* in Ner Yisroel in Baltimore before becoming the Rav in the German community in New York, so my brother Kolman and I stayed at the Rav's home for Shabbos. After having visited my father in the hospital, we went back to eat the *seudah* with Rav Schwab and his wife. The Rav asked how our father was. I answered, "I have *bitachon* (faith) that he will get well."

Rav Schwab became very serious, and taught me a lesson for life. "*Bitachon* in Hashem," he said, "does not mean that your father will necessarily recover and get well. Faith in Hashem means that we understand that Hashem has a master plan, and He knows what He is doing. It does not mean that only good things happen. Hopefully, one day we will understand His intentions."

Tragedies happen, *r"l*. *Bitachon* means having faith that Hashem knows what He is doing, and that perhaps one day we will understand. That is why we get together to give each other *chizuk*, so that we will not be broken. At the end of time, we will find out why it happened, but until then, we face the reality that difficult things occur.

A New Person

A neighbor of mine, Mrs. Gitty Lipsius, teaches in Shevach High School in Queens. She had a number of children, and then it was a few years before she was expecting another child. She went through a full-term uneventful pregnancy, but tragically, the child was stillborn. She was devastated and sank into depression.

Mrs. Lipsius told me that her father, Rabbi Gershon Yankelowitz, had lost his entire family in the Holocaust, and after the war, he and his wife had trouble having children. After years, they had their first child, a little girl — who died only four months later. He had suffered so much. Eventually, he and his wife did have a family. Now, years later, he called his daughter Gitty and asked her how she was doing. She replied that she was doing terribly; she could not find herself and did not know how she would ever be the same again.

Rabbi Yankelowitz said, "My dear daughter, you will never be the same. You are a new person. Find your newness. Get used to it, and live with it. When you accept your new situation, you will be able to go on."

> Her father then said, "My daughter, you will never be the same. You are a new person. Find your newness. Get used to it, and live with it."

When her father gave her that insight and direction, Mrs. Lipsius realized how right he was. She told me that once she accepted her new reality, she felt liberated. From that point on, she was able to return to being a functioning, accomplishing person.

That is what we must learn to accept here in Boca. We will never be the same. Once we learn to accept that, and live with that newness, we will be able to grow.

A Cup of Blessing

A while ago, I got a call from Rabbi Yisrael Rosenfeld, who had been a wonderful *mechanech* and principal in Denver, Colorado for many years. I personally have a great debt of gratitude to him because he was the teacher of my wife, Miriam, who grew up in Denver. Rabbi Rosenfeld said to me, "In the past, you have done the *brissin* of a number of my grandsons who live in New York. But now I have had my first great-grandson! Please come to do his *bris* at the White Shul in Far Rockaway."

I was honored to get that call, and so on the designated day, I arrived early to the White Shul to prepare for *davening* and the subsequent *bris*. Before *davening*, Rabbi Rosenfeld showed me the *becher* they would be using. He told me that it was very special to him, because when his parents married in Chust, Hungary, the Satmar Rebbe, Rav Yoel Teitelbaum, *zt"l*, gave them that cup as a wedding gift.

I was impressed, but Rabbi Rosenfeld was not finished. He continued and told me that he had been in Auschwitz. I was shocked. I had thought that he was born in Denver. No, he told me, he had been born in Chust, and when he was 15, the Germans surrounded Chust and turned it into a ghetto. The Jews learned that they had four days until they would be deported. Rabbi Rosenfeld's parents thought they would be sent deeper into Hungary; they had no idea that they would be sent to Auschwitz.

Yet despite the fact that he was only a teenager, Rabbi Rosenfeld wisely realized that they would not be allowed to take their valuables with them, so he asked his father to allow him to bury some of their family's precious possessions until the time when he hoped he would return and dig them up. His father consented. He took the *atarah* of his father's *tallis*, his mother's candlesticks, his father's pocket watch and the *becher*, and ran with them to the area behind his grandmother's house, where the ground was very soft (because they had chickens there). With his hands, he dug as deep a hole as he could and buried those four items.

Four days later, they were sent to Auschwitz where they were imprisoned for a year and a half. Rabbi Rosenfeld's father and brothers were murdered there. He, a sister, and his elderly mother survived. It took months for him to return to Chust, and when he finally arrived there, he ran into his home — but he was thrown out and threatened with arrest if he came back.

He ran behind his grandmother's house and tried to remember where he had buried those precious articles. The ground had hardened, but he took a piece of wood and started digging. Sure enough, he found all four of the possessions. The *becher* had been flattened by the weight of people stepping on the ground above where it lay near the surface, but sometime later, Rabbi Rosenfeld had it repaired.

"This cup," Rabbi Rosenfeld exclaimed, "has been used for *every* wedding and *every* bris in the family! Today, for the first time, it will be used for the *bris* of my first great-grandchild. That's why it's so special."

I took the *becher* and kissed it, and asked Rabbi Rosenfeld to give the cup to me before the *bris* because I wanted to address the crowd before we even started. Thus, after *davening* but before they even brought the infant in for the *bris*, I held the *becher* up for all to see and told them its story.

"I believe this *becher* represents *Klal Yisrael*," I said. "This *becher* was buried. This *becher* was trampled on. This *becher* was given up for lost — just like *Klal Yisrael*. We have been thrown out of so many countries, we've been beaten and we've been given up for dead after pogroms. But today, here we are, stronger than ever. To me it would seem that this *kos shel brachah* is so special that after the *bris*, everybody should line up to sip some wine from this precious *becher*."

Sure enough, after the *bris*, close to 20 people lined up to drink from that cup of blessing.

And that is what I believe each of us here in Boca tonight must do. We must strengthen ourselves and become like this *kos shel brachah*. That is our obligation. From tonight on, each of us must make a commitment that *we* will be a cup of blessing for others in *Klal Yisrael*. Each of us has certain talents. Each of us is accomplished in his or her own way. Tonight, we must look into our hearts and ask ourselves, "How can I become a blessing?"

Tuition Situation

None of us would have wanted this tragedy to have occurred, but each of us will now become a *kos shel brachah*, because now we will feel pain for others as never before. Now we will become more compassionate people. We will do more *chesed*. We will understand what it means when a community comes together and the people give *chizuk* to each other.

Let me give you an example.

> There is a fellow named Shabsi(*) in London who has a job as the head of the tuition committee of a local yeshivah. It is a job nobody wants. Shabsi told me that as the tuition committee leader, he called a wealthy fellow, Feivel,(*) a few days before Pesach to remind him that he owed the school £2,000, which

the school needed desperately to pay the staff before *Yom Tov*. Feivel said that he would take care of it that day and promised that he would come to Shabsi's home later that afternoon. Shabsi waited, but Feivel did not show up.

A few weeks passed. Now it was a few days before Shavuos. Shabsi made another phone call to remind Feivel of their previous conversation. Feivel protested that he had indeed come to drop off the money that day, but he had not been able to find parking, so he gave an envelope with the money in it to Shabsi's 8-year-old son who had been playing outside the house. Later, when his son came home, Shabsi asked him about it. The boy said that he did not remember any envelope.

Shabsi called back Feivel and said that it was pretty irresponsible to trust a youngster with so much money, but before going to a *din Torah* to work it out, he would go up and down his block to see if anyone found it. The block was full of *frum* families, and he asked everyone if they had found a white envelope. Finally one neighbor, Henoch,(*) responded by asking, "Do you mean the one with £2,000 in it?"

"Yes, exactly," said Shabsi. He went on to tell the finder the whole incident.

"You won't believe this," Henoch said. "A few days before Pesach, I was laid off. I had no idea how I would make Pesach. I didn't want to go home and tell my wife. I walked around, trying to decide what to do, and there on my lawn was an unmarked envelope with money inside. Like manna from heaven. That's how I covered our Pesach expenses. However, now that you tell me that it is money that belongs to the yeshivah, of course I will pay it back. But it can only be in increments as I still don't have a job."

Shabsi called Feivel to tell him what had happened. What Feivel said was remarkable. "Tell him to keep the money. I'll give you another £2,000. I was once in his position as well, and I can understand what he is going through."

And indeed, Feivel brought the money over right away. Why did he do that? Because he had gone through a similar terrible experience of being without an income and had learned from it. He had become a *kos shel brachah*.

That is how we grow. From adversity we feel pain, and that helps us relate to others in a similar situation. This, then, is a moment of growth.

Of Chariots and Horses

Finally, I believe that when a tragedy of this scope occurs, we need perspective.

I had a friend in Detroit, Elya Shoenig, who had a son named Chezky. In the winter of 1966, shortly after his bar mitzvah, Chezky became very ill. He was a wonderful, respectful child, loved by everyone. By January 1967, the doctors realized that Chezky had leukemia. Everyone was especially frightened, because Chezky had had leukemia when he was 2 years old. For ten years, it had been in remission, but now it had returned with intensity.

Chezky's father did everything he could to pursue treatments for his son. One day, someone approached him in shul and said, "Elya, I want you to know that your son will be fine! He's going to be healthy again!"

"How do you know that?"

"There is a *pasuk*," the man said, "אֵלֶּה בָרֶכֶב וְאֵלֶּה בַסּוּסִים וַאֲנַחְנוּ בְּשֵׁם ה׳ אֱלֹקֵינוּ נַזְכִּיר, *Some [the non-Jewish world] with chariots and some with horses, but we, in the Name of Hashem our G-d, call out* (*Tehillim* 20:8).

"The *pasuk* says that non-Jews rely on 'chariots and horses' to fight their battles, but we call out to

Hashem; we're on a higher level. It's the same in medicine. Your son is fighting a battle with leukemia. Perhaps for a non-Jewish child, leukemia would seem hopeless because of the limitations of medicine, but your son will get better because Hashem is fighting his battle."

Elya was moved. The more he thought about it, the more encouraged he became. Soon, he felt positive that Chezky would get better. Every day, he kept saying the *pasuk* over and over and convinced himself that this temporary nightmare would soon be over. Even after Chezky became more ill and needed a bone marrow transplant at the Harper University Hospital in Detroit, Elya Shoenig did not lose hope. Interestingly, when the doctor said to Elya, "Mr. Shoenig, your son is doing better than everybody else on the ward," he thought, *Of course*, אֵלֶּה בָרֶכֶב וְאֵלֶּה בַסּוּסִים ....

Tragically, Chezky's situation got worse, and a few months later, on an Erev Shabbos, he passed away. The whole Detroit community was devastated. They had a heartbreaking funeral, just as you had here in Boca. Every child who knew Chezky was crying, just like every child here who knew Shoshie cried.

Elya told me that for weeks afterward, every time he said that *pasuk* during Shacharis it pained him. And every day the pain grew worse. Wasn't that the *pasuk* that assured him of healing? He was distraught until, one morning, he suddenly came up with this understanding of what David HaMelech was telling us in this phrase. It is not the battle plan *during* the war, but the approach *after* the war that David was emphasizing.

After the war, when a non-Jew loses, he says, "If only I would have done something different. If I'd had a different strategy or different weapons, I could have won." — if only this, if only that ....

However, a Jew does not look back. He does not say, "If only I had used a different doctor, different hospital, different treatment ...."

Now, Elya understood the next *pasuk*: הֵמָּה כָּרְעוּ וְנָפָלוּ, *they slumped and they fell*, because they thought that they controlled the war and could have caused a different outcome. וַאֲנַחְנוּ קַמְנוּ וַנִּתְעוֹדָד, *but we arose and were invigorated*, because we knew that no matter what we would have done, the outcome, which was the will of Hashem, would have been the same.

Some people may think that maybe Shoshie should not have crossed that street, maybe she should not have been in that area at that time, or maybe she should have stayed home. But that is not how we should look at it. No matter what she would have done, and no matter where she would have been playing, it was going to happen. We can look at the Sterns and say that they raised a beautiful child. They and their precious daughter did everything they were supposed to do. We can all be proud of her, proud of her family, and proud of her community.

> **People may think that maybe Shoshie should not have crossed that street, maybe she should not have been in that area at that time, or maybe she should have stayed home. But that is not how we should look at it.**

That's why we can say with confidence, "וַאֲנַחְנוּ קַמְנוּ וַנִּתְעוֹדָד." We arise and feel invigorated, because she was raised in the most magnificent way. The Sterns did everything they were supposed to do. And if you do everything that you are supposed to do, you cannot feel inconsolable about it. You should be proud that such a child was raised in your wonderful community of Boca Raton. The family, the school, and the community should be proud.

Hashem should help all of you continue to be that *kos shel brachah*, that *lev tov* to each other, and know that though you have gone through a difficult time, you will not be broken. You will build yourselves and rebuild the Stern family; you will give *chizuk* to them and to anyone, anytime, who may find themselves in their position. May Hashem bless all of us with strength and perseverance, for they are the hallmarks of Jews through the ages.

Grieving With Others

In 1998, a small but remarkable book was written: *Friends for Life: A Guidebook for Friends of Terminally Ill Teenagers*. It was co-authored by four teenage girls: Chava Axelrod, Shoshana Frankel, Miriam Gewirtz, and Efrona Hoffman of the Yeshivah of Greater Washington High School. They had asked their principal, Rabbi Zev Katz, for extracurricular work. He suggested that since they were already involved in many *chesed* activities, they should write a book that would be practical and useful.

I called Rabbi Katz and he told me that the girls put this book together in the *zechus* that a little boy in their town, Shauli Mordechai, should have a *refuah sheleimah*. He had suffered a terrible accident while swimming and had been in a coma for years. Every day these girls and others would do exercises with him to keep his muscles from locking.

In the same vein, Yehudah (Judd) Lifschitz, a lawyer in Silver Spring, Maryland, who was a neighbor of Shauli's family, took a book written in Hebrew by Rabbi Aharon Zakkai, *Chachmei Yisrael B'Yaldusam* — inspirational stories of *tzaddikim* when they were little children— and translated it into English using the title, *Stories for Shauli*.

In the introduction, Mr. Lifschitz explains that when he visited Shauli during one of his numerous hospitalizations, he found Shauli's mother, Aviva Mordechai, clutching her *Tehillim* and crying. She told him that the nurse had suggested that it was time to take her son off the respirator. She was told he wasn't "living," wasn't thinking. But Aviva knew that her child possessed a holy soul, that he was here for a holy purpose, and that she had been put here to guard that *neshamah* for as long as she possibly could.

At that point, Mr. Lifschitz comprehended the truth of her words, and realized the meaning of Shauli's life. Shauli was here for a holy purpose. How many chapters of *Tehillim* had been recited because of him? How many prayers had been offered by Jews worldwide in his merit? How many pages of Gemara had been learned and analyzed on his account? Who among us, except for *gedolim*, lives a life that brings about the uplifting of the spirituality of the Jewish people? It was then that Mr. Lifschitz decided to translate a book that would be a *zechus* for Shauli. He thus took Rabbi Zakkai's work and translated it so that all in the English-speaking/reading world could gain from it.

Can you imagine the *chizuk* the family felt, how greatly encouraged they were, to see the work and expense that was put into that project? It showed that people cared, that Shauli and his family had not been forgotten.

A House of Mourning

We know that no one lives forever. There will come *that time* for each of us and for each of our friends. There will come a time for *nichum aveilim*, comforting and consoling mourners.

Shlomo HaMelech tells us in *Koheles* (7:2): טוֹב לָלֶכֶת אֶל בֵּית אֵבֶל מִלֶּכֶת אֶל בֵּית מִשְׁתֶּה בַּאֲשֶׁר הוּא סוֹף כָּל הָאָדָם וְהַחַי יִתֵּן אֶל לִבּוֹ, *It is better to go to the house of mourning than to the house of feasting; for that is the end of all man, and the living should take it to heart.* It is not only good for us when we go to the *shivah* house, and it is not only good for the mourner when we go. It is also good for the *niftar*. The Gemara (*Shabbos* 152b) relates that a man died with no one to sit *shivah* for him. Rabbi Yehudah gathered 10 people and had them sit in the man's house for seven days. Afterward, the deceased man came to Rabbi Yehudah in a dream and told him, "Let your mind be at ease, for you set my mind at ease."

In other words, when a person, *r'l*, is sitting *shivah*, three people gain: the visitor, because he will become serious about life; the mourner, because he is comforted; and the deceased. Rav Dovid Cohen says that because of this Gemara, even when a person is sitting *shivah* alone, it is still proper to say, "*HaMakom yenacheim eschem* (May Hashem comfort you)" (in the plural), because both the mourner *and* the deceased are being comforted.

If that is the case, then we must understand that being *menachem avel* (paying a *shivah* call) is not a reunion of old friends. Sometimes a *shivah* house looks like a party: people who haven't seen each other in years are catching up on the latest news and gossip. They are so happy; all that's missing is the beer and pretzels. That's not how it is supposed to be. A *beis aivel* is a serious place.

Once, a young widow was inconsolable during *shivah*. R' Aryeh Levin came to be *menachem avel*, but the woman could not stop crying. She said to him, "Tell me what became of all my tears; all the tears that I shed during *davening*; all the tears that fell when I said *Tehillim* day and night — what happened to them?"

R' Aryeh answered, "Every sincere tear we shed is collected by Hashem. Then, when a threat comes upon *Klal Yisrael,* Hashem takes those tears and washes away the threat. Your tears were saved by Hashem to protect *Klal Yisrael.*"

A few weeks later, the widow called R' Aryeh Levin and asked him to repeat what he had said during *shivah*, because it was the only thing from which she drew *chizuk*.

R' Aryeh spoke with sensitivity and we, too, should learn how to speak with sensitivity. The next time one of us must be *menachem avel*, talk about the *niftar*. Say what you remember about the person, or ask the mourners about their loved one; ask what the *maspidim* said. Never bring up an irrelevant topic. If the mourners ask you about school or business, you have to answer, but you should not bring up anything that is not relevant to the *avel*.

A number of widows have told me that they drew tremendous comfort from letters that people wrote. Sometimes it is difficult to express deep feelings in person, but not in writing. One woman told me that every year, on the *yahrtzeit* of her child, she takes out all the letters she received during *shivah*, and re-reading them gives her *chizuk*.

Never ask prying questions about the medical care of the deceased. It's not your business! Besides, it is too late to change anything. Don't say, "If only he had been in another hospital, with another doctor." Or, "If only you had gone to that foreign country where they have that natural treatment." Nothing can nor will help if Hashem has decided that it is the person's time to leave this world. Don't make the family feel guilty that they "didn't try hard enough."

Don't say to a mourner, "I know how you feel." If you were fortunate never to have been in that position (i.e. you did not suffer the type of loss they just suffered), you simply don't know and can't feel their pain.

> **Don't say to a mourner, "I know how you feel." If you were fortunate never to have been in that position, you simply don't know and can't feel their pain.**

I was once in Bournemouth, England, at an incredibly uplifting European Agudath Yisrael Convention. Someone there told me a great story. Dr. Shlomo Adler was a well-known doctor in London; one of his patients was Rav Yehudah Zev Segal, the Manchester Rosh Yeshivah, *zt'l*. Once as Rav Segal was leaving the office, the *talmid* accompanying him noticed the doctor's wife sitting in the front office. He suggested that Rav Segal give her a *berachah*. Rav Segal asked what *berachah* he should give. The *talmid* said, "Give her a *berachah* that she never suffers *agmas nefesh* (aggravation)." Rav Segal told him that was impossible; everyone has some aggravation in life. But he could give her a *berachah* that when she does suffer *agmas nefesh*, she should be able to cope with it.

The following week, that woman, Mrs. Ellen Adler, had a heart attack and was hospitalized. When people visited, she told them that the only thing that kept her going was the Rosh Yeshivah's *berachah*.

Of course we will all have *agmas nefesh* to varying degrees. Nobody gets off free. But Hashem should bless us that we are able to cope. That's what you can tell the mourner, "May Hashem help you with strength through this difficult time."

A woman once wrote me a painful letter describing what she had experienced when she sat *shivah*. She wrote that at one point so many of the visitors were speaking to each other that she had to ask them to stop and listen to her, because she wanted to talk.

Very often the mourners need to talk — and we need to listen to them. This woman noted that the word "listen" and the word "silent" are composed of the exact same letters. You have to be silent in order to really listen. A *shivah* house is not a place to tell your problems or your history. It's a place for the mourners to be able to express their feelings.

> **Very often the mourners need to talk — and we need to listen to them. ..."Listen" and "silent" are spelled with the exact same letters. You have to be silent in order to really listen.**

Many people don't know what to say in a house of mourning. One widow told me that she felt the worst thing was for people to come and just stare. It was agony for her. People mean well, but if you have nothing to say, say "*HaMakom yenacheim* ..." and leave. Don't sit and stare. Imagine what it's like to sit there with 30 people staring at you.

Finally, don't stay too long. Mourners may be tired; they may not have had a chance to eat. Many people come for the morning *davening* and then stay for a while. By the time they leave, the next wave of visitors has begun to arrive. The mourners don't want to excuse themselves because that's not polite, but they haven't had a chance to eat breakfast yet. Then by the time the others leave, it's already lunchtime.

I repeat, be sensitive to the mourners. Let them talk. Ask about the *niftar*. That's the purpose of your visit. The Rambam tells us (*Hilchos Avel* 13:3) how to comfort the mourners: "... and as soon as the *avel* nods his head — he is not allowed to say goodbye — acknowledging that you have come and paid your respects, it's time for you to go, so that you don't burden [the mourner] more than necessary."

It isn't easy to sit *shivah*, so do the *mitzvah*, but within limits. Tell the family that you gave *tzedakah* in the merit of the *niftar*. That is a beautiful thing and a tremendous *chizuk*. Just remember that you will never ever replace that loss. They will never forget that person. So no matter how good, how well intentioned you are, know that you are there to do a *mitzvah* and to give as much comfort as possible, but your presence will not take away their pain.

After Shivah

When my father passed away, the *shivah* was the easiest part, because the whole family was there. I felt a bond with my family and with the community. Afterward, though, the difficult part began. During the *sheloshim*, during the year of *aveilus,* the pain is felt most acutely.

The fact that someone is widowed or orphaned is not a license to pry into their private life. Try to be available for a widow, widower, or orphan, but don't be aggressive. If one of the aforementioned says, "Please don't come today," don't go. Don't push. People need their privacy. They need time to grieve.

Don't shun them either. Many people feel after they lose a spouse that they are no longer invited anywhere. Don't disregard people who have lost a spouse. Keep up your friendship. Offer to go shopping with them, or for them. Offer to take their children shopping for clothes when you take your children. Invite them for a Shabbos meal. If they refuse, don't push, but continue to invite them at different times. Eventually they will come.

After my friend became a widower, he told me, he was invited somewhere for Pesach. He refused because he still had family and wanted to spend the *Sedarim* with them. He asked, though, if he could come for a Shabbos instead. "No," the inviter said, "that's not *chashuv*." (Can you believe that?) They obviously wanted him on a prominent day so that they could tell their friends who had been their guest on the glorious holiday.

A widow told me that she made a bar mitzvah, and some people did exactly what she hoped they wouldn't: they came over and said, "Oh, this must be so bittersweet." People say that at weddings, too. Of course it is bittersweet, but that isn't what the *baal simchah* wants to hear at that moment. They want to hear, "The bar mitzvah boy's *drashah* was brilliant," or, "The *kallah* looks so beautiful," or, "You should have so much *nachas!*"

Most importantly, try to ensure, if you possibly can, that their primary source of income continues. I remember to this day the people who went out of their way to help me with my *parnassah* in *bris milah* after my father passed away.

One of the great people who helped me was someone to whom my parents were very close: Rabbi Immanuel Jakobovits, *zt'l*. My mother Mrs. Hindy Krohn and Rebbetzin Amélie Jakobovits, *a'h*, were like sisters. Later Rabbi Jakobovits went on to become the Chief Rabbi of England. Our families remained close, and I remember once walking Friday night with Rebbetzin Jakobovits — who was royalty herself — a few years after Rabbi Jakobovits had passed away. She told me something so profound yet so sad: "The happiest days of the year," she said, "have become the saddest."

She explained by asking and answering her own question. "What are the happiest days of the year? Sitting together with your husband by a *Yom Tov* table, sitting at the Pesach *Seder* led by your husband, sitting in the *succah* together. But now the happiest days of the year have become the saddest."

I am involved with an organization called Samcheinu, which was created for the benefit of widows. Over 800 women, who range in age from their 20s to their 80s, belong to this organization. And you won't believe what they consider to be the saddest holiday of all: Chanukah. Why Chanukah? Because on Pesach most everybody is invited somewhere. On Rosh Hashanah and Yom Kippur everybody is in shul. On Succos everybody is taking trips. But on Chanukah, night after night, they have to light the candles alone. Who is giving gifts? Who is receiving gifts? Think about that!

There is a wonderful man in Baltimore, Dr. Menachem Cooper, who is a geriatrician (a medical doctor specializing in treating older adults). Dr. Cooper told me that his patients were housed in various nursing homes. Every few days he meets one of his patients, a woman who unfortunately is already experiencing dementia; she has lost her short-term memory. Nevertheless, there is one thing she does remember. Every time when the doctor arrives, she recites this short poem: "Yesterday is history, tomorrow is a mystery, today is a gift from G-d, that's why we call it the present."

Each of us can be a gift-wrapped present whenever we visit someone who is ill or in mourning. That is what Hashem gives us each day that we are alive — He gives us the capacity to extend ourselves to others who are less fortunate. David HaMelech says in *Tehillim* (121:5), צִלְּךָ 'ה, *Hashem is your shadow*. If you do for others,

[Hashem will see to it that] others will do for you. We should never need it, but it is great to have that bank account of "having given to others" so that when we need it, we can draw from those "funds," as others will give to us.

Seasons
and
Reasons

Family, Festivity, and Freedom: The Essence of Pesach

R av Elya Baruch Finkel was one of the *roshei yeshivah* in Mir in *Eretz Yisrael*. This story took place when he was still a *bachur*. An American who had learned at the Mir for two years was about to return to the United States for *shidduchim*. "Before you go back to America," the young Elya Baruch said to him, "maybe you should get a *berachah* from the *mashgiach* of Ponovezh." He was referring to the great *tzaddik* Rav Chatzkel Levenstein.

The boy said that he knew Rav Chatzkel spoke only Yiddish, but he, the *bachur*, did not speak Yiddish. However, he added, he would love to go if Elya Baruch would go with him as his interpreter. Elya Baruch agreed and so the future rosh yeshivah and this American boy from the Midwest went to Bnei Brak.

They entered Rav Chatzkel's house and Elya Baruch said in Yiddish, "This *bachur* learned in yeshivah in

> Rav Chatzkel didn't realize that the boy didn't speak Yiddish, and so he said in Yiddish, *"Nu, mit vuss gaist du tzurik* (with what are you going back)?" "With El Al," the boy answered.

Yerushalayim for two years, and now he's going back to America. Could the *mashgiach* please give him a *berachah*?"

Rav Chatzkel didn't know that the boy didn't speak Yiddish, so he said in Yiddish, "*Nu, mit vuss gaist du tzurik* (with what are you going back)?"

"With El Al," the boy answered.

Rav Chatzkel was flabbergasted. What was this boy talking about? "No, no," Rav Chatzkel said, "*Vuss nemst du mit* (What are you taking with you)?"

The boy said, "Rebbe, two suitcases."

Rav Chatzkel looked at the boy, baffled.

Immediately, Elya Baruch explained that the boy didn't understand the nuances of Yiddish. With that out of the way, the boy then explained (through Elya Baruch's interpretation) that he had learned numerous *masechtos* and that he would be "taking back" a significant amount of *mesechtos* in *Shas* that he had studied with him. Rav Chatzkel of course gave him a *berachah*.

When I told this story in Yerushalayim, someone showed me a powerful thought by the Meiri who writes in his introduction to *Berachos*: At every special occasion — whether at a *simchah* or, *r'l*, a sad event — a person is obligated to ask himself, *Why did Hashem make this happen? What can I learn from this?* And he says that if a person goes through a *Yom Tov* such as Pesach, Shavuos, or Succos and is no different than when it began, then, the Meiri explains, he is like a donkey. A donkey is a simple animal. It carries the wheat in the wheat season, the barley in the barley season, and the oats in the oat season. But it stays the same donkey. It doesn't change or become elevated. An event in one's life or holidays that one celebrates should have a significant impact on one's life and outlook. You must always "take with you" something that you gained from the experience.

As we approach Pesach, we have to ask ourselves: What will we be doing so that when *Yom Tov* is over we will not be the proverbial donkey; but, rather, be on a higher level?

Cellular Analysis

When Rav Shimon Schwab, *zt'l*, was about 9 years old, he had a bronchial infection known as the whooping cough. Many years ago, this was a very dangerous disease. At that time, the Schwabs lived in Germany, and the accepted treatment was to get a huge pot of scalding water and have the child lean over the pot to breathe in the hot vapors to clear his lungs. Indeed, that is what he did. However, as he was standing over this hot pot, someone walked by and accidently knocked it over. The water scalded young Shimon's arm. His hand was black and brown for a year after.

Years later, as an adult, he wrote that if someone were to ask him if his hand was the same one that had been burned in his youth, he would say, "Of course," even though, technically, there was not one cell in that hand that had been there when it was burned. Cells live only about 120 days. (We say "you should live to 120," but we mean years!) So what makes it his arm? The answer is that the cells regenerated over and over until they became the cells in his arm today.

Based on that, Rav Schwab offered an ingenious explanation on a phrase from *Chazal* (*Pesachim* 109b) that we use in the *Haggadah*: בְּכָל דּוֹר וָדוֹר חַיָּב אָדָם לִרְאוֹת אֶת עַצְמוֹ כְּאִלּוּ הוּא יָצָא מִמִּצְרַיִם, *In every generation, a person is obligated to see himself as though he had gone out of Egypt.* "I ask you," said Rav Schwab, "were you in Egypt? Were your grandparents in Egypt? Were your ancestors five generations ago in Egypt? Of course not; so how can the Gemara say this? How can it say that we have to feel it?"

The answer is that those millions of people who were there regenerated over and over, and we are their descendants. It's the same genes, the same cells that reproduced over and over again. In a sense, we were there and we experienced the Exodus.

Thus, a person experiencing the *Yom Tov* of Pesach has to feel that he was there, but that he is now liberated and free to celebrate the fact that we became a nation.

Let Them See What They Hear

A question is asked: If we celebrate the idea of freedom, why not just hang up a sign: "We've been liberated and redeemed and now we're free!" Why is our *Seder* so action oriented, doing things such as dipping, breaking (the *matzah*), reading, drinking, washing, eating, reciting, and singing?

The *Sefer HaChinuch* (Mitzvah 16) teaches a classic lesson that provides us with an answer to this question: כִּי הָאָדָם נִפְעַל כְּפִי פְּעוּלוֹתָיו, *a person's repeated actions determine his behavior.*

Intellectually, a person may realize he must act in a positive way, but if he is constantly acting in a negative way he will become that negative person, not the person he thinks he should be. Based on this *Chinuch* my father would always give this example: A person who becomes an executioner and has to execute cruel murderers will, after a while, become a vicious person, even though he is killing people who deserve it. His repeated acts of killing will have a terrible effect on him to the point that he becomes transformed.

That's why the Rambam, in his commentary to *Avos* 3:15, writes that if you have ten dollars to give to *tzedakah* it is better to give one dollar to ten poor people than ten dollars to one poor person; not only because you are helping ten people, but because it is making you a better person. Your repeated actions eventually determine your personality and behavior.

By being active participants in the *Seder,* we teach our children by example, not just intellectually. That's why the *Seder* is so action oriented. It's not enough to hang a sign and just think about it. Action is crucial. Rabbi Samson Raphael Hirsch writes, "Children are not to be induced to the observance of Torah by mere preaching. We must show them the way by our enthusiastic example, and [thereby] teach the meaning and the sense of what we are doing" (*Shemos* 13:8).

A person can preach and tell a child to do certain things, but only when the child sees how the parent approaches the *mitzvah* — with a *geshmak* and *hislahavus,* with pride and enthusiasm — will it make a difference in how the child eventually performs those *mitzvos.* When the father shows his excitement and meticulous behavior with the various *mitzvos* at the *Seder* table — the wine, the *karpas,* the matzos, the *maror,* the leaning, the retelling — this makes the greatest impression.

The Torah tell us that at *Kabbalas HaTorah,* וְכָל הָעָם רֹאִים אֶת הַקּוֹלֹת, *The entire nation saw the [sound of] thunder (Shemos* 20:15). Rashi explains: רוֹאִין אֶת הַנִּשְׁמָע, *They saw "what could be heard."* He adds that this was a once-in-a-lifetime experience: to be able to hear a voice. A *Chassidishe* Rebbe, the Shearis Menachem, once said that these words have a deeper meaning with an inherent lesson in *chinuch*. רוֹאִין אֶת הַנִּשְׁמָע means that children have to "see" that which they "hear." If you tell a child you want them to be on time for *davening,* you have to come on time yourself. Someone who tells his son not to talk during *leining* but who does not stop talking during *leining* himself should not expect his child to be any different. That is not רוֹאִין אֶת הַנִּשְׁמָע.

As we go through life, we have to ask ourselves, *How do our children view us? Do they see us as tennis players, gym nuts, individuals defined by our occupations … or as ehrliche Yidden, honest businessmen, people who respect talmidei chachamim, people who go out of their way to help others, people who make time for learning?* Of course, we have to keep healthy, do our exercises, but we can't let ourselves be defined as something other than Jews who are true to Torah standards.

> As we go through life, we have to ask ourselves, *How do our children view us? As tennis players, gym nuts, … or as ehrliche Yidden?*

Sedarim should be memorable for their warmth, inspiration, and family *minhagim* and legacies. Interestingly, decades ago, a *Seder* took place that became memorable for a classic comment made on the spur of the moment.

> Some *bachurim* were sitting at the *Seder* of Rav Yitzchak Hutner, *zt'l,* and as one of the *bachurim* was pouring the second cup of wine, he accidentally spilled some on the *rosh yeshivah*'s white *kittel*. The boy was stunned at his carelessness. His face turned red and he was terrified because he knew his rebbi would make a comment. But what would he say? Without hesitating, Rav Hutner offered something unforgettable. He said (in Yiddish), "A *kittel* without a wine stain is like a *Yom Kippur machzor* without tears."

Rav Hutner saved the night. He elevated a moment that could have been so embarrassing. Everyone felt energized. Greatness was displayed. The great teacher defined a moment in his inimitable way. Now, decades later, we are still talking about it.

An Amazing Vort

I would like to share with you one of the greatest insights I have ever heard about the *Seder.* I heard it on a tape recording (remember those?) from Rabbi Isaac Bernstein, an Irish-born rabbi who served congregations in New York and London, and who gave his *shiurim* and lectures with incredible enthusiasm and excitement.

Rabbi Shlomo Kluger cites Rabbeinu Manoach's commentary on the Rambam (*Hilchos Chometz u'Matzah* 8:22), who gives an unusual reason as to why we dip the *karpas* in saltwater. He says, "It is because the brothers [Yaakov's sons] dipped the *kesones passim* (Yosef's coat) in blood."

But why remember that at the *Seder?*

Rav Shlomo Kluger notes that the entire night we are going to talk about *yetzias Mitzrayim,* how we left Egypt. But the *Baal Haggadah* wants us to understand right at the beginning of the *Seder* how we got *into galus Mitzrayim.* And so immediately after *Kiddush,* before any-thing else — before the breaking of the matzah, the *Mah Nishtanah,* the telling of the Exodus, etc. — we need to know what caused the *galus.* And the answer is that brothers could not get along; they sold Yosef to Arab merchants. There was a lack of *ahavas Yisrael.* That's why *Klal Yisrael* ended up in Egypt, in *galus.*

Therefore, the *Baal Haggadah* wants us immediately to dip the *karpas,* symbolizing the brothers dipping of the *kesones passim* in blood (which they did in order to have Yaakov think that Yosef had been killed by a wild animal).

Rabbi Isaac Bernstein added something incredible. The Torah tells us (*Bereishis* 37:3): וְיִשְׂרָאֵל אָהַב אֶת יוֹסֵף מִכָּל בָּנָיו כִּי בֶן זְקֻנִים הוּא לוֹ וְעָשָׂה לוֹ כְּתֹנֶת פַּסִּים, *Yisrael [Yaakov] loved Yosef more than all his children because he was a child of his old age, and gave him a kesones passim.* Rashi says the *kesones passim* was *karpas!* That is because כַּרְפַּס is a combination of two words, כַּר, "something soft and fluffy," and פַּס, "silk." That's what the *kesones passim* was: a soft, silky type of jacket.

Now we understand, said Rav Bernstein, the meaning of Rabbeinu Manoach. The *kesones passim* was *karpas* (as Rashi explains). Hence, we do the dipping of *karpas* at the beginning of the *Seder* because it alludes to the problems Yaakov's children were having in getting along with one another. That's how the terrible sufferings of *Mitzrayim* began.

Never Give Up Hope!

Rabbi Shimon Schwab teaches something significant from the text of the *Haggadah* regarding the *chinuch* of our children. He asks: Right before we talk about the four types of children at the *Seder*, we recite the word *baruch* (blessed) four times: בָּרוּךְ הַמָּקוֹם, בָּרוּךְ הוּא. בָּרוּךְ שֶׁנָּתַן תּוֹרָה לְעַמּוֹ יִשְׂרָאֵל, בָּרוּךְ הוּא. Why repeat it four times?

Additionally, he asks, why here do we use the expression *HaMakom* for the Name of Hashem, a Name that is usually used at sad and unfortunate occasions? For example we use *HaMakom* when we are *menachem avel*. We say to the mourner, "*HaMakom yinachem eschem*, Hashem should console you." *Chazal* say that if a person loses money, you are supposed to console him, "*HaMakom yimalei chesronach*, Hashem should fill your loss" (*Berachos* 16b). When we pray for those stuck in foreign lands, we say, "*HaMakom yiracheim aleihem*, Hashem should have mercy on them" (see *Shabbos* 12b). In these times of crisis a person may ask, "Where was Hashem? How could Hashem let that happen? Where is He?"

And so we say to the person thus challenged, "*HaMakom* ..." — which literally means "the Place" — as if to say, Hashem is all over. He watches everyone at all times, constantly. Hashem is with you and will protect you.

However, how does that expression fit at the *Seder*? It seems out of place.

The answer is that at times parents could be sitting at a *Seder* with their son or daughter who is "at risk." Their child is doing the wrong things, hanging out with the worst people, and the parent might think: *Hashem, how could You do this to me? How could You let my child go off the derech and waste his life?*

The answer is, *Baruch!* Every child is a blessing! Never give up! Never lose hope. If you have a sister, brother, child, cousin, or friend in that situation, never give up. *Baruch, baruch, baruch, baruch.* Every child is a blessing; everyone can change. There is no such thing as a lost hope. You never know from where and when the *nachas* will come.

And think about this. Isn't it true that when you were still in high school, there was that child that everyone expected to be the most successful and it turned out he/she was not?. But the child sitting in the back or off to the side who did not come home with the greatest marks, he has blossomed and become great? Why? Because someone did not give up on him. Maybe it was his mother, father, rebbi, uncle, *morah*, grandparent, rav, or friend, but someone believed in him. Of course, this applies to girls as well!

> **The child sitting in the back, who didn't get the greatest marks, has blossomed and become great — because someone did not give up on him.**

You cannot give up on anyone, ever, because you never know.

That's what the Rambam tells us. Rav Avraham Shmulevitz, the son of Rav Chaim Shmulevitz, makes a wonderful point on the Rambam (*Hilchos Chometz U'Matzah* 7:2), which tells us: "You have to tell your children, even if they don't ask... and how do you tell them? The Rambam continues : You start out saying, "*B'ni*, my son, *kulanu avadim hayinu,* we were all slaves ."

Why does Rambam say "*b'ni*"? Rav Avraham Shmulevitz sees *b'ni* as a sign of love: "My child," the father is saying, "I love you!"

That's what parents should do at the *Seder*: hug and kiss their children, no matter what their age. Tell them you are a millionaire, because you have them as children. Speak to them softly, with love and affection. Tell them how great it is to be a Jew. Tell them how proud you are to do *mitzvos* and how you feel elevated when you learn, *daven,* or do *chesed*. Show them your pride in being a redeemed Jew and the message will come across.

May Hashem help that we celebrate Pesach in the spirit of growth and inspiration. May we merit to give to our children and grandchildren the *mesorah* of previous generations. May the month of Nissan, and specifically the holiday of Pesach, be a time of elevation so that we merit the ultimate *geulah* speedily in our times.

Making Every Day Count

An Accounting for Life

The Torah tells us that the lands of Sichon and Moav were warring with each other. The people of Sichon knew that the main city in Moav was Cheshbon. They thus felt that if they could conquer Cheshbon, they would be able to take over all of Moav. And that's exactly what happened.

Interestingly, the Torah not only records this war between two non-Jewish nations, but even adds an epilogue:

> עַל כֵּן יֹאמְרוּ הַמֹּשְׁלִים, *Regarding this, the poets would say,* בֹּאוּ חֶשְׁבּוֹן תִּבָּנֶה וְתִכּוֹנֵן עִיר סִיחוֹן, *Come to Cheshbon — let it be **built** and **established** as the city of Sichon (Bamidbar 21:27).*

Why did the Torah find it noteworthy to record the battle cry of the people of Sichon?

The Gemara (*Bava Basra* 9b) tells us that this *pasuk* really has a much deeper significance. The Torah is not merely telling us the battle cry of a non-Jewish nation. The word חֶשְׁבּוֹן means "accounting" and the allusion is to making a *cheshbon hanefesh*, a "taking stock" of who we are; of the *mitzvos* we have done versus the losses we have incurred from doing *aveiros*. If we make this *cheshbon*, the *pasuk* continues, we will be "built" in This World, and "established" in the Next World.

We are coming to the end of a 49-day period where we should have made a *cheshbon* every night. But even if we have not, it is not too late to start. Even now we can take stock, make an account of our values, and get a handle on our goals and direction.

A Cheshbon of Time

Many years ago, Rav Avraham Pam, the Rosh Yeshivah of Yeshivah Torah Vodaath, knew someone in his shul who was very ill.

Rav Pam was a *Kohen* and could not visit hospitals (because of the problem of corpses there), but he wanted to be able to fulfill the *mitzvah* of *bikur cholim*. So he wrote the patient a short letter, noting that he would *daven* for him.

The man was so thrilled to receive a letter from Rav Pam that he kept it under his pillow, and whenever someone came to visit, he would take out the letter and show it to him. Sadly, he did not recover and soon passed away. At the funeral, many different *rabbanim* spoke. One Rav came from out of town, a friend of the man's children, but he did not really know the *niftar* (deceased) at all. But he had to say a *hesped* (eulogy), so he found out a few details and worked with them. One of the things he said was, "You can imagine how special this man was in that the Rosh Yeshivah of Torah Vodaath wrote him a letter!"

After the family sat *shivah*, a *talmid* asked Rav Pam if he knew that the man had kept that letter under his pillow and that it was mentioned at the funeral. Rav Pam answered, "On the one hand, I'm very pleased by what you are telling me. But on the other hand, I'm terribly frightened by what you are telling me."

The *talmid* said he could understand why the Rav would be pleased by the news, but not why he would be frightened. Rav Pam asked him, "Do you know how long it took me to write that letter? Maybe three minutes. And look at the *chizuk* it gave that man and the *chizuk* it gave his family. How often do we have three minutes in a day and we waste them!"

Time is the greatest gift. The first *cheshbon* we need to make is: Are we using it properly? Are we using it to give *chizuk* as Rav Pam did? Are we accomplishing positive things, be they religious or secular? Are we making the most of our time, or are we wasting it on things that are not worthwhile? If someone on the level of Rav Pam worried about this *cheshbon*, shouldn't we?

That is the first accounting, the first *cheshbon* we have to make: a *cheshbon* of time.

A Cheshbon of Middos

Another important *cheshbon* is to take stock of our *middos*. The Kotzker Rebbe once said that when *Mashiach* comes, it will be easy for him to take the Jews out of *galus*, but it will be hard for him to take the *galus* out of the Jews. What an insight!

One aspect of *galus* that we suffer from is *ga'avah* (arrogance). In fact, humility is the prerequisite for Torah. That's the reason why the Torah connects the 49 days of counting to the *Omer* offering. The *Omer* is brought from the new grain and thus represents the new prosperity of a new harvest. The Torah tells us (*Devarim* 8:11-14), הִשָּׁמֶר לְךָ פֶּן תִּשְׁכַּח אֶת ה' ... פֶּן תֹּאכַל וְשָׂבָעְתָּ וּבָתִּים טֹבִים תִּבְנֶה ... וְרָם לְבָבֶךָ, *Take care lest you forget Hashem ... lest you eat and be satisfied and you will build good homes ... and your heart will become haughty.* Prosperity can make it *easy* to become arrogant and forget Hashem.

Therefore, before we started counting *sefirah*, *Klal Yisrael* had to bring an offering of *Omer*. In effect, the Torah is saying: First bring the *korban haOmer*, show humility by recognizing the source of your prosperity, and then begin eating the new grain.

The classic *mussar sefer*, *Orchos Tzaddikim*, begins with an essay on the vice of arrogance. He writes, "The reason I started the essays with one on haughtiness is that man must rid himself of it, for it is the opening through which all evil enters. It is the worst of all [bad] character traits."

> Rav Eliezer Kirzner went to Kfar Chassidim to visit his friend of many years, the great *tzaddik* Rav Elya Lopian. Rav Kirzner woke up very early one morning and noticed Rav Elya standing in his *tallis* and *tefillin*, repeating a *pasuk* over and over. Rabbi Kirzner wanted to know what Rav Elya was saying so he tiptoed up behind him to listen. Rav Elya heard the quiet footsteps behind him and turned to see who it was. Rabbi Kirzner apologized to Rav Elya for disturbing him and explained that he just wanted to know what Rav Elya was saying. Rav Elya told him that he was saying a *pasuk* (*Devarim* 7:26): וְלֹא תָבִיא תוֹעֵבָה אֶל בֵּיתֶךָ וְהָיִיתָ חֵרֶם כָּמֹהוּ, *And you shall not bring an abomination into your house and become banned like it ....*
>
> Rabbi Kirzner asked, "What 'abomination' are you talking about coming into your house?" (The word abomination is usually a reference to *avodah zarah*.)
>
> Rav Elya answered, "We are going to go to shul soon, to *daven* in the yeshivah. Since I take a long time to *daven,* everybody waits for me before saying *Shema,* and then again at *Shemoneh Esrei.* I'm afraid that I'll become arrogant from this. Shlomo HaMelech writes in *Mishlei* (16:5), תּוֹעֲבַת ה׳ כָּל גְּבַהּ לֵב, *Those who are haughty are an abomination to Hashem.* So I am saying this *pasuk* over and over to myself so that the abomination of arrogance does not enter my home."
>
> Rabbi Kirzner asked, "Rav Elya, at your age, are you still afraid that will you become a *ba'al ga'avah*?

The *yetzer hara* is not concerned with people our age."

Rav Elya Lopian grew very serious and answered, "A bad *middah* is like a grenade. A grenade can lie there for years, but as soon as someone takes out the pin, it explodes. A person can be in control of his *ga'avah* for months and even years, but all of a sudden something happens, the pin is removed, and the person explodes with terrible arrogance. Therefore, every morning I say these *pasukim* before going to the yeshivah so that I should not become arrogant."

> A bad *middah* is like a grenade. A grenade can lie there for years, but as soon as someone takes out the pin, it explodes. A person can be in control of his *ga'avah* for months and even years, but all of a sudden something happens, the pin is removed, and the person explodes with terrible arrogance.

⸺⸺≫●≪⸺⸺

Rav Yehudah Zev Segal, the Manchester Rosh Yeshivah, was once on a train going from London to Manchester, returning from a lengthy trip. As the train rolled to a stop, the *talmid* accompanying him looked out the window and saw a tremendous crowd waiting to greet the Rosh Yeshivah. The *talmid* told Rav Segal that they were all there in his honor. As they were leaving the train and Rav Segal saw the huge crowd, he said to the *bachur*, "Look at the honor they are giving both of us!" The *bachur* said, "Rebbi, it is all for you."

"No, no," Rav Segal replied, "look at the sign. It says, בְּרוּכִים הַבָּאִים! (*Blessed are those who come* — in plural). If they meant it only for me they would have written בָּרוּךְ הַבָּא! (singular)!"

That's humility. Even though he understood that the welcome was obviously only for him, a person has to bend over backward not to become filled with himself.

In *Horeb* (Ch. 42: note 300), Rabbi Samson Raphael Hirsch gives us important direction:

> *Man has no greater enemy than success. As long as you continue to wish and to hope and to fear, you will feel that you were created by Hashem, that you are His servant, and that you are a link in the chain of mankind. But when you become a proud owner of possessions, suddenly all your feelings for your fellow man shrivel up. Instead of fearing Hashem and loving mankind, you idolize yourself, seek your own interests, and put the gifts that you now have to selfish use.*

Humility is the first step toward *kabbalas haTorah*, receiving the Torah. If you want to reach that level of *kabbalas haTorah*, refrain from arrogance and acquire humbleness. And so a second *cheshbon* is one of our level of haughtiness.

Is Kissing the Torah Enough?

The Gemara (*Sotah* 42b) describes a very dramatic scene. When David and Golias were fighting, the odds, of course, were that the giant Golias would kill David. Suddenly, says Rav Yitzchok, Hashem said, "יָבוֹאוּ בְּנֵי הַנְּשׁוּקָה וְיִפְּלוּ בְּיַד בְּנֵי הַדְּבוּקָה, *May the sons of those who kissed fall into the hands of those who attached.*"

What does this mean?

We know that on Shavuos we read *Sefer Rus*. Rus and Orpah, the daughters-in-law of Naomi, were widowed, as was Naomi. Naomi, deciding that she was a cursed person, told them that she was returning to her country and that they should go their separate ways. Orpah kissed her mother-in-law goodbye and agreed that it was right for them each to go her own way. Rus, however, attached herself to Naomi. Years later, the descendants of Rus and Orpah faced each other on the battlefield. The descendant of Rus was David; the descendant of Orpah was Golias.

Hashem said the descendant (Golias) of the one (Orpah) who kissed [Naomi] should fall into the hands of the son (David) of the one (Rus) who attached [to Naomi]. There is a deep message in this *Chazal*: Genuine attachment supersedes verbal commitment. Lip service is not enough. It is not enough just to kiss the Torah. You have to become attached to the Torah.

Each of us has to go beyond the superficial and learn how to become attached to the Torah, and each of us has his own unique way he can do so. I have a very close friend who spends, without exaggeration, six hours a day *redding shidduchim*. He happens to be the executive director of a yeshivah in our neighborhood and I asked him how he became so involved in this *mitzvah*. He said that certain people had been very kind to the yeshivah, and he wanted to help them in some way, so he decided to *redd shidduchim* to their daughters. One thing led to another, and *Baruch Hashem*, he is very successful in his endeavors. Therefore, today, when you mention this man's name, you automatically think "*shidduchim*." This man is attached to that *mitzvah*.

Another fellow I know in Monsey is devoted to the organization Tomchei Shabbos, which sends Shabbos meals to poor families. He is always busy raising money, making the packages, thinking how he can make sure the recipients are not embarrassed, where he can get food cheaper, where he can get the trucks, where he can get drivers, etc. Mention this man to anyone who knows him and the first thing people think of is "Tomchei Shabbos." He is attached to this *mitzvah*.

Certain people have dedicated their lives to Hatzolah. How many children have they helped; how many people have they saved? I know someone whose whole life revolves around Hatzolah. Everyone knows his business is secondary. Hatzolah is his *mitzvah*. Mention his name and the first thing you think of is Hatzolah.

There is a family in Borough Park who is unbelievable at *hachnasas orchim*. People come from *Eretz Yisrael* and stay with them for weeks. I don't know how the mother does it; they have about 15 children. Mention that family name and immediately everyone thinks *hachnasas orchim*.

My father, Rav Avrohom Zelig Krohn, had a special *mitzvah*: *bris milah*. There was no one who had more *sefarim* on *bris milah* than he did. No one knew more *sh'ailos u'teshuvos* on *bris milah* than he did. Medical articles, doctor's instruments — our home was like a museum of all kinds of fascinating objects relating to *bris milah*.

Many times he would tell us an insight he had on the second *pasuk* of *Tehillim* (1:2): כִּי אִם בְּתוֹרַת ה׳ חֶפְצוֹ וּבְתוֹרָתוֹ יֶהְגֶּה יוֹמָם וָלָיְלָה, *His desire is in the Torah of Hashem; and in his Torah [u'vesoraso] he meditates day and night.* My father explained that a person has to have a desire to know all of Hashem's Torah, but "וּבְתוֹרָתוֹ" — in *his* Torah, in his area of specialty — he has to be involved day and night. This was such an integral part of his life that I had this *pasuk* engraved on his *matzeivah*.

The *Mishnah* says (*Makkos* 23b), "Rabbi Chananya ben Akashya said: The Holy One, blessed be He, wanted to give Israel merit; therefore He gave them Torah and *mitzvos* in abundance." Each of us is created with a different mindset, and as the Netziv writes in his *Ha'amek Davar* (15:41), different people are attracted to excel in different *mitzvos*. Some excel in *tzitzis*, others in *Shabbos*, others in learning — and even in learning, he notes, there are different methods.

As we approach *kabbalas haTorah*, let us make a third *cheshbon*; let us analyze to what we are drawn. There are so many *mitzvos*. Everybody is unique. Try to pick out a *mitzvah* and make it your specialty or your family's specialty.

Digging a Connection

Rav Dovid Stavsky built Orthodoxy in Columbus, Ohio. He told me that he once got a call from a Russian man who told him, in Yiddish, that he was speaking with a broken heart and needed to talk with the Rav. Rabbi Stavsky invited him to come to his house.

> The man, Michel, explained that he came from Kiev and had been living in Columbus for a year. He belonged to the Reform temple. The rabbi asked how he ended up there. The man sighed and said that it was for this reason that he had to come speak to the rabbi. He had been desperate to leave Kiev, and one day his family heard that this temple in Columbus was

willing to sponsor a family. Their name was put on the list and they were chosen. The family was brought to America and this temple gave them food and an apartment and helped them find jobs. Out of *hakaras hatov*, the man explained, he became a member of the temple.

"So why come to me?" the rabbi asked.

"I'll tell you," Michel said.

"In 1944, I was just a boy and my parents were older already. One day, they were lined up with many other Jews and shot. A mass grave was dug and all the dead were pushed into it. I was young and didn't know much about *davening*, but whenever I could, I would go back there and say in Yiddish a few words of prayer for them at that site. It always bothered me that they were buried like that in a mass grave without a true Jewish burial. Therefore, before I left for America, I went to that mass grave, took a jar, dug up as much dirt as I could, and filled the jar. I said to myself, *The earth that I have from this place will serve as a memory of where my parents are buried.* I brought the jar to America, and after being a member of the Reform temple for a while, I approached the rabbi and told him I wanted to bury the jar in a Jewish cemetery. He agreed and gave me a little plot in a cemetery — and there I buried the jar in the ground."

"So why are you coming to me?" Rabbi Stavsky asked.

"Because two months later," Michel said, "I went back to the Reform rabbi and told him I wanted to put up a *matzeivah* (headstone) to my parents with their names on it. He told me it was too old-fashioned; no one in America did that anymore. He said they just put a flat slab on the grave. I told him that I nevertheless wanted a *matzeivah* for my parents. But this Reform rabbi refused to give me permission. He said they don't allow anyone to do that.

"I then asked him if I could dig up the jar and was given permission. Now that jar is in my house," the man said, "and I am coming to you to ask if I can bury this remnant of my parents' gravesite in a Jewish cemetery with a proper *matzeivah*."

Rabbi Stavsky readily agreed, assembled a *minyan*, and went with them to the cemetery. They dug a grave and right before he buried that jar, the man opened it and placed inside a moving note in Yiddish: "Dearest Father and Mother, I will never forget you. Your loving son, Michel."

> They dug a grave and right before he buried that jar, the man opened it and placed inside a moving note in Yiddish: "Dearest Father and Mother, I will never forget you. Your loving son, Michel."

After the burial Michel said *Kaddish*. When he completed the *Kaddish* he turned to Rabbi Stavsky and said, "Thank you. You don't know how much this means to me. Tonight I can sleep because I know that my parents have *kever Yisrael*." A short while later, a *matzeivah* was erected over the grave.

Michel's parents did not have a Torah education nor did he have a Torah education, but Michel wanted a connection to the Torah way of life. We are so fortunate that we have a connection to Torah. The *neshamah* of each of us was at Har Sinai. Shavuos is the time to reconnect to what our *neshamos* saw at Har Sinai. We can make that connection by being diligent in our learning and punctilious about our performance of *mitzvos* ....

And it all starts by making an honest *cheshbon*.

A Leaf ... An Arch ...
A Song of Torah

Many people have asked: Why don't we make a *sheheche-yanu* when we first begin counting *Sefirah*? We always say *shehecheyanu* for a *mitzvah* that we do periodically, such as the reading of the *Megillah*, the kindling of the Chanukah lights, or the blowing of the shofar.

The *Bnei Yissaschar* offers a very interesting reason. He writes, "Our desire [and joy] is not for the days that we are counting, but rather for the day of Shavuos when we have completed the counting. That is when we will say *shehecheyanu*." In other words, we are building up to the crescendo of the *Yom Tov* of Shavuos when that special *berachah* is recited.

Imagine for a moment I told you that you had just won a $10 million lottery, and that you would be receiving the money in 49 days. How would you count the days? One, two, three ...? Of course not! You would count backward: 48, 47, 46 (days till I can tell my boss goodbye!) ... 36, 35, 34 (days until I can buy my dream home), 10, 9, 8, 7 (days until I can learn, do *chesed*, or travel to my heart's delight) .... You would be counting backward in anticipation, just like they do at the Kennedy Space Center before a rocket launch.

Yet we don't count backward in anticipation of Shavuos. Why not? Aren't we waiting for that special day, as the *Bnei Yissaschar* writes? The answer is that the days of *Sefirah* are days of growth and development. We are not waiting for Shavuos so that we can eat cheesecake. We are striving in these days to become strengthened in our *middos, derech eretz,* and Torah learning. That is why we count upward. The 49 days of *Sefirah* are not only days of *anticipation*, but days of *accomplishment.*

As they left *Mitzrayim, Klal Yisrael* was at their nadir, the 49th level, the lowest point of impurity. Yet 49 days later, they had grown to such a lofty level that they could hear Hashem say, "I am Hashem your God who took you out of the land of Egypt." It became the ideal as to what Jews should accomplish in the days of *sefirah* leading up to Shavuos.

The theme of Shavuos is Torah. So let's learn about things that will enhance our commitment to Torah.

The Multicolored Leaf

Let me share with you a delightful story that happened a number of years ago in the town of Gateshead, in the northern part of England. A *melamed*, a teacher, was walking through a park with one of his students, a 10-year-old boy. It was early autumn. The foliage was breathtaking; the leaves were red, green, orange, and brown. The *melamed* stopped and asked the boy to look at one of the beautiful multicolored leaves lying on a park bench.

"That leaf thinks it is free," the *melamed* said. "It thinks it can fly wherever it wants to. But it doesn't realize that in two days it will wither and die. And do you know why? Because it is no longer connected to its source. Only the leaves that are still connected to the tree can continue to live, blossom, and flourish."

The *melamed* looked at the young boy and said, "My child, I want you to remember this for the rest of your life. The *pasuk* tells us, "*Eitz chaim he lamachazikim bah,* the Torah is a tree of life to those who hold onto it (*Mishlei* 3:18)." There are those who think that if they do not uphold the Torah, they will be free to eat what they want, go where they want, watch what they want, and do what they want. But that is the beginning of spiritual death. The only ones who have a life of meaning and growth are those who are connected to the source. And that source is Torah."

That little boy later told me that that walk made a tremendous impression on him. Many know him now as Rav Mattisyahu Salomon, the *Mashgiach* of the Lakewood Yeshivah. He told me that that lesson — about the importance of connection to a source — became the essence of his life. It should also be the essence of our lives.

The Arch of Titus

I have had the wonderful opportunity over the last few years to lead tours to European countries where *Yiddishkeit* once flourished. A few years ago, I was asked to lead a group of 120 people on a tour to Italy. My first thought was: What Jewish history is there in Italy?

However, I soon realized that the author of *Mesillas Yesharim*, Rabbi Moshe Chaim Luzzatto, was born there. So, too, were the Bartenura and the Sforno. The Ohr Hachaim wrote his commentary on *Chumash* when he lived in Livorno, and in his introduction he writes glowingly of the wonderful people of that community who supported him.

It became apparent that there would be much to talk about on this trip. But I knew that our visit to Rome, on the last day of the trip, would be the most dramatic. I looked forward to talking about the legendary Arch of Titus.

Titus was the ruthless general who destroyed the Second *Beis HaMikdash* and murdered countless Jews. Those he left alive were marched into exile as slaves of Rome. Many other Jews died on the long trip to Rome. As a tribute to Titus, his brother built an imposing arch, over 50 feet high, in downtown Rome. There is an engraving on the inner wall depicting Jews, bent over, broken and sad, leaving Jerusalem carrying the *Menorah*.

I often wondered: Why did Hashem put into the mind of the engraver to depict the *Menorah*? Surely the Jews carried other *klei haMikdash* as well? And why has Hashem allowed this Arch of Titus to remain whole and unbroken all these years? Other famous monuments in Rome, known as the Roman ruins, are fragmented and decaying, but the Arch remains.

In 1953, the Ponovezher Rav, Yosef Kahaneman, visited Rome. He came alongside the Arch, pointed to it, and cried out, "Titus! Titus! You thought that you would outlast us, but the Jews are still here today and the Roman Empire is gone. There is no memory of you."

My friend, Rav Menachem Gross, told me of a non-religious Jewish correspondent who was asked to write a report about Hadrian's Wall. The Roman emperor Hadrian had a wall built in the northern part of England near Newcastle and the River Tyne to defend the Roman Empire from barbarians. Hadrian (known in the Gemara as Hadrayanus) was partially responsible for the murder of Rabbi Akiva.

The reporter saw that the wall had lost much of its prestige. It was no longer 75 miles long; people freely picked stones from it. One of the locals approached him and said, "Sir, we understand that you are Jewish. Would you like to see the Jewish neighborhood nearby?"

The reporter was surprised. "There's a Jewish neighborhood in Newcastle?"

"Yes; it's called Gateshead and it's quite prominent," he was told.

The reporter had never heard of Gateshead, but agreed to have a look. He was brought in to meet the Rosh Yeshivah, Rav Leib Gurwicz. Rav Leib soon realized that the correspondent knew nothing about his heritage, so he took him to see the *beis medrash*. Never in his life had he seen anything like it. Two hundred young men debating, arguing, waving their hands, reading from big books and little books, on the shelves, off the shelves …. (Rav Mattisyahu Salomon told me that he remembers that day that the Rosh Yeshivah brought the correspondent into the *beis medrash*.)

The journalist turned to the Rosh Yeshivah and asked him what was going on. Rav Gurwicz answered, "You came to report on Hadrian's Wall. Hadrian murdered Rabbi Akiva. However, his wall is in shambles. Hadrian no longer exists, nor his memory, but these men are still debating what Rabbi Akiva said and what he meant. And not only that, but there are hundreds of other places throughout the world where men like this are still talking about Rabbi Akiva. Rabbi Akiva still exists! Torah still exists! But the Roman Empire does not!"

That, I believe, is why Hashem left the Arch of Titus standing whole. The *Menorah* represents the verse, כִּי נֵר מִצְוָה וְתוֹרָה אוֹר (*Mishlei* 6:23). Every *mitzvah* we do is a candle. Every word of Torah that we study is a light. That Arch depicts the beginning of our journey into exile. The only way that journey can continue is if we follow what the *Menorah* represents: the performance of *mitzvos* and the learning of Torah.

Interdependence

Torah represents a bond with our past and a link to the future. Torah is the reason for our existence. It is the guidepost of our lives.

Mefarshim ask why the Torah begins with a ב and not an א, the first letter of the Jewish alphabet. There are numerous answers, but I once heard the following. Once Hashem decided to create the world, everything existed in duality: Heaven and earth, night and day, sun and moon, man and woman. Only one thing exists alone: Hashem (see *Midrash Devarim Rabbah* 2:31).

Hence, the message to the world was that no person and no entity except Hashem exists alone. We need connection to another. That is the ב — two.

This idea is further expressed by the very last word in the Torah. The Torah ends with the words, לְעֵינֵי כָּל יִשְׂרָאֵל, *to the eyes of all the Jews* (*Devarim* 34:12). The *Zohar* makes a fascinating comment. The letter of the word *Yisrael* — י, שׂ, ר, א, ל — stand for "*yeish shishim riboh osios leTorah*, there are 600,000 letters in the Torah." The *Zohar* asks: Why 600,000? Because 600,000 adult Jewish males left *Mitzrayim*.

Thus, the 600,000 letters represent the 600,000 men who left Egypt. Hence those 600,000 Jews are each represented by a letter in the Torah, and therefore each of us, their descendants, has a letter in the Torah that is ours.

When I heard this, I felt that we could learn three lessons. First, what if we would come to shul on Shabbos, and during *leining* we find that one letter is missing? The Torah has hundreds of thousands of letters, and yet if just one is missing, that Torah Scroll is blemished and cannot be used. That teaches us that if there is one Jew who is not yet fulfilling Torah in an authentic way, then the whole Jewish nation is flawed. We are all blemished. And it is our obligation to "fix the letter" — to inspire and be *mekaraiv* that Jew.

The second lesson is that no two letters can overlap. If two letters in the Torah touch, the *Sefer Torah* is again flawed and unusable. That teaches that none of us overlap. We each have our own special role to play in this world. Hashem has blessed each of us with our own unique talents. I don't have to be like you, you don't have to be like me, and neither of us has to be like someone else.

We all must know that each of us is part of *Klal Yisrael*, and whatever talent we have is something we have a responsibility to share with the community. Our letter (our talent and mindset) in the Torah is unique. It does not and cannot overlap with someone else's. It is our obligation to use it for the benefit of others in *Klal Yisrael*.

> **We all must know that each of us is part of *Klal Yisrael*, and whatever talent we have is something we have a responsibility to share with the community.**

The third lesson is based on the fact that in the entire Torah there is not one word that comprises only one letter. In English you have the word *I* and the word *a*, but in the Torah the minimum amount of letters to form a word is two. That shows that no one person can do it alone. We need a partner to accomplish all we were meant to accomplish.

Write This Song

The very last *mitzvah* in the Torah, number 613, is written as: וְעַתָּה כִּתְבוּ לָכֶם אֶת הַשִּׁירָה הַזֹּאת, *And now, write this song* (*Devarim* 31:19).

The Torah is called a "song." Why? The *Ksav HaKabbalah* says something beautiful. A song must be in perfect harmony. It must be in perfect sync. All the sounds blend together. That is what the Torah is all about. It is the harmonious way that Jews can live together, the way they can exist from one generation to the next. It puts our lives in sync. It gives us an outlook on what life is all about.

We are all part of the great symphony that is *Klal Yisrael*. The letters and words of the *Sefer Torah* are our notes. Each of us follows those notes to the best of his ability. We each have a particular role to play. If we don't perform the music that we can perform — the Torah that we can learn, the *chesed* that we can do, the *tefillah* that we can pray — it makes a difference to the Conductor of the World Symphony.[1]

When it was time for Moshe Rabbeinu to leave this world, Hashem told him to write a *Sefer Torah*. "Write it on stones, in this way, that it should be very clear." Why on stones? The Hebrew word for stone is אבן — א, ב, נ. I once heard Rav Zvi Ryzman say that it stands for "*avos, banim, nechadim,* fathers, children, grandchildren." That was the final lesson Hashem wanted to teach Moshe; although he might be departing this world, his legacy and his Torah would live on. Write it on stones, because that is for fathers, children, and grandchildren.

The Short Montle

Let me conclude with a delightful story originally told by Rabbi Shmuel Blech, a Rav in Lakewood. It concerns a community that wanted to write a *Sefer Torah*.

One by one, all the men came to write a letter. The women wanted to be involved also, so the rabbi said that every woman should make a *montle*, a cover, for the *Sefer Torah*. He promised that each *montle* would be used on a different occasion: Shabbos, Rosh Hashanah, etc. But the nicest one, he said, would be used on the occasion of the *hachnasas Sefer Torah*, when the new Torah would be brought under the *chuppah* to the shul.

On that day, a long table was set up and all the Torah *montles* were displayed. Each one was beautiful in its own right, but one purple cover depicting *Har Sinai* was judged to be particularly appealing. The woman who had created it was so excited that she ran outside and told all her friends.

The rabbis picked up the Torah and put the *montle* on it — and the men were shocked. The *montle* was too short! The *Sefer Torah* was

---

1. See *Perspectives of the Maggid*, page 259, for the story about the famous orchestra conductor, Arturo Toscanini, and how that story relates to the Conductor of the World.

40 inches long, but the *montle* measured only 38 inches. The rabbis had assumed that everyone would know the standard size and make their *montle* a little longer. However, evidently this woman had not measured correctly. Regretfully, they told her they could not use her work on this day of the *hachnasas Sefer Torah*. She was devastated. She begged the rabbis to use it anyway, because she had already told her family and friends that her *montle* had been chosen and now she did not want to be embarrassed in their eyes.

The rabbis apologized, but there was no way they could use it. They tried stretching it but that didn't work. Desperately, the woman suggested they try something else. "Rabbis, it's simple," she said, "just cut the Torah shorter!"

"Rabbis, it's simple," she said, "just cut the Torah shorter!"

Obviously that is a story, but it has an important lesson. How many of us lead that type of life? Sometimes you want to do something, but we know it's against the Torah. We must then decide, *Am I going to adjust to the Torah or is the Torah going to adjust to me?* Sometimes we are like that woman who wanted to cut the Torah.

As we approach Shavuos, we have to make a commitment to the entire Torah; a commitment that we are going to live our lives according to what the Torah wants. We will adjust to the Torah, not adjust the Torah to us.

When we do so we will discover an interesting thing. We will become one with our letter — our portion — of the Torah. Our unique talents and abilities — our specially designated letter in the Torah — will find expression in a *kosher* and *kedushah*-oriented way.

Rebuilding From Destruction

Rav Elya Lopian had a very interesting custom that he started when he was young and continued into his old age. He would get up very early in the morning, sometimes before *alos hashachar* (dawn), for a special *seder* of learning. His grandchildren asked him why he arose so early in spite of it being difficult for him to do so.

He answered, "Nobody lives forever. After 120 years, we will each have to give an accounting of our lives. The *beis din shel ma'alah* (heavenly court) will open up the *Shulchan Aruch* and go through it page by page, *halachah* by *halachah*, and ask, 'Did you fulfill this *halachah*, or did you violate it?' The very first *halachah* says, יִתְגַּבֵּר כָּאֲרִי לַעֲמוֹד בַּבּוֹקֶר לַעֲבוֹדַת בּוֹרְאוֹ, שֶׁיְּהֵא הוּא מְעוֹרֵר הַשַּׁחַר, *Be strong like a lion to get up in the morning to serve your Creator, and awaken with the morning star (O.C. 1:1).* My children, do you think I want to fail on page one? That is why I arise so early."

When I heard this, it occurred to me that we should look the same way at another *halachah* in the first chapter of the *Shulchan Aruch* (1:3): "It befits every G-d-fearing person to be distressed and concerned over the destruction of the *Beis HaMikdash*."

Aside from Tishah B'Av, Shivah Asar B'Tammuz, or the Three Weeks, were any of us sad or concerned about the absence of the *Beis HaMikdash*? When was the last time we thought about it? Yet, the *Mishnah Berurah* (1:11) gives us an idea, and if we indeed undertake it, we will not fail on the first page.

The *Mishnah Berurah* cites the *Shelah HaKadosh* who says, "At every *seudah* [at which one ate bread prior to *Birkas HaMazon*] one should say *Al Naharos Bavel (Tehillim* 137), and on Shabbos and holidays, when we do not say *Tachanun*, one should say *Shir HaMa'alos (Tehillim* 126)."

In other words, before you recite *Birkas HaMazon*, say *Tehillim* 137, which begins, עַל נַהֲרוֹת בָּבֶל שָׁם יָשַׁבְנוּ גַּם בָּכִינוּ בְּזָכְרֵנוּ אֶת צִיּוֹן, *By the rivers of Babylon, there we sat and also wept as we remembered Zion*. It will make you stop and think about the destruction of the Holy Temple; you will think about what we are missing. The next time you sing *Shir HaMa'alos* on Shabbos before *Birkas HaMazon*, you will not just sing the happy tune, but think about the meaning of the words: "Hashem will return the captivity of Zion ...." You will remember that we do not have the *Beis HaMikdash* today.

By reciting and reflecting on those chapters before *Birkas HaMazon*, we will fulfill this *halachah* from the very first *siman* in the *Shulchan Aruch*. It will help us not to fail on page one.

Look Into Your Heart

The Yerushalmi (*Yoma* 1:1) teaches, "Any generation in which [the *Beis HaMikdash*] was not rebuilt is as though that generation destroyed it." There is a strong message here. We cannot blame previous generations. We must look into ourselves. What are we doing wrong? How can we get closer to Hashem so that we can merit the coming of *Mashiach* and the rebuilding of the *Beis HaMikdash*? I believe that deep down, most people really know in which area they have to improve. They know where they have failed and are continuing to fail. Shlomo HaMelech writes, לֵב יוֹדֵעַ מָרַת נַפְשׁוֹ, *the heart knows the bitterness of the soul (Mishlei* 14:10). We know, and we know that Hashem knows.

Each of us has certain weaknesses we must address. Some are weak in Torah. A whole week can go by without opening a *Gemara*. When was the last time some of us had a *seder* in *Chumash*? In *Tanach*? Shouldn't everyone have a *seder* in *halachah*? It is wonderful that people learn *daf yomi*, but the *daf* is not enough. Many of us know that there is so much *bittul Torah* going on in our own lives. If you feel that this is your weakness, you have to work on it. No one can do it for you. And, indeed, through learning Torah a person comes closer to Hashem.

Some people are learning wonderfully, but have a problem with *tefillah*. They may not *daven* with a *minyan* as often as they should, or they come late in the morning and skip half the *davening*. Nobody knows whether you *daven* with a *minyan* or not, especially if you live in a big community. If your neighbors do not see you one morning, they figure you *davened* elsewhere that day. But you know the truth. You know how often you *daven* with a *minyan* and how often you have *kavannah*. You have to work on it; no one can do it for you.

Some people have to deal with the issue of *taharah*. They learn and *daven*, but in the privacy of their own homes, they are lacking in the area of *shemiras einayim*, guarding their eyes from impure images. Those who are caught up in the trap are well aware of it. It is not for us to tell them what to do; they know. If you know that this is where you are lacking, you have to strengthen yourself and come back to Hashem. And if it takes professional guidance, get it!

Some people are so selfish that they do not do anything for any-one. They are not involved in any organization or *chesed* whatsoever. They should know that the Chofetz Chaim writes (*Ahavas Chesed*, Chapter 12) that one should not allow a single day go by without doing a *chesed* for another person. People say, "Charity begins at home." Yes, that's true, but you will not train yourself to be a *baal chesed* unless you do things for other people outside the home.

Whatever the spiritual lack is, you know it, and only you can com-mit to correct it.

A Mikdash Me'at

The Malbim (*Terumah – Rimzei HaMishkan*, p. 481) says that every person is a walking, talking *Beis HaMikdash*. He writes: "Your head is the *Aron*. This is because the *Aron* carries within it the *Shnei Luchos Habris*, the wisdom of the Torah. And it is within your head that you carry your brain, the receptacle of wisdom. Your heart is the *Lechem Hapanim*. Just as a person needs his heart for life sustenance, he needs bread for life sustenance. The *Mizbei'ach* is the stomach. Just as the stomach consumes food, so did the Altar consume food."

If we would each truly see ourselves as a walking *Beis HaMikdash*, we would be able to inspire others constantly.

> **If we would each truly see ourselves as a walking *Beis HaMikdash*, we would be able to inspire others constantly.**

What was so inspirational about the *Beis HaMikdash* in the first place? Rav Aharon Kotler, *zt"l* (*Mishnas Rav Aharon* 3:54), tells us to look at a *Tosafos* in *Bava Basra* 21a. It discusses the words, כִּי מִצִּיּוֹן תֵּצֵא תוֹרָה, *For from Zion will the Torah come forth* (*Yeshayah* 2:3). What is it that makes Tzion great? *Tosafos* tell us that people saw the *Kohanim* acting with amazing enthusiasm and excitement. That was the greatness of the *Beis HaMikdash*. It was not the *Shulchan* or the *Mizbei'ach*. It was the *people* who were so inspirational. As Rav Aharon says, "*Harei zeh ha'adam atzmo mikdash me'at,* a person is a human *Beis HaMikdash*." He writes that people used to go to watch the Vilna Gaon *daven*, and it changed them for years. People used to watch the Arizal *daven*, and it changed them as well.

When I had the *zechus* to perform the *bris* on my nephew, Simcha Zelig Krohn, my brother Rav Arye chose to have it done in Mesivta Tiferes Yerushalayim so that the *gadol hador* Rav Moshe Feinstein could be the *sandek*. I could not contain myself that morning from constantly watching Rav Moshe *daven*. I remember that during *Krias HaTorah*, he had a *Mishnayos* right next to him. The moment they finished the *aliyah*, he looked into his *Mishnayos* — until the *baal korei* started again, and then he looked into his *Chumash* again.

I remember going to Camp Agudah in Ferndale, New York, as a young teenager. There was someone I looked up to with awe. (I realize now that the fellow was all of 17.) His name was Nachum Laskin, and up until that summer, I never saw anyone *daven* like he did. He was not my counselor, so I observed him from a distance. He *davened* out loud and enunciated every word with great *kavannah*. He was so into his *tefillah* that I stood transfixed. (He later became a great *talmid chacham* and a Rav. Unfortunately, he passed away in the prime of his life.)

To me, Rav Moshe Feinstein and Rabbi Nachum Laskin personify what it is to be a *mikdash me'at*, and that is what we must all strive to become.

If we can rebuild the *Mikdash* within us, if we can bridle our desires and funnel all our energies and resources into Torah, *tefillah*, *chesed*, refined speech and purity, we will have started our own personal rebirth and rebuilding.

Cousin Nosson

A few years ago, I received a call from a non-religious fellow who lived in upstate New York. He had a son and wanted me to perform the *bris*. He told me that the baby had been born on Tuesday. I explained to him that the *bris* should be on the eighth day, which was the following Tuesday.

"That's impossible," he said. "Everyone in my family works. We have to do it the following Sunday."

As much as I tried to explain to him the importance of doing it at the proper time, he would not hear of it. He told me that if I did not do the *bris* for him on that Sunday, he would simply have a doctor circumcise the baby in the hospital.

I told him that a *bris* can be delayed at times, but that is only when a baby is ill. Here it would not be proper that the *bris* be delayed. However, he insisted that the *bris* be on Sunday. Having no choice, we began making the preparations.

I gave him the list of items that he would need for the *bris*: gauze pads, ointment, diapers, kosher wine, etc. Then, near the end of the conversation, I asked something I usually ask at the beginning of the conversation: "How did you get my name?" (After all, he lived quite a distance from me.)

"I got it from a second cousin of mine who lives in your neighborhood," he replied.

"Oh?" I said inquisitively. "Who is that?"

"Nosson Meltzer," he replied. He explained that when his wife was expecting, he called his religious cousin for a recommendation. I was shocked. I told him that Rabbi Meltzer would feel terrible if he found out that his cousin had a son and had the *bris* delayed merely for the sake of convenience.

There was a long pause on the phone, and finally the new father asked, "Do you really think he'll care? Would it really make a difference to him?"

"I am sure it would," I said emphatically.

He thought for a moment and then said, "All right, we'll do it Tuesday."

I got there on Tuesday, as planned, and was sure that Rabbi Meltzer would be there. He was not. The next Shabbos, I met Reb Nosson in shul and gave him a big *mazal tov*. He asked me what that was for.

"Are you joking?" I said. "Your cousin had a boy!"

"Which cousin?"

"The one in Westchester."

He remembered that he had given him my name months ago, but they had not called to tell him that the baby had been born.

"Nosson," I said, "do you realize that when you get to *Shamayim* after 120 years Hashem will reward you for a *bris* being done on the eighth day? Had I not just told you about it, you wouldn't understand how you justly received that reward!

"Paysach," he said, "I still have no idea what you're talking about."

I then told him the entire story and explained that without realizing it he was the cause of the *mitzvah* being done properly. Rabbi Nosson Meltzer is a *mikdash me'at*. As Rav Aharon spoke of the *Kohanim* in the *Beis HaMikdash*, Nosson Meltzer (who is incidentally a *Kohen*) has been an inspiration through his sterling character and sincere adherence to *Yahadus*.

Decision of a Lifetime

Rav Nosson Muller, *Menahel* of Yeshivah Toras Emes Kamenitz in Brooklyn, told me the story of a 23-year-old *bachur*, Chaim Schonbrun, who was learning in Beis Medrash Govoha in Lakewood. It was the beginning of night *seder*. Chaim had been learning for about half an hour with his *chavrusah* when, suddenly, he clutched his chest, fell forward, and collapsed. *Bachurim* ran to assist him, and an ambulance was called immediately. However, despite Hatzolah's quick response, it was too late. Tragically, Chaim had passed away.

Chaim had been learning for about half an hour with his *chavrusah* when, suddenly, he clutched his chest, fell forward, and collapsed. *Bachurim* ran to assist him, and an ambulance was called immediately.

Prominent *Roshei Yeshivah* and *Rabbanim* gave moving *hespedim* in Chaim's honor. Those who eulogized him spoke of him as a sacred soul, a *kadosh*, who died while study-ing Hashem's Torah. Chaim's friends decided that in his honor, they would finish the entire *Shas* by the end of the *sheloshim* (30-day mourning period). A *Sefer Torah* was written in his memory as well.

What very few people knew was that earlier that afternoon, Chaim and his friends had gathered in a restaurant in nearby Deal, New Jersey, for a *seudas preidah* for a mutual friend who was going to learn in *Eretz Yisrael*. The meal took longer than originally expected, and then, Chaim looked at his watch and realized that it was only 20 minutes to night *seder* in the yeshivah. He got up to leave.

His friends were surprised. "We haven't even had dessert yet," one of them said, implying that it was a bit impolite to leave at this time.

"I've had a great time — here, use my credit card — but my *chavru-sah* is waiting for me. I have to be on time," Chaim said as he left. Indeed, he came to *seder* on time and within a half-hour he was gone.

"Imagine," said Rabbi Muller with astute perception, "if he had stayed in the restaurant and perished there. He would always be known as the *yeshivah bachur* who died in a restaurant! Now he is known as a holy student who died in the sanctity of the *beis medrash*."

Indeed, a *mikdash me'at*.

With Smiles of Inspiration

There is a man in our shul in Kew Gardens, New York, Mr. Reuven Rosenzweig, known to everyone as Rudy, may he merit long life. He is undoubtedly one of the happiest men alive. And that is incredible because he went through the horrors of various ghettos and concen-tration camps, including the nightmare of Plaszow. He greets everyone with a jovial "good Shabbos," and Rudy dancing on *Simchas Torah* is a sight to treasure.

Rudy went through the horrors of various ghettos and concentration camps, including the nightmare of Plaszow. Yet, he greets everyone with a jovial "good Shabbos," and Rudy dancing on Simchas Torah is a sight to treasure.

One Tishah B'Av, before we read *Eichah*, I went over to him and said, "Mr. Rosenzweig, I am so happy to see you!"

"Why is that?" he asked with a smile.

"Well, first of all, because I love you," I said. "And besides that, you are the sign to me that Hashem never makes a complete *churban*. He never destroys entirely. He always leaves something to build from."

During *Eichah*, I felt that Rudy was the living example of these *pasukim*, כִּי לֹא יִזְנַח לְעוֹלָם ה': כִּי אִם הוֹגָה וְרִחַם כְּרֹב חֲסָדָיו, *Hashem will not reject us forever. He afflicts, but He will have compassion according to His abundant kindness* (3:31-32). To all of us in our shul, Rudy Rosenzweig is a *mikdash me'at*.

Look around — there are so many in *Klal Yisrael* who can be labeled as a *mikdash me'at*: Rav Elya Lopian, Rav Moshe Feinstein, Rav Nachum Laskin, Rabbi Nosson Meltzer, Reb Chaim Schonbrun, and Mr. Rudy Rosenzweig. Let's learn from them and others like them so that we can rebuild ourselves, be an inspiration to others, and thereby merit living to see the rebuilding of the third *Beis HaMikdash* in our time.

Truth and Consequences in Elul

A s is well known, the word *Elul* stands for אֲנִי לְדוֹדִי וְדוֹדִי לִי (*Shir HaShirim* 6:3): *I am for my Friend* (I have a close relationship with Hashem), *and my Friend is for me* (He has a close relationship with me). The Bobover Rebbe offered another allusion as well. *Elul* stands for אֶחָד לְעֹלָה וְאֶחָד לְחַטָּאת; literally, *One [person] is for an elevated-offering, and one [person] is for a sin-offering.*

The Rebbe explained that there are two basic types of people heading into the month of Elul. One looks back at the past year and knows that he succeeded in following through on the resolutions he made last year. He had decided to learn more, and he actually did learn more. He had decided to improve his *davening*, and he did improve it. He had determined to do more *chesed*, and he actually did. He was able "*l'olah,*" to elevate himself, and become a better person. For him, Elul is "*echad l'olah*" — it is elevating. He looks forward to the upcoming Elul in order to be able to do the same and even more.

However, then there are people who are "*echad l'chatas.*" They look back on the past year and realize that they acted inappropriately or may have even committed serious violations of the Torah. They are those who are *"echad l'chatas,"* one who sinned. Yet, they too look forward to Elul to improve themselves.

Each of us wants to be more elevated, *echad l'olah*. And each of us has made mistakes and bad decisions, *echad l'chatas*. Whether we are *echad l'olah* or *echad l'chatas*, Elul is a time for all of us to think how to better ourselves. It is a time to think about the path we have been on in the past year and the path we want to be on in the upcoming year.

At the Crossroads

There is a very pertinent comment on this subject by the *Daas Zekeinim M'baalei Tosafos* on the pasuk (*Devarim* 11:26): רְאֵה אָנֹכִי נֹתֵן לִפְנֵיכֶם הַיּוֹם בְּרָכָה וּקְלָלָה, *See, I present before you today [the choice of] a blessing and a curse*. He cites the example of a wise old man standing at a fork in the road. Young, inexperienced travelers pass and ask the old sage which path to take. He tells them that there are two paths they can choose. The first one is one in which תְּחִילָתוֹ מִישׁוֹר וְסוֹפוֹ קוֹצִים, *the beginning is [rough and] thorny but the end is smooth*. The other path is one in which תְּחִילָתוֹ קוֹצִים וְסוֹפוֹ מִישׁוֹר, *the beginning is smooth but the end is full of thorns* (*Sifri Devarim* 53).

Elul is a crossroads. The decisions that we are going to make as we approach the days of Elul are at times difficult, because change is not easy. Yet, it is well worth it, because even if the beginning of the new path is difficult and "thorny," the end is "smooth."

On the other hand, if, *chas v'shalom*, someone takes the other road — the one that looks smooth and easy at first — he will find himself in a difficult thorny situation down the road.

My dear friend Rabbi Yaron Halbertal told me an incredible insight about this. Shlomo HaMelech writes in *Mishlei* (19:21), רַבּוֹת מַחֲשָׁבוֹת בְּלֶב אִישׁ וַעֲצַת ה׳ הִיא תָקוּם, *A man is full of ideas [about the best way to approach life]; however, it is the counsel of Hashem that is everlasting*. The letters (ת-ק-ו-ם) of the word *"sakum"* (everlasting) stand for תְּחִילָתוֹ קוֹצִים וְסוֹפוֹ מִישׁוֹר. The everlasting path is the one that appears thorny and difficult at first, but is indeed smooth at the end.

Life is a path. And there are two ways a person can go. One is difficult at first, but leads to blessing. The other looks easy, but leads to curse. This correct path may seem difficult and challenging at first, but it is well worth taking because it leads to blessing

The Thirteen Attributes

The Torah tells us (*Devarim* 28:9): וְהָלַכְתָּ בִּדְרָכָיו, *And you shall go in His [Hashem's] ways.* What does it mean to "go in His [Hashem's] ways"? What are these ways? The Torah teaches that there are "Thirteen Attributes of Hashem," known as the *Yud-Gimmel Middos.* They are mentioned in *Parashas Ki Sisa* (*Shemos* 34:6-7). We say them over and over again during the days of *Selichos,* and during the *Aseres Yemei Teshuvah* (Ten Days of Repentance) from Rosh Hashanah to Yom Kippur:

ה' ה' קֵל רַחוּם וְחַנּוּן אֶרֶךְ אַפַּיִם וְרַב חֶסֶד וֶאֱמֶת נֹצֵר חֶסֶד לָאֲלָפִים
נֹשֵׂא עָוֹן וָפֶשַׁע וְחַטָּאָה וְנַקֵּה

Hashem, Hashem, G-d, compassionate and gracious, slow to anger, and abundant in kindness and truth, preserver of kindness for thousands of generations, forgiver of iniquity, willful sin and error, who cleanses ....

The Gemara (*Rosh Hashanah* 17b) tells us that when Hashem said these words to Moshe, it was as if He wrapped Himself in a *tallis,* led the congregation in *tefillah,* and said: "If the Jewish nation has sinned, let them perform for Me this order, and I will forgive them."

What is "this order"? The simple meaning is that Jews should cry out and say, "Hashem, Hashem ...." But the Alshich points out that it does not say that Hashem told Moshe that they should *say* this order. Rather they should *perform* it. They should *act* in a compassionate way. They should *act* in a way of truth. They should *act* in a way of kindness.

It is not enough just to *say* it. We have to "go in the ways" of Hashem. We have to imitate and live up to the *middos,* the attributes, of Hashem. When we do so, Hashem will forgive us.

Hashem Is Truth

The *Yud-Gimmel Middos* encompass many characteristics. Rather than explaining them all in this small space, let us focus on one of them: *emes* (truth).

We recite the words of David HaMelech in *Ashrei* three times every day: קָרוֹב ה' לְכָל קֹרְאָיו לְכֹל אֲשֶׁר יִקְרָאֻהוּ בֶאֱמֶת, *Hashem is close to all who call upon Him, to all who call upon Him sincerely* (*Tehillim* 145:18). Rabbeinu Bachya in his *Kad HaKemach* writes, "Anyone who maintains a life of honesty and integrity will have his *tefillos* answered." He deduces this from the way he understands the words of David HaMelech, which he explains as follows: "Hashem is close [and answers prayers] to all who [can] call upon him [and say], 'I am a person of אֱמֶת, *honesty*!'"

Chazal instituted a prayer that we say every day at the end of the *Shemoneh Esrei*, asking that *Hashem* protect us from speaking evil and pronouncing falsehoods: אֱלֹקַי נְצוֹר לְשׁוֹנִי מֵרָע, *Hashem, guard my tongue from [speaking] evil* — וּשְׂפָתַי מִדַּבֵּר מִרְמָה, *and guard my lips from speaking deceitfully.*

Why do we need a prayer for assistance in being honest? Because without Heavenly assistance, we cannot overcome the temptation of lying and being deceitful. Rabbeinu Bachya adds that in the first *pasuk* of the Torah, בְּרֵאשִׁית בָּרָא אֱלֹקִים אֵת הַשָּׁמַיִם וְאֵת הָאָרֶץ, we find every vowel except one – the שרק, because if you scramble these letters they spell שֶׁקֶר (falsehood), and any semblance of deceit and falsehood cannot appear in the first *pasuk* of the Torah, which is the foundation of the entire Torah.

Thus if we want to build the rest of our lives on strong and enduring foundations, there cannot be anything dishonest, anything that hints at the lack of integrity in our lives.

And, sorrowfully, that is not easy to accomplish. We need *Hashem's* help.

Examples From the Lives of the Great

Let us look at some role models: people who exemplify truth and honesty.

The wife of Rav Yaakov Kamenetzky once needed an operation. Rav Yaakov wanted to call Rav Moshe Feinstein for a blessing. He dialed his number repeatedly, but kept getting a busy signal. This was not surprising, as people called Reb Moshe constantly with questions.

Finally, one of Rav Yaakov's children asked why his father did not use the unlisted number of Rav Moshe that he gave him when he had to be able to reach him. Rav Yaakov refused, for, as he said, that number was for communal emergencies only, and this was a personal call. Rav Yaakov was prepared to wait endlessly for Rav Moshe's line to open, but he would not use the other number in a manner he considered dishonest.

———»•«———

When the Chazon Ish lived in Bnei Brak, he had a *minyan* every day for *Minchah* at 12:30 p.m. One day, they had trouble getting a *minyan*. At 12:45, while they were still short a few men, Rav Shmuel Greineman explained his quandary to the Chazon Ish (his brother-in-law). He had an appointment across town in 15 minutes. In order to make it to the meeting on time, he would need to leave immediately and not participate in the *minyan*. What should he do? He didn't want the Chazon Ish to be left without a *minyan*, but he didn't want to arrive late for his meeting.

The Chazon Ish responded that the phrase לֹא יַחֵל דְּבָרוֹ, *He shall not desecrate his word* (*Bamidbar* 30:3), obligated him to be on time for the appointment, and that the *minyan* would have to be canceled. Better for Rabbi Greineman to abandon the *minyan* than break his word and be guilty of falsehood. The Chazon Ish was sure that a *min-yan* would be formed later and he would *daven* with that group.

Coming late to an appointment is lying!

How many doctors have to hear that? How many patients? Coming late to an appointment is lying! If you are supposed to be there at 9 a.m., that means you have to be there at 9 a.m. Otherwise, everybody else after you is kept waiting. If you, as a patient, have the first appointment of the day and come late, you throw off the whole day's schedule and are stealing time from other patients who do come on time. If you cannot make it, call to cancel and reschedule. Conversely, if you arrive at your appointment at the correct time, it's unconscionable for the doctor to keep you waiting for several hours before you are seen. Too many offices overbook, with the result that the patients' valuable time is wasted.

Rav Yehudah Zev Segal, the Manchester Rosh Yeshivah, was once on a train going from Manchester to London. He was in the economy-class section, which was filled with rowdy passengers. The Rav could not concentrate on the *sefer* he had brought along, so he went with his *talmid* into the first-class section, hoping to find the conductor and pay the difference.

For some reason, during the time that Rav Segal and his student were in first class the conductor did not pass through, so when the train arrived at the London station, Rav Segal led the student accompanying him to the ticket booth to pay there. He explained to the clerk that he had gone into the first-class section without paying the difference in fares. The clerk dismissed his concern and said that he did not have to pay.

Rav Segal turned to his *talmid* and said, "It's not right. I owe them money." He then went to the stationmaster and explained the situation. The man was stunned. He took the payment, and as the Rav turned to leave, the stationmaster said to the student, "That man is one in a million."

That is honesty — as well as a tremendous *kiddush Hashem*.

In *Yevamos* (63a) we are told that Rav had a difficult wife. Whatever he wanted, she gave him the opposite. Whenever he asked for bean soup, she served him pea soup, and whenever he asked for pea soup, she served him bean soup. One night, he was sitting at the table with his son, and he asked for bean soup. Lo and behold, he was given bean soup! He was shocked.

He turned to his son and remarked, "Mother has improved her ways." Now she was serving what he requested. His son had to inform him otherwise.

"No, I just told her you wanted pea soup."

One would have thought that Rav would have been happy with his son's actions, but he was not. He said to him, "Don't ever do that again. It says (*Yirmiyahu* 9:4), לִמְּדוּ לְשׁוֹנָם דַּבֶּר שֶׁקֶר הַעֲוֵה נִלְאוּ, *They teach the people to say lies*, and הַעַל אֵלֶּה לֹא אֶפְקָד בָּם, *shall I not punish them?* (v. 8).

Of course, Rav realized that his son could manipulate her like that, and in fact, he could have done so himself. But Rav would not lie, no matter what the consequence. A person must be impeccably honest.

Rav Samson Raphael Hirsch used to say that a person must be an *adam kasher* and an *adam yashar*. An *adam kasher* means kosher in his dealings with G-d. An *adam yashar* means a righteous person, a "straight" person, in dealing with man.

Rav Hirsch was a living example of this even *after* his death. As Rav he was paid quarterly by the community. Before he passed away, he told his family that if he died in the middle of a quarter, he wanted them to prorate his salary and return any excess payment to the community. Rav Hirsch died on December 31, the last day of the last quarter.

That's a German Jew. Precise.

The $30,000 Offer

Truth, of course, is not only for great people. Each of us is obligated just the same. Let me share the story of a person very dear to me who told it to me firsthand. I'll call him Reuven.

After he had a few children, Reuven left *kollel* for the working world. One day, his firm was bought up by a new owner who decided to fire literally half the employees. All of them were suddenly out of jobs.

The vice president of the firm, who I will call Shimon, told Reuven, "You are being let go just like half of the other people in this place, but I want you to know that the boss is providing severance pay. Over the next six months, you will get paid your regular salary."

He was making $60,000 a year, so they were offering him $30,000 for the next six months.

"There is one condition, however," Shimon told him. "You can receive the money for as long as you don't get another job. If you find another job, then the severance pay stops."

Reuven accepted the terms.

The very next day, Reuven found a job. He called up Shimon and told him, "I just got a job, and I'm calling to inform you to stop the severance pay."

"Are you out of your mind?" Shimon asked him. "Nobody expects you to say that. I'm ready to give you the money."

"What are you talking about?" Reuven replied. "The condition was that I will only get the money if I don't have a job. And I got a job."

"Look," Shimon said, "everyone is doing it. Think it over."

Reuven and his wife were sitting in the car late that night. An extra $30,000 was a lot of money to give up, but they saw no *heter*, no way of justifying the lie. To be sure, they decided to ask their Rav, and they drove all the way to his house almost two hours away. They explained the case to him thoroughly, and he agreed that there was no *heter*.

> **An extra $30,000 was a lot of money to give up, but they saw no *heter*, no way of justifying the lie.**

The next morning, Reuven called back Shimon and told him, "Sorry, I just can't take it."

Two things happened in the next year. Reuven, who gave up the $30,000, made it back in bonus money at his new job. Shimon, an ostensibly religious Jew who advised people to act dishonestly, divorced his wife and eventually intermarried.

Hashem is close to all those who call to Him in truth. If you want your *tefillos* answered, be someone who can stand before Hashem and say, "I'm honest, I'm truthful."

Honesty and Orthodoxy

The *Maharsha* (*Kesubos* 67a) writes, "Many in this generation gather wealth dishonestly, bringing disgrace to Hashem's Name. They steal from non-Jews [as though that were allowed], and afterward they give from that money to a shul or a yeshivah and receive recognition. But that is a mitzvah that came through an *aveirah*, and this wealth will not last."

Hashem does not want us to earn money through the mistakes of others, whether Jewish or non-Jewish. You cannot get away with it.

Rabbi Avrohom Pam would often quote the *Be'er Hagolah* (*Choshen Mishpat* 348 note 5) who writes, "I saw many people who became wealthy from mistakes that non-Jews made, but were not successful in the end. They lost all their money and were not left with any blessing."

Dishonesty is not the way to amass blessing.

Rav Shimon Schwab (*Selected Speeches*, p. 66) said, "We must draw the conclusion that those who resort to cheating, trickery, dishonesty, and fraud, while they sometimes may have the outward appearance of being G-d-fearing Jews, are in fact irreligious; they are *kofrim* in *hashgachah pratis*."

> "... Those who resort to cheating, trickery, dishonesty, and fraud, while they sometimes may have the outward appearance of being G-d-fearing Jews, they are in fact irreligious; they are *kofrim* in *hashgachah pratis*."

A person who steals is dishonest and irreligious. I remember Rav Schwab saying this at an Agudah Convention: "The *New York Times* writes in a headline, 'Orthodox fellow caught cheating.'" Rav Schwab roared, "He's not Orthodox! If he's dishonest, he's not Orthodox!"

In summary, when we talk about "*V'halachta b'drachav*," one of the ways of Hashem is *emes*, honesty. This is one of the areas in which we have to make a commitment — in our business and in our speech. No wild exaggerations. Speak the truth and act honestly. No deception. That is what Hashem requires of us. And, indeed, if we act accordingly, according to Rabbeinu Bachya, our *tefillos* will be answered. May it indeed be so.

Indices

Index of Personalities

Note: Included in this index are those historical personalities who played a role (or made a comment about) the stories which appear in this book. Excluded are most fictionalized names, minor characters, and narrators of the commentaries cited in the text. Page numbers indicate the first page of the story in which the person appears.

All titles have been omitted from this index to facilitate finding names.

Index of Sources

Scriptural and Talmudic Index for all nine Maggid books.

Note: **MS** indicates *The Maggid Speaks*; **AMT** indicates *Around the Maggid's Table*; **FM** indicates *In the Footsteps of the Maggid*; **MJ** indicates *Along the Maggid's Journey*; **EM** indicates *Echoes of the Maggid*; **PM** indicates *Perspectives of the Maggid*, and **RM** indicates *Reflections of the Maggid*; **SM** *In the Spirit of the Maggid*; **MAP** *The Maggid at the Podium*.

Page numbers reflect the page on which stories begin.